The Mystique of Tragedy

Exploring East and West

In the same series

New Directions in Indian Drama
Sudhakar Pandey and Freya Barua, ed.

Studies in Contemporary Indian Drama
Sudhakar Pandey and Freya Taraporewala, ed.

Indian Drama Today: A Study in the Theme of Cultural Deformity
Manchi Sarat Babu

The Mystique of Tragedy

Exploring East and West

CHAMAN AHUJA

Sangam Books

SANGAM BOOKS LIMITED
57 London Fruit Exchange
Brushfield Street
London E1 6EP, U.K.

By arrangement with
PRESTIGE BOOKS
3/28, East Patel Nagar
New Delhi 110 008

ISBN: 0 86132 381 5

Composed by Pivot Computers, Delhi 110 006
Printed by Mehra Offset Press, New Delhi 110 002

Contents

Acknowledgements

The result of a long quest involving serious academic research spread over many decades, this book has certainly benefited from secondary as well as primary sources. Indeed, whatever is here has come directly or indirectly from all those critics, scholars, philosophers and playwrights whose works comprise the Bibliography at the end. All that is good here, I owe to them; for the flaws, I own the blame. To all of them, therefore, I dedicate this work—as an humble gesture of genuine gratitude.

However, it will be noticed that, in the text of the book, most of those names don't figure at all; very few of them have been actually cited and, even in those cases, there is minimal hinting regarding the sources. While offering apologies for avoiding formal documentation in the traditional way, I should wish to submit that here is a monograph, not a thesis; its aim has been to present not a learned discourse but a tentative formulation as it evolved through a series of hunches. True, the process was facilitated by reading but, in a book like this, where things proceed through adaption, absorption, even distortion, rather than direct adoption, reading serves at best as a catalyst, at time consciously but more often in an unconscious way. In any case, even otherwise, I feel that in the over-scrupulous documentation, readability is the first casualty. I have always found the scholars' game of littering the text with parentheses and note-numbers not only tedious for the author but also distracting and aesthetically unwholesome for the reader. I have deliberately refrained from using most of the material consulted over the years because any such conscious attempt to give tangible evidence of indebtedness through documented scholarship might have led to a labyrinth in which a reader was bound to get lost. Nevertheless, but for that reading, the ideas would not have crystallized into the present formulations. Hence the Bibliography. In any case, since the Bibliography contains all the relevant details, a curious reader can reach the requisite source. Occasionally, there do figure note-numbers in the text; these pertain not to references but to the Notes which may be ignored by the reader—unless he is prepared for a long interruption for additional (but by no means essential) substance.

I should wish to acknowledge the fact that the material has been collected from scores of libraries, mostly situated in Chandigarh, Delhi, Bombay, Madras, Bangalore, London. Special mention is due to the libraries of the American Studies Research Centre and Central Institute of English & Foreign Languages—both in Hyderabad. Acknowledgements are due also to the Panjab University for study leave (1988-90), to the A.S.R.C. for a spell as Scholar-in-Residence (Feb. 1990), to the British Council for facilitating my visit to U.K. (July 1990) through Charles Wallace India grant, and to the Indian Institute of Advanced Study, Shimla, for I.U.C. associateship (August-October 1991).

CHAMAN AHUJA

Prologue

What is a tragedy, and why do people laud this genre which affords an exprience that appears rooted in some of the most morbid passions? The questions are as old as Aristotle—nay, in fact, even older. The quest for answers has had such a long history that the hubris-like monomaniac tenacity to define and redefine tragedy tends to suggest a correspondence to the tenor of tragedy itself—the same pattern of mystery and paradox of creative destructiveness, the same hopeless hope and a concomitant measure of glory in the failure of the incessant pursuit! Indeed, what single definition could cover an art in which saints and criminals, victors and victims, the rebels and the resigned, men of destiny and its puppets—all can be, and have been, heroes of most representative kind? Who, pray, can define a genre that has been continually enlarging its scope so as to cover at once Greek paganism, Roman stoicism, medieval didacticism, Renaissance individualism, neoclassical poetic justice, Romantic neoplatonism and the modern plethora of 'isms'? Even if one could perform the miracle of forging a definition that may be comprehensive enough to accommodate all the tragedies to date, where is the guarantee that tomorrow it won't be rendered inadequate, if not exactly redundant, by future works? And yet—and that makes the task almost impossible—the tragedy and the tragic have had such specific meanings that some of the works labelled tragedies by their authors have been denied that title by posterity, even as some others that have established themselves as masterpieces of this genre were never conceived as tragedies! Interesting, indeed, is the fact that Shakespeare subtitled *King Lear* as 'The True Chronicle Historie' and *Hamlet* as 'The Tragicall Historie' while he included *Cymbeline* among tragedies and chose to call *Romeo and Juliet* as 'Most Excellent and Lamentable Tragedie.' It is only to be wondered what different conclusions A.C. Bradley might have arrived at regarding Shakespearean tragedy if he had gone strictly by the author's subtitles.

In such a situation, when one knows what tragedy is and yet cannot define it, and when distinctions have to be made even though no distinctions can be absolute, can the critics, aesthetes and aestheticians really help? How vague and contradictory the critical opinions tend to be becomes clear when one puts together the views of some critics about any specific issue—say, for example, what type of age would be ideally suited for tragic creativity? For Miguel de Unamuno, tragic sense of life is the prerogative of a dying society; for Michael Goldman, it is characteristic of the sick and maladjusted section of a healthy society; for Geoffrey Brereton, however, only a healthy and confident society can afford to tolerate the subversion of a tragedy because a declining culture is too afraid of being hurt and a precarious minority dare not ask questions for fear of possible answers.

For me, the fateful quest started when, in the course on literary criticism in the Master's programme, I was required to study Aristotle's *Poetics*. The diversity inhering the range of interpretations of catharsis was, to me, as intriguing as the paradox of 'plucking grapes from thorns and figs from thistles.' The Joyful Safety theory, the inoculation-therapy, the musical analogy, the Reduction-to-Scale hypothesis, the sadistic-masochistic and Schadenfreudian approaches, the tickling-with-a-dagger thesis, the dialectical alternating of illusion and disillusion, the banquet-not-hospital averment—each seemed to offer a fascinating way out and yet none appeared to clinch the issue once for all. Anyway, my real problem started a few years later when I launched my doctoral programme on Eugene O'Neill. Judged on the touchstone of the traditional theory of tragedy, his plays simply refused to satisfy me and yet here was a playwright who kept repeating in statement after statement his credo regarding his ideal of recapturing the spirit of Greek tragedy in terms of modern experience. In the face of Joseph Wood Krutch's declaration regarding the incompatibility of tragedy and modern temper, I had to make clear to myself the quintessential core of tragedy, and for that purpose I had to turn to both theory and practice.

I read a lot on the subject and managed to work out my premises by analyzing extensively the material in hand—an exercise that not only took good part of a year but also got stretched over hundreds of pages. Inevitably, I had to prune all that into a couple of chapters in my dissertation and drop almost the whole thing when it was published in the form of a book (*Tragedy, Modern Temper and O'Neill*, New Delhi: Macmillan India, and Atlantic Highlands, N.J.: Humanities Press Inc., 1984). However, a gnawing feeling that I had something really worthwhile to say and that there was a book in those discarded drafts gradually grew into an obsession and kept alive my interest in the theory of tragedy. In practical terms it meant enlarging manifold the huge pile of my notes. But before I could write out my proposed book, the newly acquired material posed new questions which clamoured to be answered. For greater clarity, I turned to the western aesthetic theory in general. As that wouldn't help much, willy-nilly, I had to turn to the oriental aesthetics, especially the Indian theory of *Rasa*. This not only meant further distraction but also greater problems fraught with serious dangers. The fact is that I do not know Sanskrit language at all—a big handicap in a pursuit like mine. Consequently and inevitably, I had to depend entirely on secondary sources, i.e., commentaries and critiques in English. The forays into Indian aesthetics did open up new vistas but answers to my questions were simply not there: after all, in the whole range of Sanskrit drama, there is not a single tragedy. In any case, my flirtations with *Rasa*-theory were interrupted time and again by long gaps caused by my preoccupations with other academic projects. Of course, thanks to the ever-simmering obsession, I kept seeking answers to my aesthetic problems wherever I could—in books and even in life-situations. To cut the story short, I have evolved a few formulations based on this personal quest in the critical and theoretical literature of both East and West. Since I do not presume to claim that the search has yielded the final key to the problem, I am offering my formulations, for whatever they are worth, as something all-too-tentative—in the hope that these might be found worthy of further pursuit by some future enthusiasts.

Under the Western Eyes

Since 'the play's the thing,' what could be a better guide (or at least a better starting point) in one's search for the clues to the mystery of tragic pleasure than plays—the plays that have been universally acknowledged as tragedies: for example, *Oresteia, Oedipus Rex, Medea, Doctor Faustus, Hamlet, The Duchess of Malfi, Phaedra, Cenci*? But, then, is there really anything common to all of them? It certainly is not the theme, nor perhaps the vision. Their action and structure are so diverse, as also their language, even endings. They are all serious plays, of course, but the quality of experience afforded is hard to generalize in terms of catharsis or otherwise. Perhaps realism demands that we should allow a measure of diversity as an inevitable part of the evolution of this genre and thus accommodate the variety under the broad categories of 'types' or 'climates' of tragedy—for example, the Greek tragedy, the Roman tragedy, the Renaissance tragedy, the neoclassical tragedy, the Romantic tragedy, or the Modern tragedy.

Obviously this does not lead one very far in one's search for the quintessence. Witness, for example, the diversity that marks the works of the Greek masters amongst themselves. Indeed, could one really generalize about the role of chorus in the Greek tragedy? The way it lost its pride of place in the plays of Euripides shows that it was not all that indispensable an ingredient, after all. Likewise, while Aeschylus's *Oresteia* ends on a note of peace and forgiveness, and Zeus and Prometheus are ultimately reconciled in *Prometheia*, Sophocles' plays invariably end on a note of unreconciled conflict. Or does the problem inhere the fact that most of the extant Greek plays have come down to us as separate plays while they were originally conceived as parts of integrally unified trilogies? What can one deduce from a group of plays that belonged to different stages of the complete trilogies? It is also worth remembering in this connection that in the fifth Century B.C., the idea of tragedy was rather vague and that, far from conforming to any specific theory, the plays just served to express the pagan zest for passionate and dangerous living. No wonder, in all the Greek plays we have a confluence of crime, conflict and suffering—and all these rooted in such horrible acts as murders, rapes, incest, infanticide, etc. That such barbarous acts in themselves don't signify quintessence of tragedy is clear from the fact that invariably the horrendous act is performed by the hero in spite of himself, as a victim of the gods' capricious ways. In a sense, therefore, the barbarism of the acts signifies the human limitation. The anguish that accompanies or follows its performance is the real measure of the unique humanity and potential of man. Since this anguish prompts the protagonists to punish the evil-doers, including themselves, it serves as an instrument to make the life yield more than what nature had determined or what those vicious gods had ordained. Thus is man seen on a pedestal higher than that of the gods who remain unchanged and unreconciled. In this way, the Greek plays humanize the irrational forces and thus suggest that human life is bitter as well as sweet because it is at once determined and glorious.

This pagan humanism, common to the Greek playwrights, cannot, however, be treated as the core of tragedy because it is by no means at the centre of the tragedies written later. For example, the Elizabethan tragedy is permeated, instead, by heroic individualism, which, as we all know, was the hall-mark of the Renassaince spirit. Here, fate is no longer the character; rather, character is the fate. The focus is not so much on gods' or God's ways to man as on man's ways to man. Passion is there, of course, but only to underscore the fact that the animal called man is by no means a mere beast; instead, his superior intellect makes him a peer of the angels. That means that in tragedy what is important is not passion but how it is treated. But, then, that accounts for diversity rather than unity of vision. The way the same old Greek myths are reworked in neoclassical French tragedy would have shocked the Pericleans—for example, the passion of love in Jean Racine's *Phaedra*. For the Greeks, love was a divine madness and heart the battle-ground of divine clashes; it was something to be celebrated. For Racine, it is something to be loathed because, as a fatal force that destroys human will from within, it signifies the tyranny of human weakness. Likewise, the passion of revenge has received such a contrasted treatment in *The Spanish Tragedy* and *Hamlet*: the blood-and-thunder heroism of Thomas Kyd's play turns out to be a most villainous attitude in the spiritual tragedy of William Shakespeare. Shakespeare's tragic heroes are slaves of passion, no doubt, but their passions serve as levers which operate the windows opening on their souls. This spiritual dimension is so conspicuous by its absence in others before and after Shakespeare—say, Christopher Marlowe and John Webster—that they look sensation-oriented melodramatists. So much so that the very idea of their sharing with Shakespeare a common umbrella appears almost preposterous. No less irritating than the absence of spirituality can be the absence of passion—as one realizes when one compares Marlowe's *Doctor Faustus* with Goethe's *Faust*. In the latter, one misses the intensity and power of great tragedies. Anyway, one notable thing about these two plays relevant to our purpose is that although one ends in the loss of soul and the other in its redemption, both are tragedies! In short, one cannot insist on any specific kind of ending or any particular type of experience: totally antithetical elements have gone into the making of tragedies. Could it be that tragedy is that which accommodates the contraries—not in the spirit of peaceful coexistence but as mutually dependent complementaries? Anyway, in the light of the plays considered above, one could say that tragedy is primarily concerned with man, with his passions as well as with the divinity inhering his humanity, and that in respect of its world-view, a tragedy is related to the ethos of its time. Maybe, ultimately, the source of tragic pleasure shall have to be traced in the context of these broad generalizations.

It might be helpful if we turn from the plays to the playwrights to see what they have said on tragedy and tragic pleasure. Of course, most of them are silent: we have nothing, for example, from Aeschylus, Sophocles, Euripides, Marlowe, Shakespeare on this art. And those who have offered their perceptions in Prologues, Prefaces, critical essays or dialogues within their plays have said things that don't help too much. In any case, their utterances are too diverse to reconcile. Some of the observations are insightful but most of them are commonplace. John Marston in his *Antonio's Revenge* urges those 'incapable of weighty passion' to hurry away from the theatre because the play would 'affright their eyes'; welcome, instead, are those whose breast is 'nailed to the earth' and whose heart is 'pierced through with anguish.' In other words, tragedy is for men with sterner sensibility. For John Dryden, on the other hand, the requisite quality is a commitment to 'the excellency of the Moral,' as the 'Preface' to *All for Love* has it. In his Preface to *Phaedra*, Racine talks of depicting vice in such a light that one may hate its deformity. In the 'Preface' to *Berenice*, he says a lot more:

> It is not necessary that there shall be blood and deaths in tragedy: it is enough that its action shall be great, that its characters shall be heroic, that the passions shall be aroused through it, and that the whole effect shall be that majestic sadness which constitutes the whole pleasure of tragedy.

These were, of course, senventeenth century writers; writing a full century after Dryden and Racine, Oliver Goldsmith, while making a 'Comparison Between Laughing and Sentimental Comedy,' declared distress as the proper object of tragedy because the great excite our pity by their fall. In the beginning of the nineteenth century, Goethe approved of heroes weeping and wailing in the tradition of the noble Greek who would say, 'Noble are the men who can weep. Leave me alone—you who have a dry heart and dry eyes! I curse the happy for whom the unhappy is only a spectacle.' By the end of that century, the concept of tragedy was undergoing revolutionary changes and thus August Strindberg declared in his 'Foreword' to *Miss Julie* that 'Life is not so mathematically idiotic as only to permit the big to eat the small; it happens just as often that the bee kills the lion or at least drives it mad.'

In our own century, almost all the practitioners of tragedy have tried to explain their art and in the process struck new notes. For example,

— A farce and a tragedy are alike in this, that they are a moment of intense life.

W.B. Yeats, *Plays and Controversies*

— Indeed, it is not in the actions but in the words that are found the beauty and greatness of tragedies . . .

M. Maeterlinck, 'The Tragic in Daily Life'

— Where there is a soul, there is a tragedy.

Eugene O'Neill

— The theatre is a school of weeping and of laughter, a rostrum where men . . . explain with living examples the eternal norms of the heart and feelings of man.

Garcia Lorca, 'The Authority of the Theatre'

— Tragedy is clean, it is restful, it is flawless. . . . In a tragedy, nothing is in doubt and everyone's destiny is known. That makes for tranquillity. . . . The spring is wound up tight. It will uncoil of itself. . . . The least turn of the wrist will do the job.

Jean Anouilh, *Antigone*

— I believe that the common man is as apt a subject for tragedy in its highest sense as kings were. . . . Tragedy, then, is the consequence of a man's total compulsion to evaluate himself justly.

Arthur Miller, 'Tragedy and the Common Man'

— Tragedy presupposes guilt, despair, moderation, lucidity, vision, a sense of responsibility.

Friedrich Durrenmatt, 'Preface' to *Four Plays*

— Wheels have been set in motion, and they have their own pace, to which we are . . . condemned.

Tom Stoppard, *Rosencrantz and Guildenstern are Dead*

Going by all these observations put together, tragedy is an art that thrives on distress, guilt, despair and moments of intense life, that deals with the 'eternal norms of the heart' and 'man's compulsion to evaluate himself justly,' that presents big eating the small and bee driving the lion mad in such action as resembles uncoiling of a spring and wheels in motion, that requires a language fraught with beauty and greatness and yet needs for the appreciation of its 'majestic sadness' a heart 'pierced with anguish' and 'weeping eyes,' that assumes the birth of a soul and preaches the 'excellency of the Moral.' Does all this help in understanding the source of tragic pleasure? I would rather not presume to make an attempt at a reply—at least, not for the time being.

Let us turn now to the theory of tragedy offered by literary critics, thinkers and philosophers. Of course, they saw the genre differently, according to their own lights. Take, for example, the question of nomenclature—tragos+ode (=goat song). Does this goat signify sacrifice and the hero's being a scapegoat; or was the prize of a goat (with prosperous hair-front and sparse tail) meant to symbolize the tragic hero's decline from prosperity to adversity? Likewise, as regards its origin, did tragedy emerge from orgiastic fertility rituals, the Dionysian rites, or Anthesteria (the Greek version of All Souls' Day) in which lamentation songs (threnos) were sung at the graves of the heroes? One can see similar diversity in respect of every issue concerning tragedy and its pleasure. However, one thing is common to most of the critics until the advent of our century: instead of thinking afresh in a totally independent framework, they would just react to the formulations of the Greek mentor, Aristotle, in the form of endorsement, echo, reinterpretation or rejection. Indeed, as has been rightly put, if the approach is not Aristotelian, it is anti-Aristotelian but never completely non-Aristotelian. It is commonly forgotten that, far from being prescriptive, *Poetics* is descriptive. Besides, Aristotle generalized from the models before him; probably, his formulations would have been different had he been writing today in the light of all the tragedies written during the last two millenia and a half. Let us also not forget that since his theory was in response to Plato's onslaught against poetry in general and tragedy in particular, the defence was inevitably determined by the tenor of the charges. Indeed, but for his master's reference to pity and fear, Aristotle might have chosen to develop his theory differently—possibly independent of these emotions, probably without laying on them the present exclusive stress. Equally worthwhile should be a reminder to ourselves that *Poetics* was only a summary of lectures prepared by some pupils. Certainly, therefore, it would be not only wrong but also unfair to Aristotle himself if, regarding the work as a flawless masterpiece, we go out of the way to defend even the pupils' lapses.

One thing more. It would, indeed, be height of ingratitude even to think of minimizing the pioneering and seminal contribution of Aristotle in the field. Still, one could say without any fear of contradiction that the task before him was comparatively easy because he had before him limited number of plays—mostly the works of the great Greek masters, viz., Aeschylus, Sophocles and Euripides. The plots of all those plays were based on the same myths even as their structures were invariably chorus-oriented. Some variations did exist but those corresponded to the individual geniuses of the writers. Besides, being almost contemporaries, they all wrote for the same stage, shared the same pagan ethos, and had a common view of man and his world. Anyone attempting to define tragedy today has before him thousands of additional plays that have been born of such divergent world-views as correspond to the spirits of different ages as well as to the geniuses of hundreds of writers. What is more, these plays have been written for varied performing situations. In addition, the critic today has to reckon with a large body of theoretical formulations which he cannot wish away. Aristotle had before him just one critical observation (Plato's) and practically no theory. True, it goes to his credit that his generalizations from limited models could hold such a pervasive sway for such a long time and even tended to accommodate, partially or wholly, such works as were born thousands of years after him; nevertheless, it was certainly easier for him to grasp the quintessence of the plays in his hand.

Aristotle could see that all those trilogies did produce pity and fear because they presented terrible, violent action (like murders, incest, massacre). They might end up in consolation, reconciliation, resignation or death(s), but at least one thing was common to all—the anguish of those who suffered. Anyway, it was suffering to which they had themselves contributed because of their own acts of omission or commission—on account of the nature of their respective characters. Those fatal qualities in their characters were not necessarily something evil and undesirable; in fact, more often than not, these were strong points, which in their given situations, turned out to be weaknesses and caused havoc. Perhaps the consequences could be less disastrous had the protagonists shown a spirit of compromise; but, made of ruthless stuff as they were, they would persist with their course, whatever the outcome. They would pursue things to their logical end and, if necessary, break rather than bend. Their suffering did bring about some realizations, but only too late—when disasters had overtaken the sufferers and completely reversed the initial situation. As such a fate was bound to touch one's heart, the response of the reader/viewer to those terrible deeds had to be qualitatively different from what it would normally be in real life. Aristotle explained this understanding of tragedy in terms of *mimesis, hamartia, hubris, agon, peripeteia, anagnorisis, catharsis*, etc. Since the later tragedies have offered different kinds of stories, numerous world-views, divers tenors of experiences, diverse aspects of characterization, varied patterns of form and structure, heterogeneous endings, and divergent nature of impact, it is not surprising that Aristotle's formulations were later felt to be rather inadequate. And yet, instead of approaching the field with an open mind, for a new formulation to accommodate the new tragedies, critics preferred to twist and distort what Aristotle had supposedly implied. Had the critics dispensed with the much-cliched Aristotelian terminology, the critical scenario today could have been entirely different.

That the Greek tragedy did not always enjoy archetypal position becomes clear when one sees how Seneca's plays, based on the same myths, lack humanistic quality. Strictly speaking, catharsis, in the musical or the medical sense, has no relevance here. Written at a time when people were interested more in amphitheatre and gladiators' fights than in theatre, these plays revel in violence and horror for their own sake. Of course, violence was not enacted on the stage but recounted in a language with a matching power of ranting and rhetoric. Evoking unalloyed fear, therefore, the plays invariably end on a note of Roman stoicism rather than redemptive wisdom or assertion of human glory. It is a pity that Latin tragedy did not inspire any contemporary to attempt a new theory. The birth of Christianity and the antipathy of the Church towards theatre explain why dark, medieval ages that followed yielded neither any plays nor any theory. The few observations that have come down clearly show that, since there had been no theatre activity for more than a thousand years, the idea of performing art had been lost and the word 'tragedy' had come to mean a form of narrative poetry. Thus, while Diomedes defines tragedy as a narrative of the fortunes of heroic (or semi-divine) characters in adversity, Isidore Seville saw in tragedies nothing more than 'sad stories of commonwealths and kings,' even as John of Garland described tragedy as a poem written in the 'grand' style, which treated of shameful and wicked deeds and, beginning in joy, ended in grief. Even for Geoffrey Chaucer it was a story of one that stood in great prosperity and fell out of high degree into misery and ended wretchedly. The medieval mind, so obsessed with Christian concern for moral sermonization, could not but think of tragedy as a warning to the high-ups that God would punish them too if they didn't behave themselves.

The Renaissance was a great movement that shaped Europe but, alas, it did precious little to recast the theory of tragedy. As late as 1589,

George Puttenham referred to the 'Poets Tragical' as those who 'set forth the doleful falls of the infortunate and afflicted Princes'—obviously an echo of the medieval concept. Even Sir Philip Sidney, the great Renaissance man, could not help bringing the medieval didacticism into his definition of tragedy, when he declared that 'the high and excellent tragedy' makes kings fear to be tyrants and, by stirring the effects of admiration and commiseration, teaches them the uncertainty of this world and 'how upon weak foundations gilden roofs are builded.' Surely, this definition does not cover Marlowe, much less Shakespeare. Even in the seventeenth century, George Chapman regarded instruction and moral purpose as the essential components of tragic experiences.

> . . . material instruction, elegant and sententious excitation to virtue, and deflection from her contrary, being the soul, limbs, and limits of an authentic tragedy.

Going by this definition, one would tend to think that either Shakespeare had also written just morality plays or else he had never existed for Chapman.

The fact is that Shakespeare had conjoined the medieval concept of 'fall' to the Greek fatalism and the Renaissance version of human nature as enshrined in the Elizabethan Chain of Being. In practical terms it meant humanizing the animal in man and by-passing the categories of black and white in favour of grey. No wonder, in his tragic world, fair is foul and foul is fair, 'to be' and 'not to be' are equally glorious, and 'None does offend, none!' Shakespeare has certainly outstripped his successors as well as his predecessors in helping tragedy scale a new peak after the Greek tragedy, but the critics of his time were still toeing the classical or medieval lines. For the first time perhaps, the dichotomy of existence had become the basis of tragedy in Shakespeare, but the critics failed to see the implications of this singularly innovative contribution. Of course, Elizabethan and Jacobean thinkers' sticking to old notions is quite understandable: for them, New Learning meant a return to the classical literature in Latin rather than Greek and thus what really influenced the tragic output of the University Wits was in the line of Seneca rather than Sophocles. If Shakespeare is an exception, it is precisely because he was not a University Wit and thus knew 'little Latin' and 'less Greek.' It is significant in this connection that he subtitled *King Lear* not as tragedy but as 'True Chronicle History'!

While Shakespeare's humanistic vision enabled him to inject spiritual glory into the passion-wrought disasters, his lesser contemporaries like Cyril Tourneur, Francis Beaumont and John Fletcher used passion to become a fountain-head of pure moralization or pure pity. Even in John Webster, death has nothing creative about it and thus his plays verge on melodrama—being veritable studies of evil, perversities, corruption, horror and suffering. If the Jacobeans saw in tragedy the celebration of pure animal in man, animal was completely ignored in the heroic plays of John Dryden for whom the essential motivation of tragedy lay in 'excellency of the Moral.' *All for Love* had to end on an unfortunate note simply because the love here was unlawful. This insistence on rewarding the virtue and punishing the guilty gradually became the order of the day and was applauded as 'poetic justice.' Subscribing to this scale of values, Thomas Rymer could not appreciate the tragic waste in Shakespeare and said very uncharitable things about the Bard of Avon. In *The Tragedy of the Last Age*, when Rymer attributed this obsession with teaching to Greek playwrights, he was only betraying his faith in hearsay or else his reading of Aristotle's *Poetics* in a poor translation. Of course, by this time, Aristotle had become better known to scholars and in Italy Marco G. Vida and Lodovico Castelverto had written books to interpret *Poetics*. In fact, the debate had already started as to what the Greek philosopher had possibly meant by Catharsis—'purging' or 'purification' of the emotions of pity and fear. In his Preface to *Samson Agonistes*, Milton refers to Aristotle's attributing to tragedy a power by raising pity and fear, or terror, 'to purge the mind of those and such like passions, that is to temper and reduce them to just measure with a kind of delight, stirr'd up by reading or seeing those passions well imitated.'

Meanwhile, in France, the neoclassical age had already started. Racine's opinion, it would be recalled, comes so close to the concept of poetic justice. Pierre Corneille's *Discourse on Tragedy* bears the subtitle 'And the Methods of Treating It According to Prabability and Necessity,' but in effect it is a kind of paraphrase, elaboration or interpretation of *Poetics*. Anyway, perhaps the best known work on tragedy belonging to this period came from David Hume who tried to resolve the paradox of tragic pleasure by bringing in the analogy of tickling. Pity and fear, he argued, are pleasurable because they are sportively administered in mild doses; with a little increase, the situation can be truly painful:

> No matter what the passion is: let it be agreeable, afflicting, melancholy, disordered; it is still better than that insipid languor, which arises from perfect tranquillity and repose.

Written in 1757, the essay came to exercise impact only in the nineteenth century after Hume's *Essays and Treatises on Several Subjects* was published in 1809.

The revolt against neoclassicism is best represented in G.E. Lessing for whom tragedy is an orgy, the emotion aroused being just pity; terror and admiration, for him, are not passions in themselves but only rungs of the ladder of pity. In his correspondence with Herr Nicolai, Lessing led the movement against didacticism by asserting that the morality of drama lies in the emotion of pity. He distinguished three levels of pity and three kinds of pity and insisted that tragic pity is the one in which misfortunes and good qualities are juxtaposed. Thanks to the Romantic spirit of the age, in the first half of the nineteenth century, emotions and melancholy came to be idealized and thus tragedy came to be treated as the highest art. No wonder, Goethe came to believe that noble are the men who can weep. Heinrich von Kleist also declared, 'Man can be great in grief, ay, even a hero.' Only a man sharing this romantic spirit of the age could declare, as did S.T. Coleridge, that he had in him a smack of Hamlet—'I am Hamlet.' It is possible to see in this declaration the seed of what followed in the latter half of the nineteenth century—tragic sense of life, which became, in this period, what didacticism was in the Renassiance view and poetic justice in the neoclassical approach. The interesting thing is that whereas, in the past, theory had followed practice or remained unrelated to the creative counterpart, in the post-Romantic nineteenth century, the two kept pace with each other. This balance was upset again in the twentieth century when tragedy was declared dead and the massive effort to revive it was matched by the profusion of varied critical writing but, alas, without any organic correspondence to each other.

The nineteenth century philosophers who practically revolutionized the theory of tragedy by bringing into it the concept of tragic sense of life were George Wilhelm Friedrich Hegel, Friedrich Nietzsche and Soren Kierkegaard. At the bottom of their theories is the assumption that man's situation is necessarily tragic because all men exist in an evil situation, whence they are not only anguished but also aware of their being anguished. While Hegel saw in this situation opposition of forces dividing man from man and man from himself, and Kierkegaard discerned in the condition a desperate need for man to break out from an imposed pattern, Nietzsche perceived in the resulting conflict the scope of joy in bringing Dionysus and Apollo together.

Hegel brought into the theory of tragedy his philosophy of dialectical process—thesis, antithesis and synthesis. Thus are reconciled such opposites as good and evil, pity and fear, attraction and repulsion. Thus seen, catharsis is a kind of synthesis. Hegel was the first to realize that, thanks to man's situation, neither of the contending forces in a tragedy is wholly damnable. Putting an ethical colouring on the conflict, he defined the tragic act dialectically as the self-dissension and self-reconciliation of the moral nature. Tragedy, thus seen, implies a conflict between two partial 'goods': good v good. That makes heroes of tragedy appear as guilty as innocent. For Hegel, *hamartia* lies in hero's identification with a single moral claim and it leads to monomaniac tendencies which accounts at once for his greatness and his doom. Tragic hero has no desire to avoid the blame that results from his choice: it is his fame to have done what he has done. Hegel is thus concerned with suffering not for its own sake but because of its causes. In the finale, the two-fold vindication of the mutually conflicting aspects is retained but the hero having suffered a physical defeat, the one-sided mode is cancelled and thus is the ideal harmony restored. Regarding tragic pleasure, Hegel avers that we but wrap ourselves momentarily, the better to enjoy the eternal sunshine.[1]

As Nietzsche quotes Hegel in *The Birth of Tragedy* approvingly, one could say that the former was influenced by the latter; but, seen more closely, Nietzschean theory tends to coalesce the Aristotelian stress on emotional core with the Hegelian emphasis on ethical conflict. It is a way of reconciling the emotive and the intellectual on the common plane of imagination. Feeling coupled with imagination amounts to ecstasy, while dream is the meeting point of intellect and imagination. Dionysus and Apollo being the presiding deities of these two realms, Nietzschean theory projects tragedy as the art that makes the two deities sit together. Under the influence of Wilhelm Richard Wagner, he seeks to resolve tragic mystery in music rather than in the plastic arts. Apollo evokes awe, Dionysus ecstasy; tragedy, like the universal language of music, amalgamates both. 'For a brief moment we become ourselves, the primal Being, and we experience its insatiable hunger for existence.' In Joseph Calarco's tragic ontology, Dionysian man is a version of the archaic man while Apollonian man is a version of the historical man. The former represents the primordial aspect of life—wild, disordered, unrestrained; the latter represents the rational aspect—restraint, harmony, balance. In a tragedy, Nietzsche avers, Dionysian and Apollonian natures are conjoint and 'whatever exists is alike just and unjust, and in both cases equally justified.'

This statement comes quite close to Hegelian conflict but Nietzsche came to this conclusion via Arthur Schopenhauer. According to Schopenhauer, the aim of tragedy is to make the spectator realize that life is vanity of vanities, an eternal strife in a thoroughly irrational world. Nietzsche joined issue by arguing that life may be a vale of tears, but the art of tragedy makes it endurable by alternating illusion and disillusion. For Nietzsche, that is to say, the action of tragedy is neither moral nor purgative but aesthetic. It is not negative and destructive but creative: it grows out of pessimistic premises but leads to the highest affirmation of life. When will is paralyzed, art approaches as a healing enchantress. It conquers the dreadfulness of the tragic fact of existence and thereby makes life endurable. And the highest art in this yea-saying game is tragedy. It is like imagining a dead leaf, when it is torn at last from its twig and whirled away by the year's first south-western gale, as shouting of the coming spring and rejoicing, even though for a moment. On Dionysian level, one becomes one with the Primordial Unity, its pain and contradiction; under the Apollonian dream-illusion comes the redemption. In a tragedy, the Apollonian illusion reveals its identity as the veil thrown over the Dionysian meanings but, at the close, the Apollonian begins to speak with Dionysian wisdom. Thus does Dionysus speak the language of Apollo and Apollo the language of Dionysus. Since both languages can be spoken in music alone, Nietzsche regarded chorus as the essential element in Greek tragedy and blamed Euripides for the death of tragedy by undermining the role of chorus.

Miguel de Unamuno put Nietzschean formula differently when he talked about tragedy reconciling the 'intellectual necessities with the necessities of the heart and the will' —the 'truth felt' and the 'truth thought.' According to Unamuno, everything vital is anti-rational (not merely irrational) and everything rational is anti-vital. And that is the basis of the tragic sense of life. Like Nietzsche, Unamuno too grows frenzied in exclamatory ejaculations. For example, when he says:

> Reasons of the heart! Loves of the head! Intellectual delight! delicious intellection!—tragedy, tragedy, tragedy!

At the end of his book, Unamuno's prayer for the reader is: 'May God deny you peace but give you glory.' For such an outcome, Nietzsche's advice is 'Live dangerously,' for 'life is good because it is painful.'

Karl Jaspers also builds his thesis on tragic knowledge—that both Existence and Action being forms of guilt, battles are unavoidable. But, according to Jaspers, the tragic hero transcends beyond good and bad and, in the ultimate result, victory is not his who triumphs but his who fails. In reality nothing conquers because men die as martyrs without being martyrs. Of course, Jaspers's basic position is that the tragic hero takes a relative truth as absolute and that brings in the turmoil of dark impulses. He would, therefore, recommend a step beyond tragedy. Hence his title *Tragedy is Not Enough*. Now, Kierkegaard also found man's existential situation to be precarious—full of fear and despondency because he has before him the hard choice of Either/Or. While the tragic hero in such a situation makes his choice between the two, Kierkegaard's preference is for a 'leap into faith.' In fact, for Kierkegaard, of the three types of existence—aesthetic, ethical and religious—the last one is of the highest value.

It is possible to explain the attitudes of Kierkegaard and Jaspers by recalling that both of them were religious philosophers who did talk about the tragic inhering the human situation but only to reject the tragic sense of life. Anyway, thanks to them, critics learnt to approach tragedy without being over-awed by the ever-lengthening shadow of Aristotle. Of course, some of the critics felt the need to aver that tragedy and theology cannot go together. Witness, A.C. Bradley, for example:

> Shakespeare was not attempting to justify the ways of God to men or to show the universe as a Divine Comedy. He was writing tragedy, and tragedy would not be tragedy if it were not a painful mystery.

I.A. Richards also asserted later:

> Tragedy is possible only to a mind which is for the moment agnostic or Manichean. The least touch of any theology which has a compensating Heaven to offer the tragic hero is fatal.

In fact, one of the main concerns of critics in the twentieth century has been to evaulate the compatibility of tragedy and religion, especially Christianity.

When one comes to the twentieth century, the survey of tragedy and its theory becomes totally hazy. Thanks to the explosion of knowledge, the academic compulsion of 'publish or perish,' and insistence on interdisciplinary approaches, countless books and articles came to be written on the subject. The problem became all the more baffling because of the fact that the intellectual sway of Marx, Freud, Jung, Frazer, Einstein, Sartre et al., opened up hitherto unknown realms of experience, new areas of exploration and therefore totally different kinds of plays. In this age, contrary to the traditional process of theory following practice by generalizing on the bases of existing plays, theory came to lead the practice. What is more, playwrights, instead of remaining content to say all they had to say in their plays, felt the need to exploit the prefaces to their works for explaining their views, including their respective understanding of dramatic theory. And, then, Hegel, Nietzsche, Northrop Frye et al., with their new kinds of theories, as also their interpreters—all prompted playwrights to explore new themes, new forms, new aesthetic values. Thus we have plays which simply don't fit the traditional notion of tragedy and yet they clamour to be so labelled because there is certainly something tragic about them. If we call them tragedies, the area of tragedy has got to be enlarged to accommodate them—something which won't be altogether unprecedented because, after all, in the past, too, the concept of tragedy had to go beyond the Aristotelian definition and the post-Periclean works. The problem, however, is that so diverse is the nature of these plays—mutually as well as vis-a-vis earlier tragedies—that any effort to accommodate them under the umbrella of one definition is bound to make the concept of tragedy so vague, amorphous, loose and imprecise that everything under the sun would get covered. So much so that we shall have to put the label of tragedy on works that tradition has always rejected as untragic. No wonder, the traditionalists who insist on the old core of tragedy have declared tragedy extinct and one of the concerns of the twentieth century critics has been to discover reasons that precipitated the death of tragedy. On the other hand, there are those other critics who would rather change the scope and definition of tragedy, and they try to convince us that our age represents a peak for tragedy, comparable to the ones in the Periclean Greece and the Elizabethan England. George Steiner's *The Death of Tragedy* and Raymond Williams's *Modern Tragedy* are classic instances articulating these opposed stances.

Ibsen, Strindberg and Chekhov, who have been credited with the fatherhood of modern tragedy, did discover new awareness of tragic experience but they were still rooted in the tradition in a broad way. What each did could be compared to the felling down of one of the several pillars of a big hall: the roof still remained. But when one pulls down too many pillars, one after another, the roof is bound to come down. This is precisely what has been happening at the hands of Pirandello, Brecht, Arthur Miller, Sartre, Beckett et al. In saying this, we are not implying any denigration of their contribution. In fact, modern plays are certainly more stimulating intellectually and more exciting theatrically and full credit is due to the modern playwrights for discovering new avenues of dramatic material, new combinations of effects, new ways of penetrating genres, and new levels of responses in the audiences, and consequently liberating drama from the claustrophobic tyranny of the limited range of pure genres. But acknowledgement of this much contribution does not satisfy those who must call these plays tragedies. Tragedy, for them, is the highest of arts and thus calling the modern plays by any other name is regarded as an insult to their creators. It is forgotten that in aesthetic criticism there is no place for such valuational hierarchy amongst genres, and that, by trying to fix the modern plays into the pigeon-hole of tragedy, we shall be not only denying the playwrights the credit for opening up new genres but also forcing them into a situation where they cannot but suffer by contrast in comparison with the Greek and Elizabethan masters. In all fairness, these works should be evaluated as realistic, naturalistic, expressionistic, epic, existentialist, psychological, sociological, mythological, poetic, Absurd or grotesque plays as they were conceived by their authors. The pity, however, is that the proponents of 'modern tragedy' ignore the fact that, at times, even the playwrights themselves resent their plays being called tragedies. In any case, so far, no one has come out with any respectable, or even acceptable, poetics of new tragedy. Nevertheless, one thing is clear—that old Aristotelian elements of drama or tragic essentials like *hamartia*, *hubris*, *peripeteia*, *anagnorisis*, *catharsis*, etc., no longer have that force of validity; nor are plot and character that important because we have had plays without either. This is not to say that tragedy cannot be written today; tragedy cannot but remain. Whether or not the modern temper and tragedy are compatible companions is quite another issue. In any case, this is not the place to indulge in that controversy and so, therefore, all that we would wish to reiterate here is that the tragedy in the twentieth century is marked by bewildering diversity in respect of both theory and practice. What is more, the output is so stupendous in each sphere that one simply cannot mention all here. Inevitably, we have to be content with broad trends with an illustration here and there.

A look at the contents of *Tragedy: Modern Essays in Criticism*, ed. Laurence Michel and Richard B Sewall (Prentice-Hall), *Tragedy: Vision and Form*, ed. Robert W Corrigan (Harper & Row), *Moderns on Tragedy*, ed. Lionel Abel (Fawcet Premier), and *Tragedy: Developments in Criticism*, ed. R.P. Draper (Macmillan Casebook) should be enough to realize the versatility of critical interest in the field of the theory of tragedy by the twentieth century. Editing *Poetics* and interpreting or reinterpreting Aristotle from different angles has been one of the major pursuits and one immediately thinks of standard editions that have come to be regarded as texts—editions like those of S.H. Butcher, Humphry House, F.L. Lucas, Gerald F. Else, etc.

The theme of maximum interest in the current century continues to be tragic pleasure in general and *catharsis* in particular. Still concerned with the emotions of pity and fear, I.A. Richards has pointed out that, implying respectively an impulse towards and an impulse away from the object, they cancel each other. For W.P. Albrecht, pity makes the audience compassionate; fear combats pride. Kenneth Burke re-evaluates pity and fear in his own way: pity, he says, is not cruel; rather it is Lord's attitude in the New Testament. Feeling pity means feeling lordly. Similarly, fear too is a noble quality (for example, if we don't fear disgrace, we should be 'shameless'). Tragedy creates situations when man is proved worthy of fearing. According to Peter B. Waldeck, pity is related to danger (hence anxiety); to this is added guilt—the catharsis-eligible factor. Harvey Birenbaum has interpreted tragedy as a kind of celebration of disaster. Catharsis, he avers, purges us not out of feelings but into them; what is purged is our resistance, anxiety and guilt. Gerald F. Else has made a singular contribution by pleading that catharsis is brought about not by pity and fear but *through* (a course of) pity and fear. A.K. Abdullah has come out with a book titled *Catharsis in Literature*. According to him, catharsis is much more than tragic pleasure/experience. It is emotional excitation leading to intellectual understanding—begins with emotional arousal and ends with cognition, which thus subsumes emotional involvement. Catharsis, he argues, is an aesthetic response which begins with the audience identification with the protagonist and leads to emotional arousal of two conflicting emotions (viz., pity and fear). These emotions are resolved by their reconciliation, bringing to the audience a sense of elated harmony, or peace, or repose, which can be thought of as understanding, whether moral, metaphysical or psychological. Abdullah thus sees seven stages in the process and argues that confusion in critical theory stems from the fact that the critics focus attention on one or some of these stages and not on all of them. In two articles in *British Journal of Aesthetics* (Summer 1972 & Autumn 1977), K.G. Srivastava has tried to plead that catharsis means the aesthetic clarification not of emotions but of events! The hint came to him from Leon Golden who translated catharsis as 'intellectual clarity.' Srivastava's contention was later (Autumn 1977) challenged by E.P. Papanoustsos who pointed out that 'pathematon' means 'passions of the soul' and not incidents. Thanks to the profusion of critical attention, the notion of catharsis has become hazier and it is so unhelpful now that D.M. Hill and F.W. Bateson have gone to the extent of demanding its excision from the dictionary of critical terms.

The interest in catharsis continues, of course—even when the word is not used. For example, in Mark Packer's 'Dissolving the Paradox of Tragedy,' the assumption is that we enjoy being excited, enriched, purged and/or sensitized. Tragedy, Packer argues, accomplishes this by placing our emotions under the aesthetic control of art works. F.L. Lucas, of course, did not think of control factor but did imply enrichment of experience through the banquet of emotions. Roy Morrell, instead, notices in the process strengthening of psyche by means of shocks from outside. A Freudian that Morrell is, he interprets the Psychology of Tragic Pleasure in terms of death-instincts and goes on to aver that tragedy is man's rehearsal of harsher realities of life; the psyche's cell is forced out of its lethargy and it adapts itself to a more complex readiness for life. Bradley Berke in *Tragic Thought and the Grammar of Tragic Myth* puts a different construction on this very idea. According to him, through the heroic ideals presented to him, the spectator learns that the attainment of non-existence being difficult, he should be content with the hope that he may ultimately achieve bliss. And that contentment is tragic pleasure in all its intensity. For W.P. Albrecht (*The Sublime Pleasures of Tragedy*), the tragedy has a touch of the sublime about it. We learn to resist evil, which is admirable; terror is rendered agreeable by enthusiasm; courage, fortitude and magnanimity inspire awe; and there is a touch of mystery in the emotions aroused. Thus terror, awe, admiration, and marvellous combine into the sense of sublime and this sublimity is the power that elevates.

Some critics, especially those with psychological and anthropological interests, trace the pleasure to the release of primitive forces; they see in the use and structure of myth a strategy to strike deeper. In 1962, Daniel P. Garcia of the University of Oregon devoted a whole doctoral dissertation to these approaches in 'Theories of Catharsis in Modern Literary Criticism: The Influences of Psychoanalysis, Anthropology and New Criticism.' In the light of psycho-anthropological insights, Francis Fergusson came out with his tragic rhythm of Purpose, Passion and Perception and T.R. Henn perceived an analogy with trigger-and-spring. For Frederick A. Pottle, tragic process is 'psychic house-cleaning'—transformation of private day-dreaming into social day-dreaming. Helen Adolf sees in the hero's death a substitute for human sacrifice: a scapegoat, the hero represents the criminal in us. For Suzan L. Cole (*The Absent One*), tragedy is a form of community mourning. As we watch an actor/character become a mourner, we undergo a similar transaction with him. He enables us to feel the universal paradox of mourning more fully than is possible in our numbed and fragmentary experience of life's losses. To the psycho-anthropological discipline belong Richmond Y. Hathorn's *Tragedy, Myth and Mystery*, Herbert Weissinger's *The Psychology of the Paradox of the Fortunate Fall*, Susanne Langer's 'The Tragic Rhythm,' even Northrop Frye's 'The Mythos of Autumn' in *The Anatomy of Criticism.*

Interest in psychological business is parallelled by interest in metaphysics and transcendence. Wayne D. Dodd's dissertation, 'The Mortal Condition,' is sub-titled 'A Definition of Tragedy.' According to him, the tragic situation inheres man's mortality; failure to reconcile to this situation leads to suffering and then to glory: the mortality remains but we transcend the mortal condition. In fact, transcendence of one kind or the other is implicit in the explanations offered by many critics. Some bring in soul, others talk generally in terms of the spiritual. For W.B. Yeats, the 'passionate reverie' of tragedy is speech of the soul with itself—a heroic cry in the midst of despair. According to John Mason Brown, splendid sinners that they are, the tragic heroes lose their necks to save their souls. And this leaves the audience spiritually cross-ventilated. Maxwell Anderson's term is 'spiritual rejuvenation.' The purification through suffering teaches us that animal though we are in many ways, there is in us all some divine incalculable fire that urges us to be better than we are. Edith Hamilton sees in the tragic heroes a true aristocracy of passionate souls; empathizing with them, the audience experience transcendental exaltation of the spirit. Going by William Van O'Connor, it implies affirming of the rational soul against the fact of passional nature. Human soul learns to endure with dignity instead of bemoaning existential suffering: 'When the mind discovered spirit, there was tragedy.' This reminds us of Eugene O'Neill's exclamation, 'Where there is a soul, there is a tragedy!' According to Ernst Cassirer, in tragic poetry, the soul acquires a new attitude towards emotions: it experiences the emotions of pity and fear but, instead of being disturbed and disquieted by them, it is brought to a state of rest and peace—a calm that is not static but dynamic. In other words, it is not a case of change in the quality of emotions but a change in the percipient's soul.

Of course, the twentieth century has abounded with Hegel's and Nietzsche's followers, especially those who talk in terms of the sense of tragedy, the tragic sense of life, the vision of tragedy, the spirit of tragedy, the tragic view, the tragic philosophy, etc. What Unamuno called the tragic sense of life, Richard B. Sewall terms the vision of tragedy—not a systematic view of life but one that calls up the question of existence and impels the man of action to kick against the pricks and state his case before God or his own fellows. For Sewall, a primitive sense of horror at the secret cause of suffering comes to grip man when he is impelled to the 'boundary-situation' and, facing the existential question, broods over his destiny involving doom, evil and disintegration of the whole society. The secret cause is also at the root of Normand Berlin's approach in *The Secret Cause: A Discussion of Tragedy*. What we know is that we cannot know. As the cause will remain a secret, it is left for us to dance to the mysterious tune as best we can, knowing that the piper will always remain invisible. For Murray Krieger, tragic vision is a vision of extreme cases, a distillate of the rebellion, the godlessness which, once induced by crisis, purifies itself by rejecting all palliatives. Charles I. Glicksberg is more positive in his interpretation of the tragic vision (*Tragic Vision and the Twentieth Century*). According to him, tragedy implies a denial of the myth of nothingness: life may be absurd but it is *not* NOTHING. Facing the appalling truth of life's absurdity, man affirms the value of life itself. His struggle against the naturalisitc chaos is the measure of his greatness. Lucien Goldmann sees not one but several forms of tragic vision but they all have one thing common—they all express a deep crisis in the relationship between man and his social and spiritual world. Tragedy is a universe of agonising questions to which man has no reply because this world is at one and the same time both nothing and everything. The God of tragedy is a God who is always present and always absent. The tragic man can therefore have one valid attitude—that of saying both 'Yes' and 'No.'

For Henry A. Myers, the tragic is neither a vision nor a philosophy; it is a view of life—neither optimistic (since it doesn't deny evil) nor pessimistic (owing to ultimate regeneration). Thus tragedy depicts inevitable relation between good and evil by fastening our mind on the two necessary sides of a value and showing specific evil in relation to the concomitant good. For Max Scheler, too, tragic is contained within the realm of values. To belong to the category of the tragic, a value must be destroyed because only then can a new value be born. The entanglement of the two in the unity of the tragic action and the tragic event is what Scheler means by 'tragic knot.'

This knot that interlocks 'Yes' and 'No,' destsruction and creation, is what critics imply when they talk of affirmation in the face of disaster and failure. Man is seen as placed in a hostile world in which, struggling to discover the significance of life, he realizes its meaninglessness and yet affirms life, now with the knowledge of its absurdity. Butcher sees in tragedy mortal will engaged in unequal struggles that end in the reassertion of moral forces. Adrian Poole (*Tragedy: Shakespeare and the Greek Example*) sees tragedy honouring the diversity of human beings: it affirms with savage jubilation that man's state is diverse, fluid and unfounded. In *The Gorgon's Head*, William R. Brashear talks of tragedy covering the negative thinker with glory—by lending to suffering a deeper significance. Likewise, E.W.L. Dahlstrom, in his 'An Approach to Tragedy,' has argued that instead of enduring pain like other animals, man tries to project his mind beyond the planes of occurrence and suffers as a consequence, but in this very suffering lies the promise of human greatness. Though crushed by the universe, man establishes his superiority in this knowledge of being crushed whereas the world does not know that it crushes him. William McCollom also sees in tragedy the relationship between self-transcending power of man and the half-recognised but recognisably persisting cosmos. Thus get interwoven fate and freedom. A conscious and free agent, the hero makes a choice which spells his disaster but that disaster is not just a personal catastrophe; it is much more—a monument to the freedom of human choice. Thus choice, not chance, is the crux of the tragic for McCollom. For George Steiner, too, man's claim to dignity is contingent on his suffering: it does not make hero innocent but hallows him as if he had passed through fire. Likewise, for T.R. Henn, the harvest of tragedy lies in the freedom and enrichment of the human spirit. The hero is led to commit evil but, in a flash of spiritual or intellectual grandeur, he makes the evil look futile. John Gassner also sees in tragedy man endowed with a perverse but somehow admirable nobility.

Cleanth Brooks in his 'Introduction' to *The Tragic Themes in Western Literature* declares that the essence of the tragic themes pertains to meaning of suffering. Man suffers but he does not know why; he cannot know it. It is a damning vision, indeed; but the very yearning to know is the source of his glory. He may never know the truth in toto but he embodies in himself all the truth there is. Of course, Aldous Huxley sees things from another perspective when he declares that the truth of tragedy is not total but partial—*sans* many aspects that won't fit the tragic vision. Timothy Reiss, in *Tragedy and Truth*, however, projects tragedy as a discourse which contributes centrally to the production of knowledge regarding individual will, power and responsibility. This gaining of knowledge has been accepted by many critics as the source of pleasure: it makes one feel wiser. This is what makes tragedy, in the words of F.R. Leavis, a positive and creative experience. What is more, this knowledge has an ennobling aspect. In 'Tragedy and History,' F. Mc Eachran has shown that the true idealism of tragedy lies in awakening men to a realization that things and events are hostile to man and that his greatness lies in this realization itself. That renders the realization into a noble act of piety and a most profound religious feeling.

Indeed, man's peculiar situation is often projected as the core of tragedy—his frailty and fragility which he cannot help *plus* his attitude of defiance towards his frailty. For Robert W. Corrigan, it amounts to accepting frailty but with a protest. According to Herbert J. Muller, such indeed is the spirit of tragedy. Tragedy, according to him, presents the mysterious, paradoxical and pessimistic ways of providence but, steering clear of cynicism, it humanistically affirms some positive values. The pleasure that it yields is neither mere relief nor moral uplift; it springs from recognition of the possibilities in a man's life. Man is an animal who is a source of sorrow to himself, to his fellows and even to his creator; but he is also the one animal with a power of conscious choice. Capable of aspiring to truth, beauty and holiness, man is the one animal who can say that he is the measure of all things and this when he knows too that he is the prey of all things. In his conflict with the fate, he goes through the worst and yet forces fate to conclude an honourable peace to coexist—a peace without victory on either side. Tragedy thus yields a pleasure comparable to the satisfaction of having played well although the game was lost. For D.D. Raphael, it is a paradoxical situation—an awe-inspiring victory for necessity on a natural plane and admiration-arousing victory for hero on the spiritual plane. Thus seen, tragedy presupposes, as Theodore Haecker has put it, not only the imperfection but also the fullness of man's existence; consequently, the fact of guilt emerges as the life-blood of human existence. Since man's imperfection and frailty are rooted in the original sin, morality and ontology tend to become one, as Laura Jepsen has argued. No wonder H.A. Mason has declared in *The Tragic Plane* that tragedy is ultimately a mystery which cannot be classified under philosophy, theology, psychology, Marxism, structuralism, post-structuralism, etc. Tragedy has to accept two contradictory propositions—being at once an affair of men and the concern of gods. Tragic paradox lies in man's dangling between two extremes: if he is a puppet at the mercy of Fate, he cannot be a hero; if he thinks he is in control of everything, he is a deluded fool.

But can one really live after such a realization and after accepting this position? In art, yes; in life, perhaps not. At least such is the contention of Lionel Abel in 'Is there a Tragic Sense of Life?' (rep. Corrigan anthology):

> We admire him [tragic writer] then for what he makes us see, a world where the highest values collide and in which we know we could not live. We recognize this when the curtain comes down and we do not know where to go. We have to become optimists or pessimists again in order to think of going home.

To put it differently, the so-called tragic sense of life cannot be a way of life in actual existence. J.C. Maxwell, on the other hand, denies that there exists any such thing as a tragic view of things: to presuppose such a vision is to place tragedy on a separate footing from the other main literary forms. Maybe, one could say with Una Ellis-Fermor that tragedy is an interim reading of life: it reveals that balance, that uncertainty which sees two worlds of being and cannot wholly accept either. The frontiers that tragedy seeks to balance are universe and man, passion and event, action and catastrophe. This balance, according to Ellis-Fermor, is essential because, without it, the play would be a melodrama.

For Oscar Mandel, tragedy is a quality, not a situation—a way of feeling in failure. Death is not evil; it is bitter only because life is good. His definition of tragedy insists on earnestness, good will, inevitability and spiritual or physical suffering. After Aristotle, very few critics have dared to offer a definition of tragedy; Mandel being one of them, his definition deserves to be quoted at length:

> A work of art is tragic if it substantiates the following situation: A protagonist who commands our earnest good will is impelled in a given world by a purpose, or undertakes an action, of a certain seriousness and magnitude; and by that very purpose or action, subject to that same given world, necessarily and inevitably meets with grave spiritual or physical suffering.

Of course, there are those who are convinced that the paradoxical essence of tragedy being what it is, it cannot be defined. Stephen Booth has an interesting point to make in this connection. In his *King Lear, Macbeth, Indefinition and Tragedy*, he asks what is tragedy and answers, 'A word.' The function of word is to fix a category, but tragedy, he argues, is something that cannot be categorized. Besides, 'definition,' coming from 'finis' (a limit, an end), sets limits; but the spirit of tragedy denies any limits. Therefore, concludes Booth, definition of tragedy would be a contradiction in terms! Thus seen, the word 'tragedy,' theories of tragedy, and the plays we call tragedies are futile (though benign) efforts to deny the existence of tragedy.

In the light of this interesting piece of logic, it becomes understandable why, avoiding the straitjacket of definition, critics in the twentieth century have been content to talk about certain aspects of tragedy—for example, essence, elements, characteristics, etc. Thus does Maxwell Anderson talk about *The Essence of Tragedy*:

> A play should lead up to and away from a central crisis, and this crisis should consist in a discovery by the leading character who has an indelible effect on his thought and emotion and completely alters his course of action. The leading character, let me say again, must make the discovery; it must affect him emotionally, and it must alter his direction in the play.

For Dorothea Krooks tragedy has four essential elements:

> (a) Act of shame or horror which precipitates suffering;

(b) Suffering which leads to the understanding of man's condition;
(c) Tragic knowledge which paves the way for the affirmation of the human spirit;
(d) Re-affirmation regarding the worthwhileness of human life.

Northrop Frye goes by quintessential phases. Of course, since he relates tragedy to the Mythos of Autumn, rather than Spring, he puts things in an altogether different (nearly reverse) order:

(1) Dignity born of courage or innocence;
(2) Loss of innocence;
(3) Passion;
(4) Fall through hybris (experience);
(5) Isolation;
(6) Loss of direction;
(7) Horror (demonic epiphany).

For Lucien Goldmann, the three constituent elements of every tragedy are: '*an essentially insoluble conflict*, resulting from the clash between a *world* which knows only relativity, compromise, the more or less, and a *universe* dominated by the need for *absolute values*, for *totality*, and governed by the law of *all or nothing*.'

In the beginning of *Shakespeare's Tragedies and Other Studies in Seventeenth Century Drama*, Clifford Leech has talked about the 'implications' of tragedy. Likewise, Karl Jaspers has expatiated on some 'basic characteristics' of the tragic in his *Tragedy is Not Enough*—for example, the tragic atmosphere; battle and collision; the individual and the universal; the clash of ways of life; men against gods; gods against one another; victory and defeat; guilt; man's greatness in failure, etc.

Most favourite[2] theme of the critics in the twentieth century has been the Tragic Hero—more so, because it is through him that the vision of tragedy is shared. In fact, it is possible to say that when critics talk about the vision, view, spirit, or sense of tragedy, they are mostly talking about the tragic hero. Anyway, much has been written on the hero exclusively. George Boas, for example, has traced the evolution of the hero through ages; Henry Alonzo Myers has devoted to it a whole chapter, 'The Heroes and the Way of Compromise.' He concludes:

> The hero takes all, gives all in one grand moment. The moderate man pays a little, lives to doze in his chair, and pays a little more. The choice between intensity and duration cannot upset the just equation whereby men pay with their lives for experience.

We have an echo of this in David Lenson's *Achilles' Choice*. Achilles' choice was either to die in the Trojan War and thus earn everlasting glory or to return home and live long but ingloriously. This choice is archetype of the decision faced by every tragic hero. Myers' Moderate Man is not necessarily a common man, for a common man, too, can be a tragic hero, as Arthur Miller has shown in his 'Tragedy and the Common Man.' A seminal contribution in the context of modern tragedy, it has rightly stressed that what is essential for the tragic hero is not status but stature.

W.H. Auden has written about the Christian tragic hero—Captain Ahab in contrast to the Greek prototype, viz., Oedipus. That reminds us of the critiques on the compatibility of religion and tragedy and the possibility of Christian tragedy by Laurence Michel, Sylvan Barnet, Nathan A. Scott (*Tragic Vision and the Christian Faith*), Helen Gardner (*Religion and Literature*), Thomas G. Rosenmeyer (*Tragedy and Religion*).

Another facet of the theory of tragedy that has frequently attracted critical attention is its relationship to other genres like comedy, melodrama, etc. Walter Kerr, for example, has devoted a whole book to the comparison—*Tragedy and Comedy*. According to him, a tragedy is a play of cleansing and transfiguration: 'It is tragedy, not comedy, which sings the praises of man.' Tragedy admires man, comedy feels sorry for him. In the words of William I. Thompson, comedy avoids evil, tragedy confronts it. Marie Collins Swabey's book is on Comic Laughter, but she talks about its antithesis, too. Comedy, she says, aims at making honest men laugh; tragedy affords a glimpse into cosmic justice beyond the earthly scales of requittal. Both further the zest for living, but tragedy only when everything has been cast in jeopardy. Comedy is skating, tragedy a voyage of the soul. L.J. Potts treats the twin genres not as antitheses but as complementaries. He projects tragedy as a bulwark of human self-respect against the superhuman and inhuman forces, comedy being a weapon against the forces of disintegration within human society. Comedy, says Potts, gives knowledge of the world, tragedy the courage never to submit or yield. Tragedy deals with the normal people in unusual situations; comedy with the eccentric people in normal situations. On the other hand, distinguishing between the two genres in *The Dark Voyage and the Golden Mean*, Albert Cook declares that tragedy deals with the wonderful, the extreme, the heroic individual; comedy, with the probable, the mean and the social norm. Maxwell Anderson points out that tragedy and comedy originated from two complementary religious ceremonies—one celebrating gods, the other phallus or the human animality. Friedrich Durrenmatt also treats both tragedy and comedy as fragments of the same aesthetic imagination, only the conditions of creation are different: tragedy presupposes a formed world, comedy assumes a world being made; tragedy overcomes distance, comedy creates it. For Northrop Frye, it is a case of different Modes—high and low mimesis.[3]

The critical literature relating tragedy to melodrama is comparatively small but very much there. Witness: Eric Bentley's *The Life of the Drama*, Robert Heilman's *Tragedy and Melodrama: Visions of Experience*, Alan Reynolds Thompson's 'Melodrama and Tragedy.' In this connection, it is worthwhile to recall Elder Olson's distinction between an experience and a significant experience. There have also been studies relating the tragic to the ironic, the grotesque and the Absurd. Even in tragedy itself, there can be types, as shown by C.E. Vaughan's *Types of Tragic Drama*. The differences get related to the differences in ages that produced them—as shown in William Van O'Connor's *The Climates of Tragedy*. Anyway, when O'connor declares that tragedy will be written again when modern man learns to see in man the astronomer rather than an astronomically negligible unit in the universe, he emerges as a participant in the controversy about the compatibility of tragedy and modern temper. The others who have written about this aspect include Joseph Wood Krutch ('Tragic Fallacy' in *Modern Temper*), John Gassner ('The Possibilities and Perils of Modern Tragedy'), Kenneth Burke ('On Tragedy'), Raymond Williams (*Modern Tragedy*), Walter Kerr ('Tragedy Now' in *Tragedy and Comedy*), Louis I. Bredvold ('The Modern Temper and the Tragic Drama'), John von Szeliski (*Tragedy and Fear*). As R.W. Corrigan's anthology shows, numerous efforts have been made to relate tragedy to our time and theorize on tragedy today. Witness, Eugene Kaelin's 'Towards a Theory of Contemporary Tragedy,' Leslie Fiedler's 'Our Country, Our Culture,' and Orrin E. Klapp's 'Tragedy and the American Climate of Opinion.' There have also been several attempts to relate tragedy to the diverse modern intellectual movements—for example, by Sidney Hook ('Pragmatism and the Tragic Sense of Life'), S.E. Hyman ('Psychoanalysis and the Climates of Tragedy'), and Wylie Sypher ('Aesthetic of Revolution: The Marxist Melodrama'). Of interest in this connection is the way Marxist view of man has been adapted into the service of tragic theory—say, by George Lukacs. According to him, man lives on two levels—as individual (specific) and as social entity (generic). In a tragic experience, when the two collide, there is a shock. This shock is what Lukacs regards as the bedrock of catharsis. Thus does he unite aesthetics with ethics.

Unabated is the modern critics' interest in the age-old issues of tragedy, like its origin (Wayne Shumaker), its metaphysics (George

Lukacs), its relationship to Myth and Ritual (Harold H. Watts), the centrality of emotionalism (W.B. Stanford), ethical dimension (John D. Barbour), language of tragedy (Moody E. Prior), etc. Of course, modern critics have not forgotten the past: the amount of critical writing on tragedy in the past ages, especially the Greek and the Shakespearean tragedy, is simply incredible. Common enough is the effort to indulge in comparisons and contrasts with the moderns—in respect of both theory and practice. Writing on tragedy in *Playwrights, Lyricists, Composers on Theatre*, Israel Horovitz makes interesting observations when he says that Hegel saw in tragedy a conflict between two goods, while in modern times the conflict is between two evils. In classical tragedy, hero discovers his mortality at the end; in modern tragedy, he has overwhelming knowledge of mortality throughout.

Obviously, the above survey is a proof (if one was ever needed) that the diversity inhering the theory and practice of tragedy is too vast to allow room for any measure of unanimity—unless one could be content with totally inane and simplistic statements. But, then, one cannot wish away the above history because any attempt at generalization must reckon with this divergence. Even if one had some brand new approach to offer, it shall have to be validated in the light of the past practice. Perhaps it is absolutely necessary to pick up from the above survey such insights as, despite their mutually clashing shades, might be least controversial and therefore broadly acceptable. The big idea is to reduce the range of controversy to the minimum so that it is possible to focus attention on the limited spectrum of near-consensus.

- — There isn't (nor can there be) anything final about the concept or the theory of tragedy which has been changing to accommodate new types.
- — There have been not only types of tragedy but also 'climates' of tragedy.
- — Reflecting the spirit of the age, tragedies of a certain age tend to group themselves together as a type.
- — Even in the same age, there may exist several variations, depending on individual geniuses of the authors.
- — There is so much variety that one may talk of tragedies, not of Tragedy.
- — Tragedy breeds a sense of mystery about life—a painful mystery.
- — Tragedy raises questions to which there are no answers, and yet it launches the reader on an exploration to find them.

— The secret of tragedy remains ever unknown and the hero seems to dance to a mysterious tune.
— Myth is not an essential element of tragedy but its use has invariably facilitated striking deep via archetypal level.
— There are no fixed tragic themes and yet the quality of experience in tragedy is assumed to be pre-determined.
— What is peculiar to all tragedies is the quality of experience and not the situations.
— Action of tragedy is serious, sober, sad and grand on the epical scale.
— The action of every tragedy has three inalienable elements—intensity, inevitability, insight.
— Tragedies have invariably depicted crimes, murders incest and other perversities.
— The most common concerns of tragedy are disaster, distress and death.
— There is always a change in the situation, a reversal.
— The episodes in a tragedy are inter-related to each other like wheels within wheels in a watch—moving at speeds so diverse as to look chaotic but actually governed by a most logical network.
— Tragedy denotes a process, not a point.
— Tragic rhythm comprises Purpose, Passion, Perception.
— In tragedy, imperfection of the hero leads to such action as breeds guilt and suffering which make life miserable but ensure the fullness of existence.
— Tragic process implies a voyage of the soul from shame to suffering to affirmation through worthwhileness of life.
— At the heart of tragedy is a vision, a sense of life, but that is by no means a systematized world-view.
— Tragedy is the most humanistic art—everything is centred around man, his nature, his relations with this world and with the cosmos at large.
— Man-centred, tragedy underlines the ultimate oneness of man: it glorifies diversity and fallibility of man.
— Hamartia is man's existence, hubris is man's will to remain human—not content to be a mere animal, but not aspiring to godhood either.
— Tragic artist may or may not have faith in God, but he must have faith in Man.
— Tragedy raises such questions as 'Is man no more than this?' and we learn to answer: Yes, he is awful but noble, too.
— Tragedy brings the realilzation that man may not know the truth

in toto but he embodies it.

- Measure of all things, man is also a puppet that pulls its own strings: an object of pity as well as admiration, a victor as well as a victim, man emerges in tragedy as a living paradox.
- The function of tragedy is to humanize the reader—to feel, even weep over, the sufferings of another fellow being as if these were his own.
- One of the paradoxes of tragedy is that, living in a world of relativity, man needs absolute values which don't exist at all.
- What every tragedy has in common is a damning world view—chaos in cosmos, in nature, in the world of man, and in the human nature.
- Tragedy thrives on demonic, anti-rational environs; it highlights what man does to man, including himself.
- Brooding over human situation, i.e., the existential position of man, tragedy shudders at the absurd and the chaotic in life, but goes on to deny the myth of Nothingness.
- Tragedy seeks to balance the positive and the negative: it says 'yes' to everything, even to the negative in man.
- Core of tragedy lies in the heroic stance of protest in deep despair.
- Tragedy shows man grovellilng in the lowest depths as well as revelling at the highest peaks.
- Tragedy celebrates disaster, but only that kind of disaster which radiates glory in failure.
- Tragedy projects the paradox of life: it is good because it is painful; it is bitter as well as sweet.
- There is tragic in life but no tragedy: what is learnt in tragedy cannot be practised in life. Tragic knowledge thus tends to be like a flash of lightning at night which dazzles for a moment but leaves one shuddering in the darkness.
- Tragedy is a discourse that yields such Dionysian wisdom as cannot be categorized under theology, metaphysics, ethics, epistemology, or psychology because it is all of these at one and the same time.
- Litmus test of a tragedy lies in the quality of suffering and the response of the spirit of man to his suffering.
- In tragedy, the role of suffering is creative—it lends dignity, meaning and significance to human life.
- A tragedy need not end in death; more essential to the close is restfulness accompanied by a lingering sense of mystery.
- A tragic hero suffers but it is creative suffering because it makes

him wiser.

— Tragic hero's suffering is disproportionate—like the huge force released at the mere touch of a trigger.
— Tragic hero has before him an Achilles' choice—glorious death or inglorious life.
— A tragic hero loses the world to save his soul.
— A tragic hero may not have high status but he must have high stature.
— Tragic flaw is not necessarily an emotional, intellectual or moral weakness; at times, it may be a most desirable virtue and a point of strength.
— Like tragic flaw and moral flaw, tragic guilt and moral guilt must be distinguished.
— Non-compromising, rejecting all palliatives, and insisting on 'All or Nothing,' the hero reveals something that is at once perverse and admirable. His consequent glory in failure leaves one baffled because one cannot decide whether to take it as a warning against man's overstepping his limits or as an exhortation to live dangerously.
— Action of tragedy serves as a warning to the high-ups to behave themselves.
— Tragic ideal is excellency of the Moral; tragedy abounds in evil only to expose its deformity.
— In a truly tragic world, relativity reigns supreme: thanks to the paradoxical outcome of everything, foul is fair and fair is foul. In its handy-dandy, hero and villain are equally guilty: 'None does offend, none!'
— In tragedy, conflict is not between good and evil, nor between two evils, nor even between partially good and partially evil, but between one kind of good against another kind of good.
— In tragedy, virtue is promoted not through reward for it but through punishment of evil. Undeserved suffering of the virtuous is accounted for as tragic waste—the necessary price paid for eliminating evil, like the sacrifice on a god's altar.
— Tragic hero moves from prosperity to adversity—a fall that is parallelled by a rise in his spiritual glory.
— The harvest of tragedy is the enrichment of spirit.
— Where there is a soul, there is a tragedy.
— The spiritualism of tragedy is related not to God or to the gods but to the human spirit.
— Physically man is doomed to defeat but, in the process, man's spirit triumphs over his fate: the hero realizes not only that he is

morally responsible because the choice was his but also the fact that the choice was worth-making as well as inevitable.

— Reinforcing one's faith in man's will, tragedy effects a kind of spiritual rejuvenation.
— Emotions are certainly stirred in a tragedy and we welcome this excitement as it is a relief from the emotional lethargy or inertia of routine existence.
— Through a plunge into primordial authenticity, tragedy affords psychic cross-ventilation.
— Pity and fear are aroused by a tragedy but not these emotions alone; it may touch our heart on other levels, too.
— Besides pity and fear, we feel admiration, sense of wonder, awe, as also aversion—in fact, the entire gamut of emotions.
— Pity, fear, admiration, wonder, all having been evoked, tragic experience belongs to the realm of the sublime.
— Catharsis is a community feeling—like communal mourning.
— By putting all in jeopardy in the crisis between man and his world, tragedy heightens the stark absurdity of human existence; but later, when the irreconcilables are reconciled in the celebration of failure, life no longer looks unworthy of living, and thus the pattern of dialectics is completed.
— The emotional and the cognitive are so blended that one feels as if one were thinking with heart and feeling with head.
— The quality of tragic experience is comparable to the satisfaction of having played well a game that has been lost.
— Essentially tragic vision is neither moral nor purgative but aesthetic.
— With emotional excitement leading to intellectual stimulation, psychic release, and stirring of the spirit, tragedy affords the most satisfying aesthetic experience.
— Tragic pleasure is the result of the alchemy of art.
— No great tragedy sends one out in morbid state of mind.
— Though aesthetic, tragic pleasure has something peculiar about it—it is born of pain.
— All passions spent, a reader feels sadly mystified and exhausted but it is majestic sadness; tragic pleasure is a species of the mystical rapture.
— Tragedy is high mimesis, comedy a low one; tragedy admires man, comedy feels sorry for him; tragedy deals with fate, comedy with fortune; tragedy is a voyage of the soul, comedy intellectual skating; tragedy presupposes a formed world, comedy assumes a world being made; comedy avoids evil, tragedy confronts it; com-

> dey gives knowledge of the world, tragedy the courage never to submit or yield; comedy is a weapon against the forces of disintegration, tragedy a bulwark of human self-respect against the superhuman and inhuman forces around him.

Is it possible to reconcile all this in a single formulation with respect to tragic pleasure? The task has tragic ramifications—a finite vision handling the infinite. Anyway, before an effort in that direction is made, we might attempt a couple of broad simplifications. One: when the details are kept out, the paradox of tragic impact inheres the fact that it has three aspects, viz., emotive, cognitive and spiritual. Two: following Aristotle, Hegel and Nietzsche, when the critics mostly talk about catharsis, tragic sense of life, or Dionysian ecstasy, they concentrate exclusively on one of those aspects and ignore the rest. The problem arises because tragedy deals with man in his totality so much so that one might say that the very essence of tragedy lies in its rejecting the customary attitude of treating head, heart and spirit as exclusive functionaries. Thus while, for the sake of convenience, one may think of the three dimensions separately, one by one, any attempt at compartmentalization should be discounted.

That the tragic experience does appeal to one's heart goes without saying. The entire range of critical theory, right from Plato (or even Socrates) centres round the 'centrality of emotionalism in tragedy' as the title of the opening chapter of W.B. Stanford's *Greek Tragedy and Emotions* puts it. Even those who want the excision of 'catharsis' do own the presence of emotions. The differences in approaches pertain to the nature of emotions or the process of 'catharsis.' Whether it is just pity, just fear, pity and fear, pity versus fear, either of them plus any other emotions, or a whole spectrum of them—that has been the point of debate. Whether it is a case of purification, tempering or reducing to just measures (Milton), controlling through right direction (Humphry House), enrichment (F.L. Lucas, or purging the tragic event (Gerald F. Else), emotions are always assumed to be present. More recently, breaking away from the obsessive stranglehold of catharsis, critics have been prompted by their growing interest in psychology, anthropology, sociology, etc., to discover deeper roles for emotions. For example, Bergson relates emotionalism to atavism and suggests that tragedy enables us to dream ourselves back into a more primitive and passionate state; Roy Morrell sees in tragedy rehearsal of harsher realities of life when the cells of psyche are forced out of lethargy by the shocking events; Edith Hamilton talks about the aristocracy of passionate souls and sees in the process of tragedy pain being transmuted into exaltation by the alchemy of poetry. There is, of course, that other trend, led by T.R. Henn—to discern in tragic pleasure something akin to exorcism. As in a scapegoat's ritualistic sacrifice, the hero's death is a kind of expiation. This notion of suffering for others (like Christ) lends to the hero's passion a Christian connotation and thus highlights in the tragic process the new element of spiritual catharsis. Indeed, it is worth realizing that, in a tragic experience, the emotions do not remain pure feelings because they are evoked only to be yoked into the service of the play's vision. Consciously aroused, they are attenuated with a matching care later towards the end so that either we find ourselves restful in a situation of 'all passions spent,' or else our sympathies are so altered, shaken or confounded that we feel totally shattered emotively. One could recall for comparison the role of emotions in a melodrama: there, they are for their own sake and survive till the end. To put it differently, although so prominent, emotions in tragedy are there not for their own sake but only to serve a pivotal role in the alchemy of art—by being related to the intellectual and/or the spiritual dimension.

Thanks to the sway of Aristotle's authority, for about 2,500 years, tragedy was completely identified with emotional churning. Even when Philip Sidney in his *Apologie for Poesie* referred to tragedy being more 'philosophical' than history, he meant its being more coherent and orderly rather than more metaphysical. It was only after Hegel that the critics started perceiving in tragedy intellectual content in the form of a way of life, a world view, a vision. Indeed, the twentieth century critics have often talked in terms of philosophy, ethics, values in tragedy. As regards the basic concern of philosophy, it is human truth, and that gets discussed under four categories—logical, moral, aesthetic and metaphysical; consequently, there are four major branches of philosophy—logic, ethics, aesthetics and metaphysics. It is possible to argue that in tragedy we have traces of all the four.

Aesthetic aspect needs no elaboration: after all, tragedy denotes the highest genre in the art of drama. Aristotle's *Poetics* was an attempt at analysing the quality of the aesthetic response which this dramatic form of mimetic poetry evokes. When critics interpret him in terms of purification or purging of emotions, getting out of the shells of personal self, sharing the universal, experiencing the exaltation, and explaining the tragic pleasure, the concern, in fact, is always with the aesthetic aspect. In their own special way have the latter-day critics analysed the aesthetics of tragedy when they have spoken of balance and harmony. However, as already maintained, the aesthetics of tragedy is a matter not of emotions alone but something deeper that touches the spiritual.

Likewise, on the level of logic, tragedy does not offer well-knit, rationally evolved arguments; its logic is not linear but multi-dimensional. Indeed, it is not dogmatic but metadogmatic because its arguments come in the form of insights rather than cerebral formulations. How could there be pure cognition in an art that is deeply emotive? No wonder, Unamuno talks of 'felt philosophy' in tragedy.

When Aristotle insisted on tragic hero being neither perfectly good nor totally evil, he was not assuming an ethical framework; but ethical aspect of tragedy has come to be treated as something all-too-obvious by every one after Hegel. Henn hints at the possibility of a tragedy accommodating any one or two or even all the three forms of evil—intellectual, moral and emotional. Even otherwise, whenever there is a talk of choice before the hero, it assumes the framework of ethics or value-system. Moral choice has to be made and that proves the seed of the turmoil. Max Scheler's tragic knot also pertains to values—destruction of one and the creation of another. William O'Connor perceives in tragic process the creation of good out of evil. Of course, as D.D. Raphael has insisted, tragic artist is a moralist who does not preach. Myers, on the other hand, observes that tragic artist sees both sides of a value and thus, instead of taking a one-dimensional, partisan stand, he highlights the relativity of human values. Hegel too is concerned with the harmony of the opposites even as Nietzsche avers that tragedy goes beyond evil and good. In other words, tragedy is concerned with good and evil but not in the way of the ethical philosophers.

As for metaphysics, tragedy does accommodate all that the metaphysicist philosophers deal with in their pursuits—the question of existence, the position of man in the world and the universe, man's relations with the self, society and the cosmos, and the scope and limits of human mind. In fact, it is possible to say that tragedy has its own ontology, cosmology, and epistemology.

The vision of tragedy being concerned primarily with man, every tragedy raises, as Sewall avers, the question of existence: what does it mean to be a man? From that poser sprout several offshoots—problem of mortality, the Original Sin, guilt, existential suffering, Free Will, man's relation with man, with other beings, with fate, etc. As Oscar Mandel puts it, man is projected in tragedy as a puppet that feels, and a puppet that pulls its own strings. Most of his problems spring from this ontological situation. But, then, the sense of tragedy also views man in relation to the world, the cosmos and even gods, and underlines how, in his effort to give himself a meaningful role, he has transcended the ontological handicap by denying the myth of Nothingness. Thus he has come to claim parity even with the gods—by first conceiving gods in his own image and then aspiring to be god-like. Man is the only animal who knows about mortality and who is trying to overcome the handicap. All this brings into tragedy its own brand of cosmology. In the battle with cosmic powers, he goes down but not without learning the meaning of suffering. Tragedy leaves one brooding over truth, about the nature of knowledge, its scope and limits, and man's capacity (rather, incapacity) to realize it in full. Tragedy brings home the realization that for the universe man may be nothing, but for himself he is everything. Besides, he may not know the truth in toto but he embodies all of it in himself. Tragedy induces, too, the Dinoysiac wisdom that living is one thing and knowing quite another. Such is the epistemology of tragedy.

Tragedy has thus all kinds of metaphysical strains. But, as can be seen easily, the question of evil and the question of existence tend to coalesce in tragedy; what is more, here ethics and metaphysics also tend to become one. The whole of tragic metaphysics is rooted in the concept of existential dichotomy and man's effort to transcend it; but, instead of bringing in a rational or supra-rational system, tragedy proceeds to affirm life through the a-rational faculties of intuition, insights and feelings.

In short, one can say that tragedy does have logic but logic of the heart; it is ethical but revolts against the ethical categories; it is metaphysical but seeks transcendence without the mediation of God; as for its aesthetics, here senses are harnessed to mirror the spirit.

As the logic, ethics, aesthetics and metaphysics of tragedy tend to coalesce, one does feel tempted to talk about tragic philosophy but, in the absence of any rational system, one can treat it, at best, as a sub-philosophy—not flowing from ideas but determining them. Or perhaps one should regard it as something comparable to pre-philosophical formulations by a primitive man to overcome the ontological terror attendant on his existential insecurity. Anyway, as against philosophy that tries to deduce a convincing logical answer to the questions posed, tragedy just raises the questions. No wonder, more often than not, tragedy leaves one's mind mystified and almost befuddled.

Religion, too, was man's answer to existential insecurity, before he could resolve his problems philosophically. Primordial man invented God and attributed the inexplicable to His will. He also created myths that would justify the ways of God to man. When all this led to codification, there came into being theology in which the fundamental tenet was implicit faith in God and His omnipresence, omnipotence as well as omniscience. Tragedy, born of the same impulse, was defiant in tone and temper and therefore placed man, with all his failings, at the centre of the universe. Since that inevitably brought in some kind of rivalry-turned-hostility between man and God/gods, glory was supposed to lie in man's defiant spirit. True, both tragedy and religion recognise the presence of evil, both strive to make life tolerable; but there the similarity ends. Tragedy has no set metaphysics, rituals or theology of its own. It does require faith, but faith in man rather than in God. Singing hymns in praise of the human spirit and its versatility, tragedy refuses to accept ready-made solutions through Faith, Charity and Hope. It has no dogma; instead, it insists on not binding life into dogmas and formulae. It urges man to realize his own potential, howsoever imperfect, and not to depend on any outside force, howsoever benign, to get out of the trap into which existence has placed him. Indeed, that explains why religion and tragedy cannot go together far enough. Religion might have been born of the sense of the tragic but, by offering the hope of divine justice, religion killed the tragic. No wonder, I.A. Richards has declared that the least touch of theology is fatal to tragedy. No wonder, too, in the so-called Christian tragedies of Corneille, it is often felt that where a play is tragic, it is not Christian, and where it is Christian, it is not tragic. In short, the experience of tragedy is spiritual, but the force here is neither divine nor superhuman; it is an intangible, immaterial something, a kind of disembodied intelligence which epitomizes the essence shared by all humans—in varying degrees, of course. While reading or watching a tragedy, one feels this spirit awakened.

From what we have said above, it should be clear that tragic pleasure cannot be explained in terms of emotional catharsis, philosophical dialectics, or spiritual transcendence; one must reckon with the emotional, the intellectual and the spiritual at one and the same time. Before we see how all these levels get involved, it is necessary to reiterate something quite obvious, almost trite—that all tragedies evoke a uniquely distinct aesthetic response, a mysterious impact which is at once painful and pleasurable. Probed further, it would be seen that the response is not just a blend of pain and pleasure but something deeper—a pleasure born of pain. A still closer peep might show that, at the end of a tragedy, a percipient finds himself emotionally shattered, intellectually benumbed but spiritually exalted.

And now, finally, a possible way out.

The tragic inheres the existential situation, of course. Created as a mere freak in nature, without claws and protective skin but with a superior brain, and continually threatened with extinction, man started evolving a small, parallel world of his own. The laws and institutions of his own making were to give him the central position in this world and thus help him escape the position of utter insignificance in the universe. To overcome his intrinsic weakness as an animal, he had to ensure the perpetuation of this world and prevent his lapsing back into a mere state of nature. With a view to circumventing the unfavourable laws of nature, he sublimated his natural urges, institutionalized his passions, and evolved such values as tended to denigrate whatever was natural. Thus each positive quality in nature came to be projected as a weakness in human terms, and vice versa. Instead of relishing the rougher animal passions, man was to cherish such qualities as liberality, affability, magnanimity, honour, humour, truthfulness, justice, etc.—qualities that are abstract and utterly independent of nature. The big idea was to reinforce the life-sustaining illusion that man, far from being a freak, is the very centre of the universe. He invented religion, art, philosophy, and other systems to foster faith in these defence measures that sought to create around man a halo of importance and indispensability. Of course, this sophistication meant less authentic living; but, then, he could do nothing else to save himself from extinction. As this world of man's making grew, gradually it came to be regarded as a sacred trust, and ensuring its continuance became the highest duty of man. The original aim got forgotten and preserving this world became the sole end of man's existence. This obviously reversed the initial situation when this world itself was created for the survival of man; now man was supposed to exist for the sake of maintaining this world.

Man's tragedy, however, lies in the fact that, despite his efforts to devote entirely to the little world of his own making, he continues to belong to the world of Nature and, try as hard as he may, he cannot completely break away from it. He continues to be an animal, and for his vital existence he is still governed by its laws. In other words, man is a denizen of two worlds—the huge world of nature, i.e., the universe, which we may call macrocosm, and the little world of his own creating, which may be termed microcosm. The microcosm is finite, relative, imperfect, even illusive; it can never acquire the infinite, absolute and universal dimensions of its rival, the macrocosm. That is to say, man's efforts are foredoomed. However, since man cannot wish away the macrocosm in order to survive in the struggle for existence, he has to persist with his labours to make the microcosm as glorious as he can. The trouble is that the microcosm is not only imperfect but also imperfectible; what is more, in his effort to circumvent nature, he has created such values and institutions as are mutually incompatible. Thus, on the one hand, man's life is beset with the existential dichotomy that results from his belonging at once to the macrocosm and the microcosm; and, on the other, thanks to its lopsided evolution, his microcosm too is full of incongruities between his ideal and his experience. This existential multivalence is compounded by man's natural, rational and spiritual levels of experience because thus he may perceive and apprehend a certain experience emotively, intellectually or spiritually.

With the passage of time, the layers of microcosmic illusions have grown so thick that ordinarily men remain preoccupied with microcosmic pursuits and thus the macrocosmic Reality and the precarious relationship between the two worlds are not perceived. However, saints and seers, with superhuman vision, see through the microcosmic layers and talk about man's intrinsic insignificance and the futility of human effort. Only on rare occasions of intense experience, when man is driven to the boundary-situation and lives authentically, and when the human values and the natural laws come into clash, a layman too is forced to shed his smug complacency and see the terrible reality regarding the illusive nature of the world that he has been creating. As this realization makes some people sad and pessimistic, they immediately discover, by way of defence measure, the means of re-entering the illusion through the ethical, social, political, philosophical or religious affirmation. Art affords an aesthetic alternative by highlighting the fact that man continues to make his effort, howsoever limited, and that he deserves a pat for being such a persevering creator. Such, indeed, is the tragic vision. In tragedy, therefore, the initial shock of recognition makes the reader sad, but as the shock is followed by the realization that man's glory lies in this dichotomy itself, pain gets transmuted into something pleasurable. This is the source of the deeper optimism of tragedy.

Tragedy, thus, represents the inevitable clash between the eternal cosmic Reality of the macrocosm and the man-made illusion of the microcosm. In his zest to denigrate nature, man has invented labels and talks glibly in terms of good and evil, right and wrong, virtue and vice—the latter being reserved invariably for whatever is natural or macrocosmic. But the fact is that the natural is essential and inalienable aspect of man, the only absolute attribute shared by all human beings, whereas the man-made qualities are, at best, of relative importance and unevenly developed in individuals. So much so that, at times, even the antitheses are equally esteemed—for example, gentleness and tenacity, tenderness and strength, innocence and shrewdness, simplicity and subtlety, frankness and diplomacy, truthfulness and tactfulness, etc. Many of man's values signify sanctification of the animal urges into human attributes—for example, lust as love, hatred as envy, cunning as cleverness, obstinacy as determination, power-craze as ambition, idleness as leisure, cowardice as humility, and so on. Consequent upon such dual value-system in human affairs, good and evil stand confounded; in everything good one may discover an element of evil, and perhaps vice versa. What is evil in Othello—unreflective rashness—could have been a saving grace in the situation of Hamlet. A tragedy points out this duality of human values, born of the dichotomy of existence on macrocosmic and microcosmic planes. Obviously weakness from one angle may be a point of strength from another angle. Such is the so-called tragic flaw. That is why audience don't dislike a hero for his flaw; rather he is admired in spite of—at times even because of—that flaw. In other words, tragedy does not deny man's being an animal living without any intrinsic purpose, but affirms the fact that he is something more than an animal. Tragedy is, thus, a form of humanism which enables one to accept in life all that is human—by nature or by choice.

A tragedy effects this artistic alchemy by leading us to a vantage point where we can view the tragic outcome of the existential situation. It starts at the macrocosmic level, but when the tragic hero, scrupulously following the microcosmic laws, does something that brings him in conflict with the macrocosmic laws, he becomes a symbol of the existential dichotomy, and in his fortunes we read the fate of all mankind. We are shocked to realize not only that our puny microcosm is in conflict with the mighty macrocosm, but also that, in being rooted inalienably in the macrocosm, it can neither survive in isolation nor ever become perfect. As a corollary comes the realization that human values shall always remain relative. Since this realization pertains to the whole human race, including ourselves, we identify ourselves with the hero and share his subsequent glory as well as the present doom. In the conflict with the gigantic macrocosm, the weakling has little chance of victory; but even as he goes down, we perceive a will rather to break than bend, to be rather an imperfect creator in his own right than a mere creature of no significance. This wresting of glory from a sure defeat is a sort of spiritual triumph which we share with the protagonist. That is what makes the tragic response so elevating.

In a tragic experience, thus, we learn to regard microcosm as a tribute to the creative ability of man who has converted an initial handicap into a glorious advantage. Having had a glimpse already into the terrible reality of human existence, now when we affirm life, we exercise an authentic choice in full awareness, rather than in ignorance, of the macrocosmic aspect of the human existence. We don't deny the animal in man but glory in the fact that, although an animal, he is more than that—almost a god. Instead of remaining a purposeless creature in the big universe, he has willed a world of his own—a world that is beautiful and meaningful despite all its imperfections and limitations. The tragic alchemy is, so to say, a humanistic experience that enables one to see man's glory as he brings good out of evil, freedom out of determinism, something divine out of animal state, the spiritual out of the sensual. Shocked earlier at man's animality, now we approve of it, for in this lies the very origin of his divinity. Perhaps there is a glory in being born an angel, but there is a greater glory in transcending bestial origin to attain position of the angels and gods. In this perception of victory-in-defeat, of order-in-chaos, of meaning-in-absurdity, of spirit-in-flesh, of unity-in-diversity lies the very essence of the paradoxical pleasure-in-pain which we call tragic pleasure.

As can be seen in the above account, the response involves at once the sensuous, the spiritual and the intellectual levels of experience. The microcosmic growth may vary in respect of individuals, but macrocosmically, all men are the same. That makes the striking of macrocosmic level an essential part of the tragic process for, otherwise, there will be no empathic identification on the one hand and universalization on the other. In this connection, it is necessary to point out that macrocosmic does not imply an evil, animal quality; it denotes the primal, sensuous and instinctual aspect of existence as opposed to the social, sophisticated aspect we usually eulogize as 'human.' Driven by the dichotomous trait, which is at once macrocosmic strength and microcosmic weakness, the hero is alienated and brought to the point where microcosm and macrocosm are chained together. Here he comes to face the choice between an imperfect human world and a perfect state of natural absurdity; he opts for the former. This choice means complete break from nature; hence physical death or something equally disastrous. Inevitably he breaks, but it is like the breaking of a vase of perfume which fills the space all around with fragrance. In tragedy, we savour the aroma of human glory. During this process, the audience response also undergoes a corresponding progression. The sharing of the macrocosmic traits of the protagonist implies the stirring of our corresponding passions. This state of empathy, once acquired, persists. Thus, when the hero is driven to the boundary situation, the shock of recognition benumbs our mind. Similarly, when the hero meets his inevitable defeat, we are emotionally shattered. But as he reaps spiritual glory from this experience, we, in empathy, share spiritual exaltation. Thus do we feel immortality in the finiteness of our existence. In this conflict with the eternal powers, the hero denies them credit of victory by raising the issue beyond defeat and triumph. For a moment, the temporal and the eternal, the material and the spiritual, the mortal and the immortal come to terms with each other. Without denying or compromising either, tragedy resolves the tension between spirit and flesh by making one look an integral part of the other. Of course, the existential ambiguities remain, but for the moment we learn to transcend them in the higher vision which reveals not only that goodness and evil coexist, but also that good is born out of the evil itself and that animalism alone is the justification of our microcosm. That is why, at the early stages when terrible questions are raised and when everything appears to be in jeopardy, we do wish that 'tragedy' could be averted, but at the end we have no such desire. There is no longer any sense of grief, indignation, anger or a wish that things should have been otherwise. Without this transcendence, which enables one to rise from narrow personal self and also above such considerations as determine normal attitudes, there could be no tragedy.

Tragedy, then, is a universal, all-embracing, humanistic experience in which, transcending the existential dichotomy, man transcends flesh and animal suffering and acquires a spiritual state wherein the terrible ambiguities are reconciled by the alchemy of imaginative treatment. It is like churning to extract cream.[4]

From what we have suggested, it is easy to see how aptly has tragedy been projected as the bulwark of human self-respect against the superhuman and inhuman forces of the macrocosm pressing from all sides. By underscoring the wonderful, the heroic and the individual in man, tragedy gives one's spirit the courage never to submit or yield. In other words, contrary to the popular belief, tragedy is deeply optimistic and sings praises of the spirit of man. Comedy, on the other hand, feels sorry for him. It offers merely knowledge of the world, especially its imperfections. It underlines the microcosmic incongruities by highlighting the contrast between the abstract ideal of what man wanted the world to be and the imperfect way that ideal has been realized. Since this incongruity does not involve the macrocosmic, comic experience does not strike deep enough to touch our emotions. In fact, comic response demands what is usually called anaesthesia of the heart—a sort of detachment which is effected by fixing the focus so much on the intellectual perception that feelings are not allowed to get involved. What is more, since the macrocosm is not involved, there is neither the sense of universality and inevitability, nor does the ideal appear unattainable. A comic hero thus battles not against any basic law, but against some part of cultural superstructure. The comic thus leaves a superficial rather than profound imapct on the mind. What makes one feel amused is the realization that the microcosm, of which man is so proud, has so many ludicrous aspects, too. The comic is, so to say, a weapon against the forces of disintegration within the human society. Our interest in the comic, therefore, is limited to the men and manners of a society in a particular age.

Obviously, whereas the tragic involves all levels of experience and is born of the incompatibility of macrocosmic laws and microcosmic values, the comic involves only the intellectual level and has for its realm only the affairs of the microcosm. To put it differently, whereas the comic is an experience in which we perceive intellectually the microcosmic incongruities, the tragic is an experience of spiritual exaltation in which we transcend the existential dichotomy.

Indeed, contrary to the intellectual skating in the comic, the tragic is akin to a voyage—a voyage of the soul through the storms of macrocosmic passions, amid the treacherous rocks of microcosmic values. No wonder, whereas the comic is often confused with laughter, the tragic is not identified with any one particular mood or passion, for it is by no means one-dimensional. What is more, whereas in a comedy, the comic spirit pervades throughout as we view the whole thing with detachment, in a tragedy, our responsive moods vary from stage to stage. Thus what we call tragic pleasure is climactic result of what is perceived and experienced, through empathy, in the course of tragic action. Before we reach that stage when we can affirm life spiritually, we pass through a terribly emotional experience. That is to say, the tragic pleasure is not simple reaction but the end-product of a process that involves numerous perceptual responses.

Now, the microcosmic incongruities not only change with the evolution of an ever-developing human world but also vary from society to society and from time to time; the macrocosmic laws, on the other hand, are eternal, inexorable and universal. Thus it is inherent in the very nature of things that the comedy of a particular age would be related to its peculiarities. In a tragedy, too, the spirit of the age plays a major role because the conflict lies between a certain variable factor in the microcosm and a corresponding, although invariable, feature of the macrocosm. That is why in the Greek, the Elizabethan, and the French tragedies, the conflicts are different in nature. Nevertheless, in all cases, one of the conflicting factors represents the macrocosm, and the other the microcosm. Indeed, not all but only such of the conflicts can be tragic as, on the one hand, involve macrocosmic forces and, on the other, yield spiritual victory to man. Since an experience that shows man in conflict with a microcosmic force, however disastrous, cannot suggest inevitability, it can never produce the impact of tragedy proper. Nor can an experience that ends in an inglorious defeat of man be called tragic in the true sense. To be truly tragic, a play must show man's depths and heights, his spirituality as well as his animality, his perverseness and nobility—and these polarities intertwined with each other. A play that suggests one without the other, or depicts both but without relating them as inalienably interdependent, may be a great drama, but it cannot yield tragic pleasure. It is, therefore, desirable that such a play be treated as distinct from tragedy.

This caution is necessary because, often enough, the presence of just one element of tragedy in a certain play might prompt one to stick on it the label of tragedy. Indeed, a play might evoke emotive response and yet not be a tragedy—for example, melodrama in which, properly seen, the realm of experience is either microcosmic incongruity or purely macrocosmic passion rather than existential dichotomy. Consequently, either it lacks universal touch or its intensity moves one excessively and so exclusively as to shut out the spiritual appeal. Likewise, quite a number of the modern plays deal with existential dichotomy all right but the quality of the impact is by no means tragic because the mode of perception may be purely cognitive. Take, for example, irony. Here the area of experience may be existential dichotomy which overwhelms one in tragedy when that is perceived emotively, but the mode of perception is intellectual which, in comedy, evokes laughter. Consequently, encompassing both tragedy and comedy, irony refuses to settle in either the tragic or the comic mould and thus places the percipient in a state in which head and heart fail to agree. Juxtaposed on the line of interaction of the tragic and the comic, irony projects the microcosm and the macrocosm in the relationship of contrast rather than conflict. While the fusion of the opposites is effected in comedy through laughter and in tragedy through catharsis, in irony, feeling is held in check by thought, intuition by reason, and the spirit by flesh. No wonder, with irony is associated emotional discord when something is at once funny and painful. Indeed, while tragic is eternal truth experienced in a state of transcendence and comic is temporal truth perceived in a state of self-consciousness, ironic is eternal truth perceived in a state of self-consciousness.

These distinctions, we repeat, must be borne in mind; else, we might be in for generic confusion and declare such plays as tragedies as are essentially ironic dramas. Such clarity is particularly necessary in the assessment of modern plays. Struggling for a tragic revival, the moderns, whose ancestors had long ago lost the key to tragedy, have been all-too-keen to hail as tragedy anything and everything that has something of the tragic in it—be it the emotive mode of perception or the quality of experience. The fact is that we in the twentieth century have no pure genres and that the tragic and the comic have often tended to intertwine themselves. Irony is only one such result; there are the absurd and the grotseque, too. In the Absurd plays, the tragic and the comic are so balanced against each other that the whole thing appears to be at once painful, terrifying, and yet funny. Here we see Man living in a world that is not only dichotomous and imperfect but also nightmarish—without any value or logic at all. As man's sufferings remain unredeemed, the vision of the wretchedness of life is not followed by tragic exaltation. In such a world, nothing is good or bad, moral or immoral, for everything is seen to be Absurd. We do have in tragedy a moment when all seems meaningless, purposeless, and absurd—when Lear may ask, 'Is man no more than this?,' when Hamlet might wonder about the worthwhileness of life and contemplate 'to be or not to be,' when life might appear to Macbeth as a tale told by an idiot full of sound and fury but signifying nothing. But, then, that stage marks in tragedy a halfway house; a lot follows to enable Lear to realize that ripeness is all and to prompt Hamlet to see Providence in the fall of a sparrow—and so on. In tragedy, the Absurdist vision is transcended; in the theatre of the Absurd, it is the thing itself and thus here tragic and comic lose distinction.[5]

To sum up, tragedy makes one wonder what a wonderful creature man is. The way he wrests glory from his suffering compels our admiration for him and our affirmation of the microcosm. Tragic glory may be illusive but we learn to affirm it with all the responsibility of a conscious choice. When we face reality and see the absurdity that lies at the core of human existence, we realize the imperfect nature of the microcosm and the inevitability of the macrocosm; yet, notwithstanding all this, we affirm human values all too willingly. After a tragic spectacle, we return to the mundane life as a more committed and a wiser member of the microcosm.

The last paragraph is by no means meant to offer a definition of tragedy. We do not propose to offer one because a definition always tends to act as a straitjacket. Perhaps a more sensible approach would be to underline what, according to us, are the quintessential aspects—not just elements—in the absence of which the response evoked falls short of tragic impact/pleasure.

First and foremost, it has to be a humanistic play in the sense that it deals with man and his world, is concerned with the fate of man, affirms the human microcosm and humanizes the hero as well as the audience. A play that gives primacy to gods or animals cannot be called a tragedy nor the one that ends up indicting man, his microcosmic effort and his institutions. In a tragedy, we must feel the relevance and sway of man despite all odds and, at the end, exclaim, 'Wow, how very human!'

Of course, the action of tragedy is not restricted just to man and his world on the social/microcosmic plane; nor to man in relationship with the macrocosm. It has to be related to both. In fact, both are equally important and indispensable. What is more, they must come into conflict with each other. This is a very important aspect because it is such a conflict which enables the percipient to see man from different angles and realize his ontological insecurity in the context of the fragile and precarious position of microcosm vis-a-vis macrocosm. As this negative aspect of man's existence shows him in an unenviable light and projects him as unworhty or unheroic in certain ways, he appears all-too-human like ourselves and therefore some one with whom we can identify ourselves. If this aspect is not highlighted, we may not be able to identify ourselves with the hero. Its absence could make the play a heroic drama rather than a tragedy. Anyway, this negative aspect is not an avoidable error or lapse but something inevitable that should make us exclaim, 'What a pity it had to be so!' But besides the negative, there is quite a lot positive, too. Of course, the positive is not as powerful as the negative; nor is it inevitable. But it has to be there. Any play that is lacking in this aspect will fail to afford that touch of humanization.

Now these two essential aspects, one positive and one negative, must be seen as related and the label of a play's genre would depend on how these are related. There are several possibilities. The two can remain isolated; they may be juxtaposed in a spirit of coexistence for comparison and contrast; the twins may accommodate each other on terms of equality or as complementaries; they may clash and cancel each other; one of them may be rejected completely to yield supremacy to the other; or either of them may come to be affirmed. In a tragedy, (a) they must come into clash with each other and (b) there should be affirmation of both or at least of the positive (microcosmic) aspect. If there is no clash or if it is a clash without any affirmation, or if the negative (i.e., macrocosmic) alone is affirmed, the result would not be fully satisfying.

Again, our perception of the phenomenon presented must not be either purely intellectual or purely emotive; it has to be both. In the final stage of affirmation, the intellectual and the emotive are transcended with some kind of spiritual response. In case the response is one-dimensional, if there is no emotional dimension or if there is no spiritual touch later, the play cannot pass muster as a tragedy proper. The conflict has to be intense; what is more, it must have about it a measure of shock or disgust. A goody-goody conflict at superficial level does not involve; nor does it yield the suffering which every tragedy must have. The shock followed by suffering is indispensable because it is through that shock that the character-percipient identification is accomplished; but for it, the audience/reader won't experience the pain of tragedy, nor therefore the glory that follows. It is during this suffering that the hero gets a chance to show heroic fortitude and thus become a symbol of the human spirit. In the assertion of this spirit lies the creative role of suffering. That is for the percipient; for the hero, the suffering is creative in the sense of not being for its own sake: it must yield some wisdom to the sufferer. Thus does suffering humanize both the hero and the percipient. A suffering for its own sake, however pathetic, would not serve the purpose. Broadly speaking, this Dionysian wisdom pertains to the fact that man can neither do without the microcosm nor wish away the macrocosm.

As a corollary, the wisdom yielded pertains also to the relativity of human values. Like the hero making his choice before inviting suffering to himself, now it is the turn of the percipient to make a choice between the microcosmic and the macrocosmic. If the tragedy is successful, he will affirm the microcosm or both the microcosm and the macrocosm. If the choice falls in favour of macrocosm alone, the result would not be, as averred earlier, satisfactory. In making the choice of the microcosm, one opts for something that is neither universal nor final; the problem, therefore, remains. And the consciousness of this fact keeps one wondering about all that has happened. For a moment, a harmony had been restored but now the doubts rise again. Hence the sense of mystery persists when one leaves the work. A play ceases to sound tragic if it ends on a note of finality, be it totally happy or totally unhappy.

When there exist all these possibilities at different stages, it is not surprising that so many plays do have macrocosmic and/or microcosmic dimensions, conflict, shock, suffering, wisdom, affirmation, etc., and still do not satisfy completely. The reason is that somewhere, something vital might be wanting or the balance might have tilted in favour of an uncongenial alternative. For example, when macrocosmic is not involved and the concern is with the microcosm alone, the clash is obviated and the result approaches a comedy, especially if the whole thing is viewed cognitively. Similarly, viewing the incongruities of the microcosm emotively could mean a melodrama. On the other hand, if microcosm is seen both emotively and intellectually, or microcosm and macrocosm are related without creating an intense conflict, it might be a case of tragicomdey. Likewise, if the play ends on the note of confrontation between macrocosm and microcosm, when microcosm seems precariously situated vis-a-vis macrocosm, the outcome is Absurdist if things are viewed intellectually, and grotesque if perceived emotively. If at the final stages, there is just balancing without any affirmation, we have irony which can materialize also if the microcosm is seen emotively or macrocosm is perceived intellectually.

In the light of the above, we suggest that whenever the play fails to satisfy as tragedy, for grasping the core of its failure, we should subject it to the touchstone of the following questionnaire:

— Is the play man-centred in the sense that it makes one think about man in relation to his world and the cosmos?
— Do we perceive in the action assertion of the macrocosm in the form of passion or natural urges?
— Is the macrocosmic dimension of man's existence seen not in isolation but in relation to the microcosmic, i.e., human values?
— Do the macrocosmic and the microcosmic aspects collide?
— Can we say that the conflict is between one good against another?
— Does the conflict afford a frightening glimpse of negative position of man—absurd and helpless?
— Does this glimpse breed a shock for the hero?
— Does the conflict lead to the suffering of the hero?
— Do we, as audience, suffer empathically?
— Does the suffering raise questions about the relativity of human values?
— Is the suffering of the hero creative in the sense of facilitating self-realization?
— Does the hero's suffering induce a corresponding wisdom in the audience, too?
— Does this Dionysian wisdom imply heroic glory of human spirit?
— Is our perception of the action more emotive than intellectual?
— Does our perception have some spiritual dimension towards the close?
— Does the hero die or meet some disastrous fate to find himself redeemed in some way?
— Is there any positive glory perceived in the hero's fall?
— Does the experience leave one emotively shattered?
— Does the experience leave one intellectually benumbed, bewildered?
— Is the end marked by spiritual exaltation for the percipient?
— In the last stages, is there any feeling of transcendence from narrow personal self into something universal?
— At the end, are we affirming microcosm—with or without macrocosm?
— Does the overall picture of man fill one with confidence in his future and thus prove deeply optimistic?
— Is the total impact pleasurable rather than depressing?
— Does one leave with a sense of deep mystery, still brooding over the complexity of human situation born of the incompatibility of macrocosm and microcosm?

Perhaps it would be in the fitness of things if we look at some plays and see what made them great tragedies or else what prevented them from making that grade. In the case of plays that have been called tragedies with some reservations or else denied that label, we shall look for the reasons of their comparative failure. Anyway, the basic aim of this exercise is going to be to test the validity of our formulation on the touchstone of representative plays. In the process, we might also get the chance to evaluate the spirit of certain types of tragedy. Let us, therefore, take up the plays both individually and collectively (period-wise).

Despite its happy close, Aeschylus's *Oresteia* answers all the questions enumerated above in the affirmative. Here is the story of humanizing the passion of revenge not through a hero but through a House. A new and higher law emerges from the sufferings of the Atreus family. What triumphs at the end is not Apollo's argument but the civilized ideal, the Athenian state—the achievement of man. If one takes the three parts of the trilogy individually, as three complete tragedies, one finds no common pattern at all. The first half of *Agamemnon* is expository—choral narrative with no action; the protagonist appears just for a short time and the close is horrible. The second part, *Libation Bearers*, is full of exciting action—comprising regicide and matricide—but the close is demonic in the sense that the Furies take over. *The Eumenides*, taken as a complete play, lacks the tragic tempo, tragic motivation, etc., but it has the right redemptive notes in what appears at surface to be a kind of reconciliation. Taken together as a trilogy, there emerges everything that a tragedy should have. This fact makes one feel very uncomfortable when talking about the plays by Sophocles and Euripides because, more often than not, we have to treat as complete tragedy a play that might have been only the opening part, the middle bit, or the closing section. Where may one place *Oedipus Rex*, for example? And yet this play was Aristotle's model—the paradigm of his entire theory! Maybe, Sophocles' trilogy presented tragedy of the House of Thebes; or possibly, he conceived of trilogy not as a tragedy with three parts but as a set of three complete tragedies.

Be it what it may, *Oedipus Rex*, too, answers all our questions in the affirmative. There is so much negative in the play and it is possible to see the core of the play in the swollen footedness of man, in his ignorance, in his limitations that make him commit evil even when trying to escape evil. But these questions are perfectly balanced later and we are in a position to record the negative statements in such a way as to sound most positive. For example, it could be said that since man was physically handicapped, he has become spiritually strong; man's knowledge might be all-too-limited, but he has immense desire and capacity to learn, even through suffering; to act may mean inviting gods' disproportionate ire but man has high potential of accepting such fate and asserting his free will in defiance of the gods' will; here may be a case of humbling the greatest, but it also underscores man's being the measure of all things. What the play clearly says is that man's situation might be bleak but it is not without god-like glory. Indeed, it is possible to take an optimistic view of Sophoclean fatalism and say that gods cannot do anything without man and that, even to punish him, they depend on him. This humanism is summed up in Sophocles' exclamatory declaration in the play itself: 'Wonders are many but none is more awesome than man!'

In the case of Euripides' *Medea*, at first the positive and the spiritual seem to be absent and quite a few of the posers in the questionnaire receive negative responses; in fact, in view of multiple deaths, one feels tempted either to label it as a melodrama or else to plead its being an opening or a middle part of a trilogy. But it should be possible to discern at a deeper level a truly tragic pattern if we see closely and perceive the tragic dichotomy in woman's nature: the gentler sex is sterner in wreaking vengeance. Mysterious, indeed, is the heart of Man who may be at once life-preserving and life-destroying—as a mother and as a mistress, respectively, in the case of Medea. In her, a very thin margin separates love from hatred. The fact that children remain in the focus from the beginning to the close is a subtle hint to what Euripides meant. He wanted us to see Medea not merely as a jilted mistress but as a mother. Indeed, it is worth noting that her spiritual conflict pertains to her children and not to Jason: about the prospects of leaving him she utters not a single word of regret. Perhaps that also explains the profusion of all those speeches about child-bearing and woman's position. A woman's real fulfilment lies not as a beloved but as a mother; and yet Medea kills her children. This is a most painful act but absolutely necessary because it is a kind of sacrifice to facilitate the redemption of a lost soul, viz., Jason. Towards the end, when he is itching just to touch his children about whom he was least bothered earlier, except in respect of their financial security, it is a different Jason before us. A new Jason has been born—Jason with a soul. That is what Medea's sacrifice has wrought. She had to suffer—and suffer the maximum possible in the act of sacrificing her motherhood—to make life spiritually richer.

Putting together the three Greek tragedies discussed above, it is possible to say that violence, crimes, infanticides, rapes, revengeful murders, incest and other heinous acts of all sorts were accommodated in Greek tragedy just to show that although men are animals they are not beasts, after all: they punish the evil-doers, including themselves. In fact, although they are proved physically weaker than the gods, they emerge stronger spiritually—thanks to that physical weakness itself. We realize, too, that while capricious gods will the murders and other crimes for their amusement or out of mutual rivalry, the human beings commit murders for some microcosmic values. So very barbaric and yet so human—that is the essence of pagan situation which serves as the bedrock of Greek tragedy.

Although Roman tragedies were a rehash of the same myths, Greek humanism became a most conspicuous casualty in the treatment. Thus while Euripides' Medea has to commit crime to achieve her purpose, Seneca's Medea creates designs that she may commit crimes. No wonder, the spiritual aspect of the Greek tragedy yielded place to sensationalism and thus what goes in the name of Roman tragedy borders on the melodrama—romantic turmoil sans classical serenity. Here is, indeed, brutalizing and barbaric rather than humanizing experience. Since such a tragedy was the model for the University Wits and Renaissance writers, it is not surprising that passion in the sixteenth century tragedy lacks spiritual dimension altogether and tragedies of the period are content to depict just the fall of a man of prosperity into adversity. Death is all—without any suffering, wisdom, spiritual regeneration, etc. Witness Thomas Kyd's *Spanish Tragedy* and Christopher Marlowe's *Tamburlaine* or *The Jew of Malta*. Doctor Faustus does touch spiritual chords but he is not redeemed. Jason regains his soul, Faustus loses his. Of course, the last moments of Faustus's struggle to save his soul touch the reader's heart and one may hear in his cries the birth-pangs of spiritual tragedy which Shakespeare was to produce shortly, but in itself *Doctor Faustus* remains a good pageantry entertainment suffused with sportive pranks of devils, shapes and spirits as well as a lot that is farcical, parodic or trivial. No wonder, here, almost half of the posers in our questionnaire receive a negative answer.

Shakespeare's *King Lear* would, on the other hand, get full marks on that scale for here is the flowering of the Renaissance humanism. Most shattering, it is also a tragedy that humanizes the audience through the redemption of the hero. Operating at once on the physical, moral and psychological planes, it brings the microcosm and the macarocosm so close to each other that, when they clash, in the handy-dandy that gets created, it is difficult to tell who is to blame. Perhaps, 'None does offend, none!' It is a typical clash of two goods. Like Oedipus, Lear learns through suffering. Of course, there is a moment of stark despair. He stumbles when he sees the truth—the absurdity of existential dichotomy—and goes mad; but he comes back to sanity to radiate divine light of a purified soul. The new Lear knows now; he has learnt through suffering. So has Hamlet when he returns from the voyage to England. Having learnt the difference between a scourge and a minister, he has reconciled the contrary pulls from macrocosmic laws and microcosmic values. Instead of brooding over 'To be or not to be,' as he used to do once, he is confident and clear enough to declare, 'If it be now, 'tis not to come; if it be not to come, it will be now; if it be not now, yet it will come: the readiness is all.' Of course, he has been a slave of the passion of revenge but he is not a Senecan hero who would sacrifice his humanity for animal craving. That kind of revenge Shakespeare left to Laertes; his own hero would rather lose his life to save his soul. As in other Shakespearean tragedies, here, too, a passion spins the plot; but the way the macrocosmic dimension is made to serve as a grist to the microcosmic mill, one cannot help wondering if man would have been so noble a creature if he had not been what he is, an animal. Such humanistic affirmation is what makes Shakespeare so great a tragic playwright.

The pity is that never again has any playwright succeeded in recapturing such a perfect fusion of the positive and the negative, the demonic and the divine, the microcosmic and the macrocosmic. And thus one cannot think of any tragedy after Shakespeare that would shout 'yea' as answers to all our questions: maybe, 70 or even 80%, but never cent per cent!

John Webster's *The Duchess of Malfi* is a classic example. Here is a fascinating study of evil, darkness, perversion, corruption, horror and suffering, but it lacks affirmative touch. Thus here we have macrocosmic shudder sans microcosmic humanism. A typical Shakespearean tragedy, too, rings the curtain down on numerous corpses; but there death—at least that of the hero—is a fulfilment rather than a punishment; here death is a retributive step as if the villain's death itself would redeem the sufferings of the protagonist. That is a false note which the Greek playwrights and Shakespeare would eschew. With them, a hero's death is a creative act: his mortality eternalizes certain human values. In Webster we have no such feeling. An opposite but equally inapt effect may be created when to highlight the human the macrocosmic is completely ignored—as in Dryden's heroic drama. Being a hero, the protagonist cannot do anything wrong or evil—as if evil were something that belongs exclusively to the realm of villainy. The next logical step in that direction was to insist that even while the villain is punished, the hero must be rewarded for his virtue. That is the concept of poetic justice which dealt an almost fatal blow to the tragic spirit. No wonder, throughout the eighteenth century, England could not produce a single worthwhile tragedy. Even in the Romantic age, the spirit of tragedy eluded the great poets. P.B. Shelley's *Cenci* does have a truly tragic situation—killing of an incestuous and tyrannical father by a gentle soul—but the play fails to afford a universal, humanistic experience because what follows is physical agony rather than spiritual anguish.

The concept of poetic justice was one of the many misinterpretations of the Greek classical drama which the neoclassical writers abounded in. What happened at their hands is best illustrated in Racine's *Phedre* as it underlines how the same myth may undergo sea-change, because of the injection of a new world view. A Jansenist, Racine could not possibly see anything divine in the pagan passions. Thus while the Greeks depict passions to probe the human soul and to show human heart as a battleground of divine clashes, Racine projects passion as something loathsome—a fatal weakness that destroys one's will. If Euripides' *Hippolytus* laments excessive asceticism as violation of the laws of nature, Racine sees in the passion of love a tyrannical force that corrodes one's soul. He is therefore opposed not only to indulgence of love but also to the very thought of it. Racine's Phedre does not commit any crime; the sin of intention is enough as it breeds such weaknesses as jealousy, falsehood, anger, impulsiveness, etc. Thus, impregnating Greek myth with Jansenist morality, Racine came to replace tragic guilt by moral guilt. Becoming a moral disease that consumes Phedre, passion of love loses its tragic potential because one fails to see anything spiritual behind the moral wreckage. Consequently, Phedre's suicide comes to be viewed not as a measure of her moral superiority but as a well-deserved punishment for her depravity. There is no glory in her death. Her suicide cannot be seen as a heroic, redemptive self-punishment because salvaging of a soul is, according to Jansenist theory, the privilege of God's grace. Man has no will to exercise in this matter: 'The evil I would not, that I do; the good I would, I do not.' By denying man Free Will, by injecting both morality and theology, Racine has killed the tragic. The play does retain passion, conflict, even suffering, but, having lost the creative role of suffering, Dionysian wisdom, spiritual glory, transcendental quality and deeper optimism, it has been reduced to a moral sermon. Somewhere above, it was seen that tragedy is ethical but rejects the ethical categories; it is spiritual but without the mediation of God. Racine has tied the pagan myth into the stranglehold of not one but two straitjackets of morality and religion.

Racine's importance in the history of tragedy lies in the fact that he is the first 'modern' who anticipated the dispossession of soul and search for its repossession and the consequent chaos within an individual, who showed life on the verge of disintegration, and who projected unsatisfied women as harpies. No wonder his plays, like the modern plays, leave one emotionally strung, intellectually distraught, and spiritually lost. His contemporary Corneille, too, struck a 'modern' note when he concentrated in his tragedies on a conflict between two human relationships (i.e., two microcosmic values) rather than between a microcosmic value and a macrocosmic urge. Victor Hugo took the first step towards the Absurd theatre when passion assumed grotesque form in his plays. The German playwrights could also claim the dubious distinction of taking such innovative first steps: for example, when Georg Buchner projected in his *Woyzeck* a pitiful man from the lowest class as a tragic hero. The fact is that the age of anti-tragic tragedies had started. Even the great Goethe failed to strike the right balance. His *Faust* is certainly more brilliant than *Doctor Faustus* but it lacks the verve and poignancy of the Marlovian finale. Margaret's seduction, desertion, child-murder and madness should touch the reader, but the grandiose and poetic style on the one hand and the philosophical monologues on the other spoil the effect. While Part I is marred by Faust's philosophical monologues, Part II has little of conflict or suffering. Here is a proof that not all kinds of poetry help enhance the poignancy of the existential dichotomy and that excessive exuberance of romanticism can be be as fatal to the tragic spirit as the shackles of classicism. Tragedy is neither pure poetry nor purely ideational; in it, ideas must be subsumed by poetry. *Faust* may be good poetry but it doesn't impress as a drama. Friedrich Hebbel's *Maria Magdalena* and John Schiller's plays about English Tudor history are not only more dramatic but also more tragic. Indeed, judged on the touchstone of our questionnaire, Hebbel and Schiller score more than Goethe.

Now, we have reached the stage when tragedy could be seen entering its own 'tragic' phase of confusion, unending struggle, torment and dismemberment. It is said that Henrik Ibsen's *A Doll's House* was the first modern tragedy and that the slamming of doors at the end of the play resounded in the whole of Europe. Indeed, tragedy, too, like Nora, left its artificial doll's house in which this all-sacrificing genre had been kept as a mindless toy for amusement. It, too, went out in the open to live a different kind of life—a life of greater social responsibility. But, alas, it realized too late that, like a divorcee, it also belonged nowhere. Even after this realization, sheer force of hubris has kept it from re-entering the door of protection that it had clammed shut upon itself. And till this day, it has been leading a nightmarish existence, moving about on existential plane, prostituting with strange bed-fellows, trying various experiments on itself in naturalistic localities, looking grotesque, behaving absurdly, revolting neurotically against its breaking illusions, or seeking in vain moments of terrible passion. Here is a case of an animal at large—animal castrated, animal herdified, animal lost in antics and mimicry but never animal humanized. This is not to say that its present state is any worse than the listless, languishing and spineless existence it had led for centuries since Shakespeare, but certainly it is not a high moment of glory either. It has changed so much that it cannot be recognised by its old admirers like George Steiner who has come to believe that it is no more. There are, of course, others like Raymond Williams who declare its every manifestation as its authentic identity.

Tragedy, of course, is not dead; it can never die so long as man's life is riddled with the existential dichotomy. That it need not always be in focus is borne out by the fact that so far it has had only two (or at most three) 'peaks.' That each peak-age had its own kind of tragedy has been used as an argument to insist on accommodating each and every serious modern play as a tragedy—by changing the definition, if necessary. But if that is done, tragedy becomes a faceless entity with no identity of its own. In short, we must not presume, on the one hand, that tragedy can no longer be written in our age, nor must we, on the other hand, distort the basic concept of tragedy into something amorphous. The fact is—and that is what our questionnaire serves to underline—that most of the plays written during the last hundred years do have some tragic aspects; but, thanks to the want of other vital aspects, they fail to satisfy as tragedies and thus appear at best truncated, incomplete, even antitragic. Indeed, it is time it was realized that a play can have tragic elements without becoming a tragedy.

Ibsen's plays are certainly not what G.B. Shaw would have us believe—comedies of ideas. They are certainly concerned with sociopolitical issues but they don't concern themselves with the incongruities in the microcosm. But, then, are they tragedies, really? Let us take *Ghosts*, for example. True, here is a tale of disaster suffused with irony because the best of intentions yield the opposite results, as in *Oedipus*; here, too, there is a conflict of very intense nature between facts and ideals; Mrs. Alving does learn to affirm the joy of living; and at the close, as Mrs. Alving fumbles for the deadly medicine we do start wondering if she would really administer it to her own son—and thus we leave more mystified than we came. Some critics use all these facts to argue that it is a tragedy, indeed. But there are those others who refuse to accept it as a tragedy because here are individuals challenging not the universe and the inexorable laws of nature but human institutions. Thus seen, the conflict here is not between microcosmic reality and macrocosmic reality but between two microcosmic forces—man and his own values or institutions. Since it is not possible to instil in such a conflict a sense of inevitability, the theme does not have the power of universal appeal. What is more, the human spirit is not affirmed and thus here is no spiritual transcendence. No wonder, at the end, the overall impact falls short of tragic elevation. There is, of course, intensity of conflicts but the turmoil is intellectual rather than spiritual. It is possible to argue back that here is a new brand of tragedy in which Ibsen has brought a new deterministic force (viz., society) and in which man gets projected as a victim not of the gods' will but of his own irrational powers. This being a new tragedy, it must not be judged by traditional standards, it is argued.

This kind of arguing and counter-arguing brings back that unenviable choice between rejection and redefinition. But, maybe, if we look a little closer, a third alternative is discernible: it is neither a comedy nor a tragedy but something in between—an ironic play. It debunks Christian morality of Pastor Manders, places the roguish Engstrand on a higher pedestal, projects ideals as ghosts—'dead that walk again,' as the original title had implied. The overall outcome of Mrs. Alving's sacrifice is not heroic sublimity but ironic ridicule; the dark night of the soul has yielded enlightenment in making her aware of the joy of living but, in practical terms, it amounts to killing her son! What Ibsen seems to say is: as social norms kill one's soul, an individual should try to be true to himself; but since too much of individuality can make one a troll, life can become chaotic. To bring home this point, Ibsen has placed an individual and the society against each other in such a position that, seen emotively, it looks a tragic situation but it turns into something funny too when it is perceived intellectually. In short, treating this play as 'new' tragedy would be contrary to the intentions of the writer and therefore a case of misplaced sympathy.

Likewise, hailing August Strindberg's plays uncritically as tragedies must be resisted because here again, if we see things closely, the writer's intention is different. If Ibsen discovers tragic counterparts in the realm of comedy, Strindberg uses the comic paraphernalia in the realm of tragedy. The battle of sexes has always been a theme of comedies, but Strindberg has projected it as a Dionysiac orgy. Instead of dramatizing the conflict in terms of social institutions, he seeks it in personal relationship—in *The Father* and *Miss Julie*, for example. As Strindberg's interest is not in what the conflict would do to the antagonists' souls, the whole thing gets reduced to the level of nerves. It is a neurotic problem, not a tragic dilemma. The overall realization of the audience—how like hate it is to love—is an ironic dig which stifles both the potential comedy and the inherent tragedy of the situation. Passions unite; neurosis separates. No wonder, we cannot empathize with Julie. According to

Strindberg, life is not mathematical or one-dimensional but complex and multidimensional. Julie's fate was precipitated by numerous factors—environment, heredity, chance, class-struggle as well as the battle of sexes. This complexity yields many perceptual strings which one finds difficult to strand together, and thus one's response too acquires the characteristics of neurotic behaviour. Indeed, our involvement in the play can be compared to one's involvement in a nightmare—intense but undefined. No wonder, the play leaves one not only emotionally shattered and intellectually baffled but also psychologically strained and spiritually depressed. All told, there is nothing redeeming in the suicide of Miss Julie; it affirms nothing. It makes her victor neither in the battle of sexes nor in the class struggle. Nor, of course, against the forces of environment and heredity. There is no Dionysian wisdom for the audience. By putting things like this, we are not trying to denigrate the art of the playwright who fathered naturalism, expressionism, and existentialism in modern drama. His contribution is monumental, indeed, but only if we judge the plays as plays. By trying to stick on them the label of tragedy, we shall be distorting his art and even belittling it because, as pointed out earlier, it would necessarily imply unfavourable comparisons with tragedians like Sophocles and Shakespeare. Anyway, does a playwright become great only if he writes tragedies? Attributing such value judgement to a genre has been a most unfair practice. We shall judge Strindberg fairly only for what he did—exploring the naturalism of human psyche.

Perhaps on no one has the mantle of tragic creativity been thrust more forcibly than on Anton Chekhov who minced no words in declaring his plays as comedies. *The Sea Gull* actually bears the subtitle, 'A Comedy in Four Acts.' Chekhov was shocked when *Three Sisters* was received by the artists of the Moscow Art Theatre as a tragedy; he insisted at the time of rehearsals that *The Cherry Orchard* be treated as a comedy. It is a wonder that, despite all these disclaimers, critics continue to call his plays as tragedies of inaction, of life's trivialities, etc. Perhaps it is possible to resolve this riddle by saying that as a writer of funny short stories and vaudeville sketches, he had learnt to approach life from the comedian's end; but, being a keen observer of life, he saw life in its entirety, including its pain and misery, and thus when he presented life 'comically,' in effect it meant modifying laughter through pity and neutralizing the pathetic with the comic. For him, being flat, featureless and inconsequential, life is basically wanting in drama but it is there, nevertheless. Since his plays are about this *is*-ness of life, Chekhov is a kind of naturalist who carves out a slice of life without touching it with any dramatic gloss, tragic or comic. In fact, it has been argued that Chekhov's is undramatic drama that makes him a precursor of the Absurd theatre. But, surely, it has nothing comparable to the vision of a Beckett or an Ionesco. True, there is something absurd, painful, and hopeless in what we witness in Chekhov; but, then, at the same time, we ask: is life that meaningless and pathetic, after all? As we start brooding over this question, Chekhov counters with something ludicrous and thus we cannot help the urge to chuckle. We laugh but with a lump in our throat. That is certainly something neither tragic nor comic; it is more akin to the dry mock of irony.

Chekhovian characters may be frustrated but they are not neurotic like Strindberg's nor symbols of shattered idealism like Ibsen's: they are just shattered fragments of human reality—self-absorbed, impractical, stunted, outmoded and therefore eccentric. Those being the prerogatives of the comic characters, the tragically explosive material peters out in bangless whimpers. No wonder, while a tragic hero's death leaves the sense of vacuum, Chekhovian characters leave no void. It is possible to say that Chekhov shades together effects of the pathetic and the comic through ironic naturalism. In any case, Chekhov's plays don't attempt to strike a note of tragic affirmation. Thus in *The Cherry Orchard* we do not know whether we should be sorry or happy at the sale of the orchard. True, it comes to symbolize all that was terrible in old Russia; but must it go? Though no longer useful, it was beautiful; we may be able to dispense with it, but its going is no joy. At the end of *Three Sisters* again, the three sisters are holding their hands while affirming their faith in future, but we know that it is a hopeless hope—a pipedream that is taking the place of the earlier one about their return to Moscow which has been finally thwarted for good. It is a world where Natashas thrive, where scholastic ambitions end up in pushing prams, where Kulygins alone can live in peace. Sensitive people like the sisters must stifle their souls if they have to live here. In a sense, we do feel the stirring of their souls, but it is not an affirmative vision. Anyway, there is in the play no conflict, no existential dichotomy; suffering is there but nothing creative in its yielding an insight into life.

That every affirmation is not necessarily tragic is endorsed by *The Power of Darkness* in which we have a mystic kind of affirmation. In fact, it is possible to say that the moralist born of 'conversion' having elbowed out the artist in Leo Tolstoy, here sentimentalism has snorted out the tragic. In Maxim Gorky's *Lower Depths*, we have the right kind of affirmation. When Luka leaves after creating a temporary impact, things return to the old pattern. Indeed, men must go on living, even the same bestial way—committing murders, adultery and crimes—for even in the animalism of theirs, one can see the hope of a superman; after all, what other animal can do things like that? The assumption is that horrible reality in man's world is environmental rather than spiritual, and therein lies the hope for mankind.

The dramatist who ranks beside Ibsen, Strindberg and Chekhov among the pioneers of modern drama was Luigi Pirandello. He is the most seminal of all and, as Robert Brustein has shown, he challenges comparison with almost all the modern playwrights. What he initiated and others followed was the refutation of the myth of tragic hero and, therefore, indirectly, the possibility of a tragedy. Tragedy assumes the reality of a character with a strong, unified ego, capable of accepting his plight as well as his responsibility for all actions, good or bad. Pirandello could not conceive of man as intrinsically noble enough to be tragic or, for that matter, consistently ludicrous enough for pure comedy. Pirandello performed the feat of dissolving this ego itself by making it more complex and by disintegrating personality into states of mind. So in his 'Theatre of the Mirror,' following Bergson's lead, Pirandello presented life as something fluid and evanescent; devoted to appearances and under the impact of ever-changing personality, the hero plays ever-new roles. At each step, the image in the mirror of the play is distorted until he is forced to adjust his own position; when the balance is about to be restored, the image is distorted again. That makes his plays grotesque: the statement about the way we live is in terms of comedy but it is proved in an experience of tragedy. In the words of J.L. Styan, Pirandello 'conceives a tragedy and writes it as a comedy.' Indeed, *Six Characters in Search of an Author* is dramatization of a 'potentially tragic situation within the circle of the comedy of illusions.' It starts with the process of viewing the truth of a certain character in a given situation from different angles (as seen by himself, by wife, by son, by daughter, by actors, etc.); then we pass through a gamut of responses extending over the tragic (when enacted by characters) and the melodramatic (when enacted by actors). In fact, the overwhelmingly tragic and fantastically comic elements are so intermingled that they acquire a touch of hallucination about them—gripping, terrible, fantastic and farcical. Seen properly, far from writing tragedies, the 'fathers' of modern drama were pulling down one after the other the different pillars that supported the edifice of tragedy. Thus Ibsen underplayed macrocosmic inevitability, Strindberg subverted the role of microcosmic values, Chekov dispensed with dramatic intensity, and Pirandello took away the character itself.

Empathy was the next pillar to fall—at the hands of Bertolt Brecht whose 'epic[6] theatre' was avowedly anti-Aristotelian, anti-heroic, anti-naturalistic, anti-Stanislavski, anti-individualism. In a sense, Brecht represents in modern drama a new classicism in which intellect must hold the reins of emotions. Aware that emotional straitjacket usually keeps the audience bound to the object of their empathy and that such involvement is an enemy of cool thinking, Brecht, as a playwright, does his best to ensure that we, as audience, do not fall into the trap of sympathy and sentiments. He obviates any such possibility of involvement through what he calls Alienation-effect (V-effect in German)—through epic proportions, through masks that undo hypnotic effect, through music which breaks the rhythm of prose-dialogues, through direct preachment by actors who abandon the illusion of role-playing for a while, through extravagant theatricality that keeps reminding that all this is happening on stage and that all this is a fiction rather than reality. The big idea is that response may come not from heart but from head.[7] Surely, all Brecht's tricks notwithstanding, his drama continues to attract the label of tragedy which was contrary to his intentions. Such plays that tend to suggest the tragic in spite of the author's professions are at best aborted tragedies. They leave us emotionally uninvolved and suppressed, intellectually stimulated and spiritually bewildered. Moreover, in Brecht's theatre, the basic problem is social and not human; that is to say, man is not worth a moment's thought, society is. That practically implies utter denial of the macrocosm in favour of microcosm. Anyway, when all is said and done, the net result of the conflict between the desired alienation and the half-way empathy does not belong to the realms of tragedy, comedy or tragicomedy; it hovers somewhere between irony and grotesque—like celebrating at one and the same time funeral and wedding, as do the guests in *The Caucasian Chalk Circle*.[8]

G.B. Shaw was another playwright who scorned emotions and yet attempted a tragedy, *Saint Joan*. It has all the elements of a tragedy. Here is a moving struggle of a girl against mighty forces leading to her inevitable doom which is helped by the hubris of her character, overconfidence acting as a tragic flaw. In her fall from great heights of glory, we have Hegelian dialectics of good v good (for murders are committed by people who are not murderers), the paradox of victory-in-defeat, and a sense of mystery at the close. Epitomizing the fate of all geniuses, the story has a universal colouring, too. But, then, Shaw could not help his genius and the tragedy of execution is followed by the comedy of society making amends in the form of canonization in the Epilogue. Perhaps the Epilogue can be justified by being referred to as a counterpart of the Greek satyr play; but when one looks at the play closely, one may see that, instead of a tragedy, we have in *Saint Joan* a travesty of tragedy. The elements of tragedy are there but they refuse to coalesce into one integral whole: it begins as melodrama, resolves into a discussion, and ends as an extravaganza. In this heterogeneric work, we do have pity, fear and terror but they are all isolated; a Hegelian balance is there but, instead of the balance of emotions, we have intellectual pity against intellectual terror. In fact, in this 'dialectical extravaganza,' as Arland Ussher says in his book on three great Irishmen, we have a feast of reason and intellectuality just as we have a riot of emotionalism in melodrama. Shaw knew that the anticlimactic Epilogue shattered whatever tragic intensity the play might have mustered, but he retained it deliberately because, more than artistic necessities, he was concerned with the communication of his thesis which was partly Marxist, largely Ibsenian and mostly Nietzschean. He chose *Saint Joan* for dramatization not because her heroic life climaxed into a tragic death but because she too embodied his favourite Life Force––a concept that mutilates against the tragic vision which asserts, instead, essential macrocosmic imperfectibility of man. For Shaw, man is not imperfectible, only he is taking too long to become a superman, as the poignant cry at the close of the play clearly implies.

In any case, it is worth noting that Joan is contending not against macrocosmic forces (which instead are on her side) but against microcosmic factors of man's own making. It is not a case of human sufferer and secret cause; the source of her suffering is bigotry and ignorance of her contemporaries. That makes her a superhuman spirit from one angle and a rustic wench from another. In neither case can one identify with such a creature. Perhaps all this vindicates the general feeling that a saint cannot be a tragic hero. Even T.S. Eliot in his *Murder in the Cathedral* could not perform that miracle. In his case, concentration of the emotional experience is there; poetry is exploited for the purpose. If the potential remains still unrealized, it is because characters have woodenness and artificiality of the 'morality' plays and that prevents our identification. Action is as good as non-existent and the four knights' self-justification has the touch of Shavian verbosity. Thanks to rationalization in poetry, there gets created a kind of dissociation of sensibility in the spectators as well as in the characters: thoughts and feelings do not correspond to each other. As for the spiritual gain, it might be there for Thomas Becket, there is none for the spectators.

Like sainthood, revolution is another field where tragedy has failed to find a congenial environment for its growth. The reasons are obvious. Revolution insists on a change for the ushering of utopian society; tragedy assumes the impossibility of such a utopia and is therefore content with all kinds of changes that evolutionary forces yield. Revolution starts with dividing people among right and wrong, pro-revolution and anti-revolution, the rebels and their adversaries, the white and the black; tragedy is against such compartmentalization, its favourite colour being grey. Revolution rejects all that exists and wants all changed; the typical mood of tragedy is acceptance—'yea' to everything. There is a lot of suffering in both, but while the most characteristic feature of a revolution is destruction (eclipsing whatever construction it might have to offer as a consequence), the typical mode of tragedy is creativity which, born of suffering, transcends destruction itself. Besides, revolution is an affair of the masses, not of an individual hero. In short, being incompatible, tragedy and revolution are hard to yoke together. No wonder, more often than not, the plays about revolutions, even strikes, end upon a note of melodrama or irony rather than tragedy.

John Galsworthy's *Strife* has a lot of suffering for both the parties and there is tragic hubris in the intransigence of the two opponents, but the conflict yields nothing creative because it is a conflict between microcosmic forces. On the contrary, the parting kick—reconciliation on terms agreed to even before the start of the strike—comes as a painful shock which makes us feel uncomfortable about the unnecessary turmoil, loss, and misery which could have been avoided. It is an ironic outcome. The close of Clifford Odets's *Waiting for Lefty* is equally ironic: the motives of all types of workers are not only different but at times even mutually conflicting; but when the unconfirmed news of the death of a long-awaited leader reaches, they forget all. Since it underlines the crudity and lowered rationality of a mob rather than integral unity of the masses, there is little to affirm. Indeed, when the conflict is between social forces without involving the macrocosmic, the tragic impact is hard to effect: it may be sensational, activistic, ironic, depressing, but it cannot be tragic in the sense of being affirmative and transcendental. Ernest Toller's *Machine Wreckers* is a study of the mass-frenzy of the strikers and, like all expressionistic plays, it affords a nightmarish experience in which you are gripped in spite of yourself, without any empathy. The protagonist is a sort of quizzical antihero; you cannot identify yourself with him; so far as the workers are concerned, their activities are such that identification with them would mean succumbing to the mob-instinct.

That was the positon in G. Hauptmann's *The Weavers* also: there is no central character nor any central scene and the close comes at a stage when the struggle is still on. The curtain comes down on the death of old Hilse but he is not a hero: he opposes the strike and yet has sympathy for the cause of the weavers. How insignificant is his life or how ironic his death is suggested by the fact that the machine gun keeps booming as he lies dead. Anyway, identification with a group of persons is possible on macrocosmic level, not on microcosmic level, because human nature is too diverse to conform to a particular set of values with the same degree of intensity. Indeed, we are all one in passions but as many in humanity. That is why mass-drama is effective on mob-level only. Tragedy, on the other hand, insists on identification not only on the macrocosmic level but also on the human level. Sean O'Casey knew this and therefore his plays about Irish revolts related the struggle to certain characters. That is why his mass-dramas retain the tragic 'feel.' His *Plough and the Star*, like *The Weavers*, ends on the death of a character by a stray bullet but this time the character is one with whom we have been empathizing. But, then, what O'Casey gained this way, he frittered away by letting comedy jostle with tragedy. Uproarious laughter and bitter despair succeed each other in *Juno and the Paycock*; 'it's a darlin' amalgam, as Joxer would have put it. In each situation, we have a tear for Juno and a guffaw for the Paycock; and as the title implies, both are equally important.

Besides the saints' fate and revolution, the other favourite hunting ground of the twentieth century playwrights were the Greek myths—of course, for reinterpretation in terms of modern experience or contemporary view of life. True, Jean Cocteau employed them for farcical purposes, too—e.g., in his *Orpheus* and *The Infernal Machine*—but most of the time the employment of myth has been prompted by serious purposes. Jean-Paul Sartre used the Orestes myth in *The Flies* to impregnate it with his existentialist philosophy. Of course, it was a ruse to address his compatriots in the theatre and urge them (without arousing suspicion) to rise against the German Occupation Forces. Aegisthus stands for Nazi dictatorship; Orestes, the son of the soil, seeks to give meaning to his otherwise empty life by wreaking vengeance. He realizes that the directive for vengeance can be no one else's but his own—an existentialist choice, indeed. Since Sartre's chief concern was his philosophy, the situations are used to illustrate his theory of commitment. Thus do his characters tend to become his mouthpieces. As an aesthetic experience, it stimulates the head rather than the heart, and what comes home is not the tragic situation of man but the existentialist situation in which existence precedes essence and idealism. It is a powerful, engaging philosophical play but, as a tragedy, it leaves one rather cold and unexalted. In Jean Anouilh's *Antigone*, the French were to see the Nazi dictator in Creon. Anyway, being a playwright rather than a philosopher, Anouilh has gone beyond the political situation to explore as well the complexity of human personality and the human soul. Hence greater depth in this play. However, it is worth noting that Antigone goes to death not because of her natural love for brother but because of her dissatisfaction with the crass society around. Thus the revolt is against the microcosm and does not involve the macrocosm. That makes the play another modern amputated tragedy. Tragedies these can be but only with lots of reservation—tragedies of sorts.

Some of the modern tragedies have such anti-tragic dimensions that the only way to accommodate them as tragedies would be to concede the concept of antitragic tragedies—the Absurd plays, for example. The Absurd theatre assumes not only incongruities in the microcosm but even its purposelessness. True, Absurd, in this sense, is at the root of existentialist philosophy, but it is also a stage in every tragedy. Driven to the 'boundary situation,' when the tragic hero finds himself turning from the cosmic chaos to a microcosm which is equally chaotic and even purposeless, he is facing the Absurd. But, then, as shown earlier, that stage is subsequently transcended in tragedy. An existentialist playwright's concern with the Absurd is a starting point for presenting his philosophy; the Absurdist playwright stops short at this point without effecting any tragic transcendence or proceeding with philosophical theory. Camusian hero, on confronting the Absurd, revolts against it. Caligula realizes that no one can judge him because no one is innocent. He shows, in his symbolic search for the moon, the utmost limits of the absurdity of living. In such an irrational world, the reader finds himself gripped with horror and shock—and that is all. There is no microcosmic affirmation and therefore the total effect of the play is an undefined sense of shock rather than exaltation. Of course, Caligula is not really mad: only he knows the Absurd. His tyranny is a substitute of the war to make himself famous: he replaces the plague, as it were. This way, he is a symbol of the antiheroic absurdity of existence which, in the theatre of the Absurd, is the thing itself.

While Sartre and Camus presented the Absurd in a rational and realistic style, the Absurdists are more theatrical. Instead of discussing the Absurd, they present the absurdity of the Absurd—and absurdly, too. The Absurd plays thus do share the existentialist anguish but in a style that combines verbal nonsense with clowning, fantasy, dreams, acrobatics, circus-like juggling, etc. What ritual is to myth, the Absurd theatre is to the traditional tragedy: the latter helps you know; the former makes you experience it. The Absurd experience is neither comic abandon nor tragic catharsis; it is poetry mixed with grotesque. It leads not to the tragic pleasure but to a tragicomic horror. The Greeks too underlined the precarious and mysterious position of man in the universe but, then, at least there was a system of values in the man's own world. Instead of explaining the inexplicable ways of God to man as tragedy does, the Absurd presents the irrational, nightmarish aspect of human existence. Here is, in short, a farcical expression of the predicament of tragedy.

In Samuel Beckett's *Waiting for Godot*, meaninglessness of life is conveyed through purposeless waiting for a Godot who won't come, whose identity is unknown, and whose very existence is in doubt. It could be the waiting of Man for a meaning of life that is essentially meaningless, illusive and elusive. The way Vladimir and Estragon persist with their waiting has something of the touch of hubris about it and, maybe, it is possible to say that hamartia lies in man's seeking to bring meaning into something that is absolutely purposeless. One might even treat this long, long waiting as an endless suffering, but then what is the realization that it yields? None, except that life has to be lived with all its absurdity: you can neither live it nor leave it. Even as Vladimir and Estragon decide to go, they cannot move. The whole situation is balanced like that beautiful sentence about the two thieves: 'Do not despair: one of the thieves was saved. Do not presume: one of the thieves was damned.' A tragedy would have chosen one of these two alternatives and shown that although the consequences of the choice (whatever it was) were disastrous, the choice had to be made and had its own worthwhileness and heroic consequences. In *Waiting for Godot*, no choice is made; the Absurd remains. Here Abel and Cain are one and the same; there is nothing heroic or tragic. In fact, here, the distinction between horror and laughter, logic and illogic, tragic and comic ceases to exist. That is true of all the Absurd theatre: in Arthur Adamov where life is a childish game of Pingpong, in Eugene Ionesco where life is sound and fury signifying nothing like the oratory of a dumb man, in Jean Genet where life is an illusion-mongering and role-playing masquerade, in Edward Albee where life is onion-peeling until you find nothing at the core, in Harold Pinter where life is nightmare itself. It is, let us repeat, all these in tragedies, too, but it is transcended there; here it is the be-all and the end-all.

Theatre of the Absurd marks the very dead-end where the pursuit of tragedy in terms of modern terms could have led—a play without plot, character, passion, drama, inevitability, even language. In the pre-Absurd modern plays, one could still see remnants of the tragic; hence the temptation to call them tragedies of sorts. In our terminology, some lacked existential dichotomy, some macrocosmic dimension, others conflict or suffering; else, it was the case of the absence of creative aspect of suffering, spiritual affirmation, or humanistic core. In Theatre of the Absurd, practically everything associated with tragedy is absent. One by one, all the pillars having been pulled down, the whole edifice has collapsed.

Of course, there are some twentieth century plays which do retain some or most of the tragic aspects, but their tragic power is proportionate to their return to the traditional. That, in a way, goes to reiterate the incompatibility of tragedy and the modern temper. These are plays that turn to myths, to history, to such areas of experience as get related to nature (say, sailors and foresters), primitive life, war, etc. J.M. Synge's *Riders to the Sea* is a powerful tragedy: we have sons in conflict with nature and suffering, and their mother's heroic acceptance of the situation, including their deaths. The secret lies in the fact that Irish people live so close to nature. Maybe, that explains why the best British drama has always come from Ireland. Of course, the role of genius cannot be denied. For example, W.B. Yeats's plays do have simplicity and passion but they do not strike the right note possibly because his imagination had lost the innocence of the primeval life. His problem probably was that he was too learned to keep out theory and abstraction. Another writer of great power was the Spanish bard, Frederico Garcia Lorca, whose *Blood Wedding* has blood passion, conflict between love and honour, affirmation of both microcosm and macrocosm, and a lyricism that is overwhelmingly elevating. Eugene O'Neill's early sea-plays and later farm-based plays like *Desire Under the Elms* confirm the tragic inhering the life that is nature-oriented.

In fact, in the United States, we have had a lot of striving after tragedy but, in terms of real achievements, the record is not commensurate with the incessant, endless pursuit. There is about these attempts a touch of forced effort which cannot be a substitute of true genius or of genuine authentic experience. Writing of tragedy was perhaps a psychological necessity of this nascent nation which wanted to excel in a genre that enjoyed the reputation of representing the best literature of all times; but, then, for fear of being dubbed as backward-looking traditionalists, the playwrights wanted also to accommodate the best in the contemporary intellectual trends in the fields of philosophy, psychology, sociology, literature, etc. In their effort to revive tragedy in terms of modernism, they wrote a lot but failed inevitably as the two refused to coalesce into each other. The American Dream was so very materialistic that it seldom allowed free play to macrocosmic factors and thus, on the level of experience, the success-worshipping America had little tragic in life—excepting such preserves of primitivsm as the Negroes, the Red Indians, the Frontiersmen, the sailors, etc. Had the American playwrights just dramatized their experiences, they might have recaptured the spirit of tragedy; but, having got into the habit of aping Europe in interpreting life in terms of the Freudian, Jungian, Marxist, Frazerian theories, they lost the tragic essence in favour of 'cases.'

In this connection, Eugene O'Neill's progress as a playwright epitomizes, as it were, the goings-on in the entire United States. True, he made statement after statement about his ambition to resurrect the spirit of Greek tragedy, but his insistence to do it in terms of modernism resulted in his producing plays which are certainly fascinating experiments but at the same time such poor tragedies that he himself never felt satisfied enough to explore an experiment in hand any further. Even when he dealt with sailors (*The Hairy Ape*), Negroes (*Emperor Jones*), history (*Fountain*), Greek myths (*Desire Under the Elms*; *Mourning Becomes Electra*), he allowed the modern thoughts to eclipse the tragicality of the themes in hand. Only when, towards the end of his career, he gave up his ideal of writing tragedies and concentrated on just dramatizing the life as he had known it, he produced two of his masterpieces, viz., *The Iceman Cometh* and *Long Day's Journey Into Night*. These plays were not conceived as tragedies but they are some of the most powerful plays of our time. It is possible to say that we have a new kind of tragedy in *The Iceman Cometh*—tragedy not of a hero but of a whole civilization. Thus seen, pipe-dreaming serves as a kind of a tragic flaw shared by all mankind, and the way man sticks to pipe-dreams smacks of hubris, too. What is more, these tragic traits lead the human race to rockbottom where there is nothing really worth affirming, and yet man always prefers to affirm the illusive pipe-dreams. As all this follows the pattern of tragic process, one could say that *The Iceman Cometh* has dramatized tragic vision itself. But as a closer look should show, the stress is not on conflict, suffering and spiritual outcome; what is more, O'Neill operates on the level of contrasts and thus evokes an ironic rather than tragic impact. Ironic, indeed, is the painful realization towards the end of *Long Day's Journey* when the unmasked souls of the four protagonists appear in a very poor light. There is hardly anything affirmative about the Dionysian wisdom thus gained. O'Neill would call the response evoked as the right kind of pity but it is certainly not the tragic kind of pity.

The other major American playwright who consciously attempted tragedy and even theorized about it is Arthur Miller. His chief concern has been to project common man—like a Salesman, for example—as a tragic hero. But *The Death of a Salesman* is concerned more with what is happening to the psyche rather than to the soul of the protagonist. And at the end, Willy Loman's suicidal accident affirms nothing: being no wiser for his experience and his suffering, he dies illusion-mongering still. We cannot interpret it as the affirmation of human spirit, and well might we cry with Linda in the Requiem, 'I don't understand it. Why did you ever do that? . . . I search and search and I search and I can't understand it, Willy.' It is possible to argue that, in creating his last illusion, he has, in a way, affirmed the game of illusion-making that man's life essentially is; it is possible also to interpret audience-bewilderment as an equivalent of the tragic mystique. But, then, do we approve of what he has done: is it an affirmation that exalts us spiritually? All that can be said is that here is a classic case of accommodating all the relevant threads without being able to create the tragic strand.

In Tennessee Williams's tragedies, we have an altogether different kind of response: we suffer but cannot empathize; shocked, we revolt. In his world dominated by women, we have sex without passion, fragility without tenderness, pathos without pity, failure without struggle. Williams's heroines do have a tragic potential but his focus on their neurosis and psychosis makes their fate pathetic rather than tragically heroic. In fact, they sound more like case studies in abnormal psychology than living characters. In *A Streetcar Named Desire*, the situation may make us sympathetic towards Blanche, but is it possible to empathize? And where is the spiritual dimension in her being declared a lunatic? Disintegration of personality does have a tragic power but the bizarre motivations in Blanche render her portrayal unconvincing. Perhaps her sickness can be believed in but certainly not its inevitability.

In the same way, 'modernistic' treatment of material with tragic potential has invariably thwarted other American playwrights. Because of violence and bloodshed, war can be the right background for a tragedy, but only when accompanied by an equally compelling tenderness; in the absence of the latter, the result is brutalization rather than humanization. On the other hand, while suffering is certainly a necessary part of the tragic action, it cannot be just any type of suffering. In the 'Red' plays, in the absence of macrocosmic terror, the 'human' peters out into the pathetic. In short, while elements and aspects are important, even more important is their proper integration.

Perhaps it is no use going on and on with this underlining of the untragic in the so-called modern tragedies. From what we have said so far, it should be clear that every modern playwright has perverted the genre in his own way and thus perhaps there are as many types of 'modern' tragedies as the playwrights. They are serious plays all right, but they do not always assume existential dichotomy; if the dichotomy is there, it may not precipitate into a conflict, or that conflict may not be between the macrocosm and the microcosm; even if the right conflict is there, it may not involve anything shocking or produce suffering; else the suffering may not prove creative in the sense of yielding the Dionysiac wisdom or affirmation of the human spirit. In the absence of one or some of these aspects, the overall impact fails to crystallize into the humanization of the auidence; instead, all this manipulation of our responses may fizzle into sentimental tears, farcical amusement, or ironic laugh at the futility of human effort to reap glory out of nothingness. Indeed, in almost all the modern tragedies, one discerns the presence of something or the other which is basically untragic. What single definition can accommodate the so-called tragedies of Ibsen, Strindberg, Chekhov, Pirandello, Brecht, Yeats, Eliot, Shaw, Galsworthy, Anouilh, Sartre, Camus, Beckett, Ionesco, Genet, O'Neill, Arthur Miller, Tennessee Williams, Edward Albee? As we cannot find any way of amending or emending our understanding of tragedy to accommodate them, we propose to call their works 'tragedic' plays rather than tragedies.

At this stage, perhaps it would be interesting to raise again those oft-asked questions for possible answers in the framework of the formulations offered by us.

First and foremost, what is the essence of tragedy? It is, as we take it, affirmation of the imperfect microcosmic values even after realizing the inalienability and absoluteness of the macrocosmic laws which tend to reduce man to a position of absurd nothingness. In simpler words, the essence of the tragedy lies in endorsing affectively the transcendence of the natural/animal within man. From this, it is easy to deduce the function of tragedy. It implies (a) stripping of the illusive masks covering the macrocosmic Reality; (b) letting man see, from the vantage-point of authentic existence, the vital dependence of the microcosm on the macrocosm; and (c) inducing man to affirm, even after realizing the relativity of human values, the human effort at transcending the existential limitations which can never be overcome. With respect to the audience, the function of tragedy is (a) to rouse the natural self through empathy, (b) to help share the macrocosmic as well as the transcendental, and consequently (c) to facilitate feeling purified and exalted because of the catharsis of the natural/animal in man. Catharsis thus may be regarded as the purgation of animalism in the act of affirming the human microcosm.

Does tragedy signify a clash between Fate and Free Will, Necessity and Freedom? The answer would be in the affirmative if Fate or Necessity is the name of the eternal laws of macrocosm from which there is no escape, Freedom standing for human will to transcend the existential limitation. In case Fate is interpreted as a blind, superhuman force and will as an individual's spirit, the endorsement cannot be all that unequivocal. It is worth noting that we are not using the word macrocosm as an equivalent of the Greek gods; macrocosmic laws are eternal, absolute and non-partisan. A tragedy that makes one perceive the real relation between Nature and man, surely affirms not only microcosmic human values but also macrocosmic laws. This is certainly different from what the Greeks termed as divine justice.

Must a tragedy end in death? Mortality being the easiest way of perceiving the absoluteness of macrocosmic laws, it is most commonly used, but it is by no means an essential attribute of tragedy. What is indispensable is the inevitable, ultimate triumph of the macrocosm and man defying it with dignity. In place of death, unhinged mind, stupor, physical violence, resignation might do as well. What is more essential in the close of a tragedy is a sense of mystery. Exploring the mystery of human existence, a play does give the impression of approaching a neat formulation by way of an answer but, towards the close, it wraps up its pandora's box as if to declare that the human spirit is too eclectic to be shackled in the bonds of ethics or any formula. That versatility also answers the question about the view, vision or philosophy inhering tragedy.[9]

Is tragedy nihilistic and/or atheistic? Nihilistic it is certainly not. As for atheism, it is, in fact, both antigod and religion-substitute. To overcome the fear of existence, man had created gods; when the gods too failed, the cosmically uprooted man invented a substitute, viz., tragedy. It serves the same purpose as religion—of overcoming existential limitations, of holding man in a meaningful relationship with macrocosm which crushes him. It is not for nothing that tragedy originated in the worship of Dionysus—a god whose divine status was suspect. Both strong and tender, majestic and coquettish, Dionysus was neither man nor woman but woman-in-man and man-in-woman. Indeed, as Thomas G. Rosenmeyer has shown, Dionysian state means an ambivalent state of being superhuman and subhuman, a savage as well as a demigod—conducting bloody orgies in the Paradise of milk and honey.

What and who is a tragic hero? The answer is quite obvious—a man who is at once natural enough to represent macrocosmic laws and social enough to embody the microcosmic values. Clearly, each man has in him the making of a tragic hero, though not every body is animal enough to force the confrontation or human enough to affirm the microcosmic imperfections. It is not the question of social status: tragic hero is superior to the common man in that he belongs to the aristocracy of passions. What it means is that the hero is not a man dehumanized but an animal humanized. The animal in a normal man is dormant; in a hero, it is fully aroused but on a leash, as it were. This strong point can prove to be his weak point, too—his *hamartia*, so to say. The *hubris* lies in his insisting on remaining human—i.e., being attached to both the macrocosm and the microcosm, despite their mutual incompatibility. The noncompromising and monomaniac aspects of a tragic hero are nothing but the assertions of the *hubris* that is persistent and unchangeable. When the conflict between the human values (born of microcosmic illusion) and the macrocosmic Reality befuddles the mind and touches the hero deeply, *agon* is the result. *Peripeteia* signifies the erosion of the strong passion, even as *anagnorisis* implies the dawning of the realization regarding the inevitable and vital dependence of the microcosm on the macrocosm.

Coming to the 'action' of tragedy, one can only echo McCollom: it is all-too-purposive. In fact, everything in a tragedy is purposive—be it plot, action, form, structure, language, or hero. They are all interrelated because they are there just to help the formal cause or the essence of tragedy to realize its function. In a truly dramtic situation, plot, character, language promote one another; being the most dramatic of all the genres, tragedy has to have such plot, character and language as are so mutually dependent on one another as to appear one.[10] After all, the basic *purpose* governing plot/action, structure/form and language of tragedy is harnessing of the tragic view of life in the service of purgation, revelation and elevation. Indeed, there need not necessarily be a story with fixed motifs but it must accommodate microcosmic and macrocosmic attributes, the conflict between the two, the shock resulting from it, and the affirmation of the existential dichotomy. The action has to be emotionally exciting, intellectually stimulating and spiritually exalting. The range of form and structure is not pre-fixed; but it has to accommodate shocking events, hero's suffering and affirmation, and audience-epiphany—in a manner that would vouch the validity of Henn's analogies about 'nets' and 'trigger.' The organic development must take care of relating the microcosm to the macrocosm in such a way that the particular becomes universal. Besides, it must create the right empathy and go on to facilitate the alchemy of transferring the passion and glory of the hero to the audience.

The language also has to be purposive—one that can manipulate the emotive, the cognitive and the spiritual. That it necessitates the employing of emotive language goes without saying. But, obviously, it has to be more than the language of the heart; it must also help express the cognitive aspect. But, then, the metaphysical or ethical contents are not to be just articulated but to be communicated in the form of vision wherein mind and imagination interact. Besides, to lend the plot a universal touch, use of figurative speech, imagery and symbols is most helpful. This is to make a case not for versification or poetic drama but for a language that can, even if in prose, raise the play above the level of everyday experience and thus help transcendence. Only such a language can effect the fusion of character and action, words and meaning. As for the spiritual dimension of tragedy, the right medium should be music—the language of the soul. No wonder, chorus had such an important role in Greek tragedy that Nietzsche accused Euripides of killing tragedy in the process of reducing the role of chorus. In this connection, one could also refer to the role of myths in tragedy. Myth is ideal for organizing collective experience, for accommodating in an experience the philosophy, ethics, theology, sociology, jurisprudence and history of the people, for universalizing the particulars, and for striking deeper into one's psyche via archetypes, images, symbols, etc. Even otherwise, since myths afford pre-historical history, pre-theological state of religion, pre-traditional art, pre-scientific reality, pre-logical philosophy, and since the vision of tragedy is also a kind of sub-philosophy or pre-philosophy, myths and tragedy can be ideal companions.

As regards the question of tragedy being related to the spirit of the ages, the answer is quite obvious. The macrocosmic laws are, of course, the same and man by nature remains unchanged; but the microcosmic values keep undergoing continuous changes, depending on the evolution of civilization and the temper of the times. Every age has its own problems in relation to Nature, even though the latter is fundamentally the same. That accounts for a different kind of conflict in each age and therefore potentially different kind of tragedy, too. Thus tragedy of a particular time depicts dichotomy uppermost in the minds of the artists of that time. For example, it asked the Greeks, the pagans, if their gods were really as good and powerful as they were supposed to be; it made the Christian Elizabethans, who had faith in the Chain of Being, wonder if the animal in man was really despicable; for the seventeenth century French, the question posed was whether man is really as rational as they believed him to be. What applies to time applies to space, too. Hence such distinctions as Renaissance, Elizabethan, Jacobean, Modern tragedies on the one hand, and Greek, Roman, French, Irish, Spanish, Russian tragedies, on the other.

The inevitable corollary to all this is the question: why has tragedy not thrived in all ages and why has it been a monopoly of certain ages? The answer lies perhaps in the fact that there are times when man is too preoccupied with his microcosmic problems to bother about his relationship with macrocosm—the moderns, for example. That it thrives in comparatively primitive milieus is undeniable; that is why Negroes, sailors, foresters are being exploited by the modern tragic artists. Indeed, as civilization advances, not only poetry but also tragedy declines.

True, the animal or natural within man does not, and cannot, die altogether and thus a most civilized man can also be touched macrocosmically, but it does affect the capacity and degree of intensity. What is more, since tragedy requires awareness of dichotomy in human nature, involves conflict with Nature and disaster of man, and insists on the assertion of the human dignity in failure, the world-view has to be not only humanistic but also optimistic at a deeper level. Obviously, not all ages have that—at least not equally. In any case, how different and how deeply tragic the experience afforded by an age can be would depend on its perception of the relationship between the macrocosm and the microcosm. The nature of conflict would also depend upon the temper of an age. Take, for example, the relation between individual and society. In Hellenic Greece, society and individuals were inseparably one—interchangeable terms, as it were; in the sixteenth century England, the Renaissance did project individualism as a great value but it went hand in hand with the social values and thus we have the situation of society-and-individual, both being represented by kings and generals as heroes; in the seventeenth century France, it was a case of either individual or society; in the late nineteenth century Europe, it became society versus individual. Because of these various factors, it is not surprising that tragedy has had such a chequered career during the last twenty-five centuries.

It should be interesting to have a look on the one hand at the tempers of those civilizations that witnessed the high peaks of tragedy (viz., Periclean Greece and Elizabethan England) and on the other at the geniuses of those literary epochs which have yielded lots of dramatic literature and yet proved barren in respect of truly tragic creativity (e.g., ancient India and modern age). Let us, first of all, take the peak ages together to see what is common between them. Answer comes from Edith Hamilton: neither was a period of darkness and despair; in both, life was exalted, each being a time of thrilling and unfathomable possibilities. Both held their heads high after their respective victories over their neighbours. This joy of heroism made the world appear a place of wonder and mankind beauteous. Indeed, an age of darkness and defeat cannot yield a tragic outlook.

For Lane Cooper, the Hellenic traits were three—direct vision, a high degree of sensitiveness and an extraordinary power of inhibition, i.e., restraint: they saw clearly, felt keenly and refrained from much. Besides, they could see parts individually, parts related to each other as parts, parts related to the whole, and the whole as a whole. These qualities enabled them to live fully on both macrocosmic and microcosmic planes and thus experience the conflicts and their outcome, which could not but be humanistic and deeply optimistic for those known for pagan joy of living. Sir R.W. Livingstone has pointed out that the Greeks regarded life as a human problem and they gloried in the imperfections of man. H.D.F. Kitto's study of the Greek mind has revealed that the Greeks possessed a sense of wholeness of things, a firm belief in reason and rationality of the universe, a simplicity that facilitated the discovery of unity in diversity, a strong sense of form, and Logos that enabled them to see things with the eyes of mind. No wonder, for them, their theology was one with their morality in the form of mythology. Their ideal was not refraining from authentic living but acquiring serenity through the control of passions. They did not despise biological urges; instead, they lauded eros for tingling every nerve. Besides, as E.R. Dodds has highlighted, for the Greeks, the greatest blessings came to man by way of madness—the prophetic madness of Apollo, the ritualistic madness of Dionysus, the poetic madness of the Muses, the erotic madness inspired by Aphrodite, etc. It was, indeed, typical of the Greek mind to lend divine dimension to the irrational and to see the whole thing as tragic anomaly. Tragedy is an achievement possible only when mind and spirit, the particular and the general, are balanced; then alone can one individual symbolize the whole humanity on both macrocosmic and microcosmic planes. Instead of submitting to reality, the Greeks resisted, rejoiced and turned full-face to life, knowing full well how bitter life is, and how sweet, with all its joys and sorrows. For them, Truth was Beauty and Beauty, Truth. To such people comes the glorious vision of tragedy—only when the spirit of enquiry meets the spirit of poetry. Indeed, the Greeks affirmed the microcosm without denying the macrocosm.

As for the Elizabethan age, its character was epitomized in the Queen herself—sensual, artistic, pleasure-seeking, at once extravagant and sordidly mean, possessing cool and calculating intellect and yet governed by the blindest passions, both compassionate and cruel, affectionate and vain. Marking the close of the medieval times and the dawn of the Renaissance, it was an age of wisdom as well as of darkness, full of hope as well as despair. Bristling with a new outlook, new aristocracy, new literature, new religion, new spirit of humanism, newly acquired sense of nationalism, new geographical boundaries, new fields of trade, new learning, it was also an age in which people were still superstitious and revelled in bloodshed, cock fighting, violent warfare, etc. In this 'Merry England,' the exuberant joy of life was evidenced in their heavy drinking, boisterous singing, love of glitter and pageantry; but in the firmament of this 'nest of singing birds,' there also played a network of menacing lightnings. Copernicus, Luther, Machiavelli and Montaigne had struck discordant notes by posing uncomfortable questions. Humanism of the age tried to reconcile the old and the new, the general and the particular, the mind and the spirit, the sensual and the ethereal in the Chain of Being. No wonder we have in this age a balance between worldliness and otherworldliness, individualism and respect for authority, Christianity and Machiavellianism, Catholic faith in God and Protestant urge for individual soul. One step further towards Puritanism would—and it did, in the seventeenth century—upset this delicate balance. In the Elizabethan age, the old was not turned out as undesirable; it was accommodated with the new. Marked by unity, concord and proportion, the age recognised in the microcosm as well as in the macrocosm, a unity in diversity—that the Universe is like a body with diverse organs. Like the Greeks exploring the possibilities of human experience, the Elizabethans were ever-seeking something new. To suck the marrow out of life and find all that was worth the feeling—such was the ideal of that age. To be a good animal and yet never make a beast of oneself—that was a part of the life's philosophy which the Elizabethans, like the Greeks, cherished. No wonder, tragedy suited so ideally the temper of this age. The Elizabethans could see clearly both microcosm and macrocosm and how they were related to each other—both vitally and precariously.

And now to the incompatibles. As regards the complete absence of tragedy in Sanskrit drama, the reason can be traced to the Hindu view of life. Tragedy, as we have maintained, thrives in humanistic cultures and its chief motivation has always been to restore confidence to man when his position in the universe is menaced. Faced with a threat from macrocosm, man turns to microcosm in which he would rather be a petty something than a mere nonentity. The Hindu view of life is not man-centred; on the contrary, the Absolute Nothingness which the Western man seeks to avoid at all costs is the very thing that an Orientalist seeks in the form of *Moksha* or *Nirvāna*. As the Absolute is Nothing, being something means being less than Absolute. Thus, in the East, instead of being satisfied with a little of material progress, one would rather aim at achieving the highest acme of perfection by becoming one with the Absolute, i.e., Nothing. Brahma created Himself out of Nothingness and later, feeling bored, created the Universe. It was His *Leela*, His *Maya*, an art in which man is a creation like others—created not for the glory of man but for God's own amusement. Thus, Nature, Man and Society having been created simultaneously, no permanent feud among them is to be assumed. The why and wherefore of this *Samsāra* is not known; nor is it knowable. People come, play their roles and die. In this context, obviously, death is no evil as a Westerner would treat it; it is rather the potential gateway to salvation. Being a man is nothing either good or bad intrinsically. It is just an opportunity wherein by playing the game of life fairly, one may earn *Moksha* (salvation); otherwise, one will be reborn to play yet another role. Unlike the Greek gods, the Hindu gods are always just. Once one has earned suffering, one cannot escape it—one must suffer for it now or later (maybe, in one's next incarnation) when it might appear inconsonant with the *Karma* of one's life then. Being punished now means settling the account and thus slashing down chunks of debit-side. In other words, out of suffering, man emerges a lesser sinner, a purer being, and therefore nearer *Moksha*. Suffering is, therefore, to be treated as a welcome state of existence. Worldly pleasures are no sins; rather they are permissible; only their excessive indulgence is not in one's own-interest because the consequences might thwart or delay one's ultimate aim of *Moksha*. Even eroticism is not a curse so long as one lives within the framework of *Dharma* (i.e., duty or right-doing).

Governed by the laws of *Dharma* and *Karma*, Hindu view of life obviates any conflict between one's duties towards the society on the one hand and towards the family on the other. Such are the conflicts which serve as the staple basis of tragic dilemmas in the Western literature. Far from ignoring or denying the natural instincts, Hinduism relates them to social and spiritual aims and makes them dependent on one another. All the four ideals of human life, (viz., *Dharma, Artha, Kāma*, and *Moksha*) are based on the natural human urges—for common good, for power and wealth, for sex, and for communion with the Unseen, respectively. By relating *Dharma* to *Karma*, the Hindu concept of *Honi* (destiny) is saved from becoming a sort of pessimistic fatalism that might lead to surrender or else induce inaction; instead, it urges one to good action. Because of this perfect blend of Fate and Character, there is no clash between what the Westerners would call Necessity and Free Will. Similarly, what the Westerners call evil is an ingredient of health here: *Rajas* and *Tamas* are needed to effect an amalgam with *Sattva*, or else there will be no equilibrium in nature.

How could there be a tragedy in the Hindu literature where gods, instead of being capricious and wanton, are absolutely just; where individual, social and natural desires are incapable of entering a conflict; where even Wealth, Power and Phallus are idealized; where suffering is a desirable thing and never meaningless; where personal flaws are mere errors and never existential evil; where, in short, human valuation is totally dispensed with? In a religion that bestows divinity on all creatures and in which the subject and the object, I and Thou, are phases of the same spirit, there cannot be any existential dichotomy, for it denies validity to nothing. With such a faith there can never be a sense of mystery or questioning the ways of God, and therefore there can never be a tragedy!

And now, finally, the modern age vis-a-vis tragedy. Never before has tragedy been the centre of so much critical concern, theoretical attention and determined pursuit as in the twentieth century, and yet there has been so little of genuine tragedy. Numerous attempts have been made to explain this phenomenon.[11] To us it appears that the source of failure lies in the modern temper itself. As civilization advances, the struggle of culture to keep pace implies a shift in values. That change signifies the modernity of an age. At the turn of the century, this modernity became 'modernism' when the usual cultural lag became a cultural vacuum. Owing to technological, psychological and sociological discoveries, most of the current values were discarded one by one; that necessitated a cultural reconstruction of a radical nature. But the birth of that new culture did not materialize for decades on end and thus the usual phoenix hour stretched into a whole age of one-dimensional evolution. Here was a civilization without culture; having rejected all traditions, traditionlessness became the only tradition. This dissociation of culture and civilization implied an ontological insecurity and alienation for man: he found living more comfortable but life more meaningless. It appeared as if there were a kind of conspiracy—which Joseph Wood Krutch termed 'Grand Strategy'—to dispossess man of his position of significance in the world of his own making.[12]

The diverse pulls resulting from the dissociation of culture and civilization lent the modern man's personality a touch of paranoia because the sense of superiority derived from technological progress was matched only by the lack of confidence in himself. In short, here was a creature rich in intellect but weak in rationality, morally bankrupt, spiritually anguished and emotionally desublimated. Having rejected all faiths, laws and traditions of the past, he was, as it were, decrystallized. Lust without love, defeat without loss, and victory without hope came to characterize his spiritual state. It was a most unenviable situation, indeed. Not content with the existential insignificance, man had revolted against the macrocosm; must that very man now accept a similar position of insignificance even in the microcosm of his own making? This was a tragic dilemma, but since affirmation of this situation would mean living like a robot, the modern man could not affirm life tragically. That is to say, the modern man's experience looked tragic but could not afford tragic exaltation. No wonder, in modern drama, we have tragic melancholy without its imagination, tragic revolt without idealism, tragic wisdom without its experience.

Tragedy needs mythology, modernism offered pathology; tragedy insists on experience, modernism could supply problems; tragedy demands robust yea-saying, modernism prompted protean acceptance; tragedy breaks illusion to induce an authentic reaffirmation, the modern man knew only too well the intrinsic absurdity of accepting tragic consolation. An age that had perverted humanism could not breed tragedy which must sing hymns in the praise of man. Tragedy is a mode of hero-worship; it could not thrive in an iconoclastic age that took pride in breaking idols. Certainly an age that consecrated faceless masses and hallowed quantity and materialism could not be an age congenial to an art that celebrates individualism, quality and idealism.

The literary output of an era corresponds to its temper; an age like ours may produce debunking naturalism, schizophrenic expressionism, faceless cubism, mechanistic futurism, neurotic surrealism, the grotesque and the absurd, but not tragedy that exalts, synthesizes, affirms, glorifies and restores one's faith in man. No wonder, too, instead of Promethean image, in the modern protagonism, we have an antihero. Inhuman, perverse, moronic, hysterical or sterile, the typically 'modern' heroes are minimal men. A tragedy does have moments when one asks the question, 'Is man no more than this?' but later one learns to offer an affirmative answer. In the Absurd theatre, we only keep repeating the question. In the existentialist literature, what we learn to admire is man's role and not his tragic place in the universe. The existentialist's distrust of idealism is matched by the naturalist's craze for the petty and the trivial. Expressionists abolish time and space and effect nightmarish distortion instead of tragic exaltation. In the psychological literature, instead of experience that one may share or empathize with, we have 'cases' and obsessions. In short, the literature of the twentieth century highlights only the absurdity, triviality, abnormality and perversity of human life. All this could yield good plays, even great drama, but, when all is said and done, the overall result is antithesis of the tragic.

Eastward, Ho!

About the formulation discussed in the preceding section, gradually I started having reservations. I had a growing feeling that the relationship between the macrocosm and the microcosm, which has been treated as the very pivot of the theory, is more of a myth than a fact. Besides, tragic pleasure being basically an aesthetic response, the key to this phenomenon cannot be sought outside the framework of aesthetics. However, when I turned to the western aesthetic scholarship for answers, the exercise left me more baffled than before. The philosophers' minute hair-splitting being too subtle and abstruse, in the long run, I found myself surrounded by posers rather than answers.

Indeed, the entire range of aesthetics is littered with controversies. There is no unanimity on anything, not even about the starting point, viz., the concept of beauty. If Plato sees in beauty a shadow of the archetypal Beauty, a manifestation of God, for the Aristotelians, it is something altogether mundane: it owes its existence to its perception by man who is the measure of beauty. Likewise, while the Middle Ages felt convinced of the divine origin of beauty and Renaissance traced it to nature, for the French materialists, it is no more than a natural property of objects and phenomena. If, for the classicists like Nicolas Boileau-Despreaux, beauty inheres goodness, for a romanticist like John Keats it is another name of truth. For Benedetto Croce, life is aesthetically neutral and beauty emerges when man emotionally penetrates his inner wealth to life. For Immanuel Kant, whatever pleases without interest is beauty, even as George Santayana defines it as pleasure objectified. Michelangelo Buonarroti, on the other hand, sees it in the purgation of superfluities. Despite all these theories, one might as well wonder still whether it lies in the object or in the beholder's eye. Is it subjective or objective, natural or divine, sacred or profane, a means or an end, a fact or a value? Above all, can one analyze beauty, or is it something inexplicable?

Variety with regard to the interpretations regarding the nature of art is equally bewildering and so also the other related questions which clamour for answers. Plato would banish artists from his Republic because, for him, art is not only hedonistic imitation of imitation but also irrational in every way. Aristotle's defence only helped raise art from the sphere of sensuality to that of morality. If for Plotinus it is a form of mystic ecstasy, for the intellectual aesthetes of Renaissance it is reason in sensuous form. While Leonardo da Vinci and Shakespeare project art as a mirror held up to nature, George Wilhelm Friedrich Hegel believes that it is a superstructure built on the basement of nature. For Johann Wolfgang Von Goethe, on the other hand, art is art because it is not nature. According to Denis Diderot, art cannot imitate nature because nature is always changing. For Croce, it is intuition; for Joshua Reynolds, it is imitation under the direction of imagination; for Roger Fry, it is perception of purposeful order and variety; for Dewitt H. Park, it is a thing made by man for his pleasure; for Jacques Maritain, it is a virtue of practical intellect; for Leo Tolstoy, it is a means of communicating emotions. In vain does one ask whether the quintessence of art lies in content or in form, whether it signifies illusion or reality. Likewise, is art in creator's imagination, in the process of creation, in the artefact, or in the percipient's response? Is it a thing created or imitated, a concretization of an idea or an emotion? Does it lie in parts or in the whole? Is its aim hedonistic pleasure, knowledge, communication, enrichment of life, or therapeutic outlet of surplus energy? Is it universal or something individualistic? Is it subservient to morality or is it something for its own sake? Is it art that is expression or expression that is art? Interestingly enough, Yuri Borev, in his text-book on aesthetics, talks about the genealogy, ontology, sociology, psychology, morphology, semiology, gnoseology, even exiology of art.

As for the aesthetic experience, does it belong to the realm of creation, perception or both? Do the twin experiences of poiesis and aesthesis belong to the same field or would it be more sensible to treat the psychology of creation as entirely different from the psychology of perception? Echoes of the earlier questions one hears in different forms when it is asked whether aesthetic creativity is something mundane or divine, a case of involvement or detachment, a matter of creating forms or values, determined by intention, execution, inspiration or perspiration. Again, is artistic activity a mode of presentation or representation, an exercise in selection or integration, product of impression or expression? Likewise, from the angle of reception, does the aesthetic experience belong to the realm of emotions, philosophy, psychology or spirituality? Is aesthetic perception a matter of intellection, suggestiveness, inference, recollection, introspection, illusion, revelation or transcendental communion? Indeed, is the aesthetic experience a mode of awareness or escape, a matter of empathy or distancing, an affair of intellectual enlightenment or divine madness? Is it a hedonic indulgence, an experience loaded with deeper meaning, or a form of desublimation? Is one's response to a poem, a novel, a piece of music, a dance performance, a play production essentially of the same nature?

Indeed, is there really anything common in one's reception of Pablo Picasso and Michelangelo, Shakespeare and Samuel Beckett, an art film and a popular entertainer? Above all, is aesthetic experience always pleasurable, and does a work of art have to be beautiful necessarily?

While Hegel regards aesthetics as the science of senses and emotions, for Croce it implies knowledge—of course, intuitive rather than logical. For the latter, art being expression of impression, aesthetic feeling is more apparent than real. For Kant, it is a case not of perception but of apperception. For John Dewey, every work of art is a complete experience involving a perception of relationship between what is done and what is undergone. For Hunter Mead, however, it is relational experience—a matter of perceiving two or more sensations in relation to one another. Theodore Adorno, on the other hand, sees beauty in what he calls 'homeostasis of tension.'

The vast diversity of opinion inhering the western schools of aesthetics is brought home in *The Foundation of Aesthetics* by I.A. Richards, C.K. Ogden and James Wood. Indeed, following the different aestheticians, anything and everything can be accepted as beautiful if it possesses the simple quality of beauty (Roger Fry), if it has a special form, if it is a work of genius (Kant, Arthur Schopenhauer, Henri Bergson), if it reveals truth (S.T. Coleridge), if it leads to desirable social effects (John Ruskin), if it is an expression (Croce), if it causes pleasure (Santayana), if it embodies the spirit of nature/the ideal/the typical/the universal, if it produces illusion, if it excites emotions, if it involves the process of empathy, if it heightens vitality, if it brings one into touch with exceptional personalities, or if it conduces to synaesthesis. Indeed, these attitudes have yielded theoretical paradigms which trace aesthetic response to beauty, form, medium, genius, expression, imitation, empathy, revelation, etc. Perhaps one can group these paradigms under the functions of art. In this connection one recalls James K. Feibleman's five functions—ontological (art for its own sake), logical (creating harmony out of parts), epistemological (increase of knowledge), psychological (increase of experience), and social (art as a means of communication).

True, all these are important insights but, unfortunately, none of them explains all. For example, the Imitationist approach judges artistic product by standards of literal truth; the Expressionist approach reduces everything to biographical components; and the Formalists' exclusive concern with form bypasses altogether the broad matrix of human experience. Likewise, the Emotionalist theory ignores intellectual tensions and even complexity of emotions. The proponents of Communication, on the other hand, tend to forget that the core of aesthetic experience lies in experience rather than in its meaning. No wonder, in *The Aesthetic Field*, Arnold Berleant refers to these approaches as surrogate theories. According to him, aesthetic experience is meta-aesthetic—a direct communion in which senses, imagination, awareness, values, etc., get fused to yield a total situation involving the object, the activity, and the experience of art. In this experience, art gets bound to life and one lives a life that is richer and more complete; after all, in its totality, it embraces at once biological, psychological, historical, cultural and even technological factors. In the aesthetic field thus created, the artist, the art object and the percipient interact mutually in all possible permutations. Consequently, the quality of the aesthetic transaction can be described neither as cognitive nor inferential, nor even discursive. It is presentational rather than representational, immediate rather than mediate, intuititve rather than analytical, contextual rather than fragmented. In the totality of such a transaction, the role of art is not teaching and yet it is educative, experience is not evaluative and still it is evaluational, aesthetic value is experienced as intrinsic and yet judged as extrinsic.

Indeed, it is possible to go a long way with Berleant when he stresses the experiential totality. By no means an anti-intellectual approach, it is primarily a protest against the reductionism of the others. One feels uncomfortable, however, when he starts talking about aesthetics in terms of the 'modes' of experience without relating them to the substance. Besides, in his keenness to accommodate the experiential totality, he forgoes the uniqueness that goes with art. What is more, his approach is too empirical to be concerned with the quality and the dynamics of the aesthetic experience—how exactly the immediate communion gets effected and what the overall impact of the response yields. For me, in Western philosophy, Berleant served as a dead-end. If even such an eclectic approach is inadequate, one must give up or turn elsewhere, I argued to myself. Thus did I direct my probe Eastward.

In nothing perhaps does the polarity between the spiritual East and the rational West appear more crystallized than in their respective arts, cultures and aesthetic formulations. Believing that the reality lies in what is visible, the anthropocentric occidentalist is ever concerned with the realm of the senses; priding in the superiority of his own intellect, his obsession is with the ideas. For the mystical orientalist, on the other hand, Reality is within and thus his concern is with the invisible, inner world of the spirit. Indeed, as someone rightly put it, Buddha seeks within, Archimedes without. Orientalist lab. is within him: as against observation in the West, in the East it is always self-examination. Instead of asserting the egoistic 'I,' the eastern mind aims at primordial unity wherein 'I' is by no means an independent entity. Eastern man sees no permanent feud between man and the universe, between the self and the world around, between feelings and thoughts. The Western and the Eastern aesthetics, therefore, present a study in contrast with regard to their exclusive concerns—form against formlessness, parts against the whole, diversity against unity, imitation against ritualism, realism against idealization, individualism against totality, empathy against participation. Not surprisingly, while the West talks in terms of art-versus-life, in the East, art subsumes all aspects of life. So much so that one of the most cherished oriental ideals is to make living itself a veritable art. In fact, art, religion and metaphysics being intimately interrelated, the aesthetic and the spiritual values tend to coalesce in the East.

However, in the East, the attention received by aesthetics proper is not extensive enough—except in India where, too, the context is invariably theatre or poetry. After all, the Eastern mind is not too concerned with analytical theories. Interestingly, however, whatever the East has said is conspicuously different. Most characteristically, its soul-oriented explanations steer clear of the Western obsession with such ideational categories as cognition, perception, etc. Seen closely, it is possible to say that in certain ways, the diverse approaches of the East and the West complement one another. Possibly, therefore, the tapping of the perspectives could help arrive at a better understanding of the aesthetic problems.

The Islamic world has little to offer—because of the well-known antipathy of Islam towards the fine arts. The two arts which did receive some patronage were architecture and calligraphy—both yoked into the service of religion via mosques and scriptures. Understandably, the principle of monism which governs Islam is reflected in the realm of their aesthetics, too—vis-a-vis these specific arts. Art is supposed to clarify; it must help the spirit to detach itself from the disturbing multitude of things so that it may climb again towards the Infinite Unity.

In China, the scenario with respect to artistic creativity is more varied, but the contribution to aesthetic theory is not too impressive. The Chinese mind is practical and proverbially known for wisdom rather than for abstract theories. Anyway, it is easy to see that the traditional art of the Chinese was rooted in their typical world-view which discerned transformative power in the rhythmic vitality of the universe. To conform to that rhythm, an artist tries to recognize the centre of the cosmic forces. Once he has identified the rhythmic vitality in his own feelling, even the simplest form becomes evocative. Thus gets established a unity between the subject and the object—the artist, the art object and the percipient. No wonder one of the most characteristic images of the Chinese art is a waterfall in which the fusion of mountain and water signifies the union of 'Yang' and 'Yin'—the male and the female principles which represent, respectively, the static sameness of the object and the dynamic change in the subject. Another characteristic expression of the Chinese art lies in the perfect beauty of lotus. Being a modelled image of the Buddha, it prompts the viewer to look inward to see the Buddha there and thus to recognize the Buddha in one's own nature.

In fact, the Chinese aesthetics is ultimately linked to the Buddhist practice of *Dhyāna*. Here, the cardinal principle is—'the less done, the clearer is reality; the less said, the more direct our apprehension.' The mindless-mind state sought in the meditation is that blissful condition of *Nirvāna* when everything in the universe looks nothing but the original mind, viz., Buddha. Only in a similar state of original mind does one create true art, which has, in turn, the power of inducing a comparable state of original mind in the percipient as well. No wonder, in China, the right to paint is traditionally denied to those who, in their love of luxury, power or money have lost the innocence of their mind.

The '*Dhyāna*' Buddhism of China became Zen Buddhism in Japan. That is why the practice of concentration has come to be idealized in all the Japanese arts—even the martial arts like swordsplay, judo, karate, etc. An artist's mind, it is believed, is a mirror to reflect things as they are: that is possible when the mind becomes one with the object. For this, the artist must practise mental training. By focusing his consciousness on a certain phenomenon, he can experience the Reality itself. In other words, as in the Zen practice, the artistic creativity implies emancipation from the worldly worries. The big idea is to achieve a tranquillity of mind when it is possible to grasp the core or the essence of Reality. In the Zen terminology, it is called *Satori*-experience—a dive into the depth of cosmic unconscious so as to reach the pure experience of pre-knowledge innocence. The aesthetic counterpart of *Satori* is what Zeami calls '*Yugen*'—*Yu* (faintness, shadowyness, negation of solidity) plus *Gen* (darkness caused by density). In *Yugen*, the empirical world becomes intangible and mysterious—after losing solidity and pointing to the presence of the primordial reality underlying there. In the practical terms of aesthetics, this fusion of 'mystery' and 'depth' implies a focus on certain phenomenon in such a way that its spirit is derived before giving that flash a reality. An artist must gaze intently at the invisible underneath the visible; he must go beyond the sensuous limitation until he reaches that stage of nothingness which the object had before it was polluted with a 'being.' That explains why the Japanese invariably write very short poems. The idea is to chisel the words and fill them with an ineffable and undefinable beauty. Since the Japanese are practical rather than abstract in thinking, this quality of *Yugen* is at the heart of such typically Japanese arts as the flower-arrangement and Way of the Tea. Needless to add, the fusion of mystery and depth is best realized in Noh and Kabuki.

Zeami has described nine stages[13] in Noh acting—ranging from crude realism to mystical beauty. This evolution, in fact, corresponds to the emergence of metaphysical meaning in the practice of the Zen—from density to nothingness. What is more, the four levels of contemplative experience which Zeami describes sum up the processes of both the Zen and the aesthetic experience. On the first level, the cognitive focus ceases to be cognitive and thus turns into the awareness of the contemplative field. Thus, instead of the subject and the object of cognition, we have the field as well as the awareness of the field. On the second level, the distinction between the field and the awareness vanishes and consequently images and forms are wiped out. Next, image of a physically visible extension gradually changes into an image of unfathomable depth; awareness gets dissolved and what remains is only the field illuminating itself. Lastly, on the fourth and final level, both the awareness and the field disappear and we witness something beyond imagination. The unfathomable darkness itself becomes suddenly transformed into a boundless dazzling light.

Traditionally, the Zen/*Dhyāna* meditation has come to be identified inalienably with Buddhism so much so that invariably people treat it as the very point of its distinction vis-a-vis other faiths. But the fact is that it is by no means altogether alien to the spirit of Hinduism. Seen closely, *Dhyāna* is *Yoga* with a difference. The *yogin* seeks transcendental joy, *Brahmānanda*, in the merger of soul with the Supersoul by controlling his ego; the practitioner of Zen aims at killing that very ego so as to reach that zero-stage called *Nirvāna* where even the soul stands annihilated. Anyway, what *Yugen* is to *Satori*, *Ānanda* is to *Brahāmananda*. And that brings us to the Indian aesthetics.

To understand the distinctive features of the Buddhist and the Hindu fall-out in the realm of aesthetics, perhaps it is necessary to bear in mind the fundamental difference between the ultimate ideals of the twin faiths—viz., *Nirvāna* and *Moksha*. While the sole concern of the latter is the purification and awakening of the soul, i.e., *ātman*, the former aims at realizing the *anātman* state—i.e., the negation of soul or self. One wants to light the lamp, the other to extinguish it. Both treat time, space, ego, desire, thoughts as delimiting forces; but while Buddhism would eliminate all of them, Hinduism sees them as essential parts of an organic whole. In the organistic Hindu world-view, each and every person is a manifestation of the same Absolute force, *Param-ātman*, i.e., Supersoul. What is commonly called 'life' is a kind of detour from that Cosmic Life to which a living being returns after 'death.' Thus seen, an individual's life is a period of darkness when one's soul has come astray. During this spell, surrounded by sheath after sheath of senses and ignorance, one's soul is so deluded that it starts accepting as reality what is, in fact, an illusion—*Māyā*. In the course of this game of deception, one is constantly enslaved by gross materialism, natural passions, imperfect knowledge and egoistic selfishness. Consequently, one commits at every stage such acts as cause grief and bewilderment. After death, a man's soul may merge again with the Supersoul; but that is possible only if it has remained untainted. Ordinarily, to atone for the follies committed during one's 'life,' it has to be reborn. The cycle of birth and death goes on and on until a soul earns through disciplined 'life' the right to be free. That stage of liberation, deliverance, or salvation, is what the Hindus call *Moksha*. When this happens and soul merges again with the Cosmic Supersoul, the exhilarating experience of reunion yields a supreme bliss called *Brahmānanda*.

Such a union is possible even during life-time, here and now. For that, the soul must be enabled to release itself from the shacklesome nescience of senses through their purification and refinement via sublimation. This is what the Hindu would call *Jīvan-mukta*. But it is not given to an ordinary mortal to reach that state. In fact, he is so deluded by *Māyā* that more often than not, he attributes ultimate reality to the world of senses, boasts of his own rationality, and denies the very existence of soul. Only seers and savants can see through the delusive veils of *Māyā*, detach themselves from the life of the senses, return to the state of pure consciousness and thus experience something of the supreme bliss. Rising above the limitations of time and space and thus entering Eternity and Infinity, a soul feels as if it were one with the *Brahmān* (Absolute Consciousness). Now alone it can say, 'I am I.' In this transcendental state of union, unity is regained, ego is humbled and grief disappears. With tension yielding place to harmony and serenity, soul experiences a joy that has the thrill of an ecstasy. It is not exactly a pleasure, nor even an emotion as we understand by that word; it is a state, an enjoyable situation. It isn't something that one may be able to define or explain; it is something that one can only experience. In fact, one does not experience it; one can only have an experience of it. In this state, the experience and the experiencer tend to become one. It is a state of pure consciousness but it cannot be attained through intellectual exercises, howsoever rigorous. On the contrary, for this experience, one must, first of all, release oneself from one's intellectual apparatus. After all, the rational mind of man is bound by time and space.

Brahmā, the creator, is *Ānanda*. Holding the key to the inner harmony of the universe, he alone sees unity in diversity, perfect order behind the apparent chaos. Return to the Supersoul restores to the merging soul that sense of harmony and therefore that joyfulness of *Brahmā—Brahmānanda*. So long as our senses and mind are active, we can see the multiple parts but not the integrated whole. Unless there is dissociation from *buddhi* (mind) and purification of senses, we cannot see the method behind the madness of the bewildering facade. In other words, we must decondition ourselves before we can hope to reach the stage where the knower and the known become one. That total, transcendental deconditioning is possible through the rigorous exercises of *Yoga* which literally means joining—joining of body and mind and, by extension, the union of soul and Supersoul.

In ancient India, in the traditional Hindu way of life, invariably, everything got related to, if not exactly reduced to, religion. Even cooking, eating, bathing, sleeping, etc., were supposed to have spiritual dimensions because *Ātman* pervades everything and determines all. Being tainted, however, its presence is generally too clouded by *Māyā* to be perceptible. However, just as the Supersoul may be experienced through yoga, it is possible to experience the sway of *ātman*, too—an experience that leaves one thrilled as if one had tasted of *Brahmānanda*. Such is the *Ānanda* afforded by art. In other words, aesthetic pleasure is a form of temporarily experienced *Brahmānanda*. It is not exactly a spiritual or religious experience but has a close family affinity, as it were. Aesthetic *Ānanda* is, so to say, a kind of brother to *Brahmānanda*. Even otherwise, religion and aesthetics are sort of twins; each is rooted in senses but experienced by the spirit. Just as meditation leads to self-realization, union with cosmic forces and ultimately a perfect bliss, a *sahridaya*—Indian aestheticians' word for the percipient—also passes through similar stages of detachment, contemplation, perception and blissful joy. In art, too, mind expands and, as *Sattva* comes to dominate, *buddhi* itself is transcended. Of course, not for good. Although, intrinsically, both the experiences involve negation of senses, desires, cognition, etc., the overall effect is positive rather than negative. It is there only for a moment because detachment is not complete. After a spell of transcendence, one is back in the world of daily experience and finds oneself ensnared by *Māyā* once again. In any case, at least for one glorious moment, one experiences a unitary feeling in which there are no opposites.

Commonly, obsessed with appearances of the world around us, we see it through our senses and have fragmentary view of things. Transcending our individual sensuous self in art and viewing ourselves harmoniously related to the universe, we acquire an enlightening insight—very like a *yogin's* tearing of the veil of *Māyā*, mystical illumination, and union of soul with the Supersoul. Inherent in the experiences of both *yogin* and *sahridaya*, there is a paradox: in each case, detachment leads to alienation which turns out to be a form of union. In short, aesthetic pleasure (*Ānanda*) is a cognate of *Brahmānanda*—a joy awakened when one is enabled to perceive a relation between the universe and something within us.

From what has been said above, it is obvious that, in the Indian aesthetics, the key concept is neither beauty nor imitation but such joy as has a touch of the spiritual bliss about it—something comparable to the state of *Sacchidānanda* in *Yoga*—when *Sat* (Is-ness), *Chid* (=Pure Conciousness) and *Ānanda* (=bliss) conjoin into a triune. Here, too, the joy has no independent identity; it also represents one facet of the trinity comprising Truth, Bliss and Beauty—*Satyam, Shivam, Sundaram* ('I am Truth, I am God, I am Beautiful'). As everything in the world is a manifestation of the Supersoul, it is beautiful. In the state of Pure Consciousness, when one sees one's Reality related to the Supersoul, one experiences blissful joy. In the twin experiences, on the one hand, one discovers that, besides the spiritual aspect, the ethical and the metaphysical have beauty about them and, on the other, one discerns a spiritual touch in the natural, the physical and the mental. With physical and metaphysical becoming undistinguishable, the distinction between beauty and joy also disappears. In the aesthetic experience, too, when *Sattva* (purity) comes to dominate, everything looks beautiful and joyful.[14]

In the Western aesthetics, cognition is envisaged in terms of senses and rationality; in the Indian framework, it is in terms of soul also. Of course, the advent of soul does not make aesthetic experience superhuman; instead, it is because of this spiritual element that it becomes fully human. Indeed, it is on account of this soul-factor that (a) aesthetic experience is exclusively human (and perhaps most human of all experiences) and (b) art is an unending reservoir of bliss. In any case, to obviate the chances of aesthetic bliss (*Ānanda*) getting completely identified with the spiritual bliss (*Brahmānanda*), it is customary in Indian aesthetics to use the word *Rasa* for aesthetic pleasure. That *Brahmānanda* through *yoga* for the *yogin* is not the same thing as *Rasa* through *bhoga* for the *sahridaya* would become clear when we add that

Rasa-ānanda makes no sense for one who has already attained *Brahmānanda*. 'After knowing that, nothing remains to be known,' says *Bhagavad Gītā* about God-realization. But a *sahridaya's* lust for knowledge, experience, bliss continues unabated. His position is that of a man who, after a flash of lightning, finds himself readjusting his eyes to the ordinary light.

But what exactly is *Rasa*? It has been translated into English variously as sentiment, disposition, aesthetic enjoyability, emotional mood, bliss, etc. But, in fact, this is a term from dietics which means relish, taste, juice, flavour. That is the literal meaning of the word; as for its spirit, the nearest expressions would be essence, spirit, soul of a thing. Thus viewed, in the culinary framework, it would mean that quintessential juice, taste or flavour of the food which you keep relishing after the meal is over; in the aesthetic context, it would imply the overall feeling after the aesthetic event is over. After witnessing a play, for example, one may feel like exclaiming to oneself, 'How heroic!', 'How comic!', 'How horrible!', 'How disgusting!', 'How wonderful!', 'How pathetic!', 'How romantic!', or 'How terrific!'. In exclaiming thus, one is summing up, as it were, the *Rasa* of the play. Since, in the Western aesthetics, it is customary to refer to the total impact in terms of emotions, perceptions, pleasure, etc., the common practice of translating of *Rasa* as sentiment is quite understandable. But, in doing this, one is missing the fact that the real thrust of the Indian aesthetics is distinctly different—more spiritual than sensuous or intellectual. Properly speaking, *Rasa* is neither a feeling nor a mental construct; it signifies soul of the experience presented in a work of art. Like the soul, it is something that can be neither explained, defined nor even experienced; one can have an experience of it. Manifestation, representation, communication, cognition, suggestion, inference—all these concepts from the Western aesthetics are pathetically inadequate in describing the experience called *Rasa*; basically, it is an affair that belongs to the transcendental phenomenon. As discussed earlier, in the metaphysical aesthetics of the Hindus, aesthetic pleasure is a surrogate *Moksha* and a cognate of *Brahmānanda*. One could say that *Rasa* represents a ray of that *Ānanda*.

To the Western mind, this might sound esoteric nonsense and well might one question the wisdom of making an experience sound so fuzzy or ethereal when it is known to be within the reach of even the commonest of laymen. Such a demur is a reflection not so much on the oriental tendency to overdo the spiritual as on the occidental impatience with anything spiritual. It is time the West realized that it is because of its exclusive concern with body and mind that it has failed to resolve the mystery of aesthetic pleasure. Anyway, the theory of *Rasa* does not keep the mundane out; it not only takes cognisance of the emotions but even makes them the very basis of the entire theory. The only thing is that it insists not on emotions *per se* but on their quintessential spirit. The basic assumption is that, thanks to the alchemy of art, emotion itself undergoes a transcendental transformation. In real life, emotions are earthy, personal, subjective, patternless; with a view to retaining their essence, an artist subjects them to disinterested selection and imaginative reassimilation and thus lends them not only a pattern but also a superterrestrial dimension. That invests these with a beatitude that we never associate with the sensuous apparatus. In saying this, we are, of course, implying purification of the emotions, but not in the moral sense. It is a purification on the spiritual plane. Ordinarily, feelings are experienced through mind; in the aesthtic experience, mind either melts or burns away, according to the nature of the basic feelings. The disappearance of mental limitation prepares the ground for spiritual experience.

To get into the spirit of *Rasa*, it would be worthwhile to turn to *Nātyashāstra*, the great Indian classic on theatre arts. In this connection, first and foremost, it must be realized that theatre was conceived as a kind of worship, *yajna*,[15] rather than a mere pastime. No wonder, too, the Fifth Veda, *Nātyaveda*, was enriched with the teachings of *shāstras* and its aim was to offer good counsel and practical guidance to the people at large. Its role was to be the same as performed by all the four main Vedas put together—attainment of the four human ideals called *Purushārtha*, viz., *Dharma* (duty), *Artha* (wealth), *Kāma* (satisfaction of senses), and *Moksha* (liberation of the soul). Of course, it had two additional ideals—*Yasha* (fame) and *jnāna* (wisdom through perception). Anyway, with the passage of time, in the course of its evolution, drama absorbed at different stages dialogues from the Vedas, narratives from the *Upanishads*, myths from epics, and rituals from sacrificial ceremonies. In the spirit of *yajna*, the stage was treated with reverence as a sacrificial-shed. The play would start with the invocation of the gods, sprinkling of holy water in all the corners of the stage and reciting of *mantras* to drive away the evil spirits. Also, as in a *yajna*, the performance would end with *Bharata-vākya*—pleas to the deities for blessing the audience. Just as, after a *yajna*, there is sharing of the sweets as *bhoga* to betoken the receiving of the gods' benediction, the audience in theatre would accept *Rasa* as the shared *prasāda*.

Comprising 600 couplets and spread over 37 chapters, Bharata's *Nātyashāstra* is a veritable guide manual on the arts of drama, dance and music. Indeed, it covers the whole ground of theatrical presentation—composition, plot-construction, types of drama, types of heroes, conventions, use of language and dialects, theatre architecture, spectacle, diverse aspects of presentation (rituals, theatre companies, gestures, modes of representation, styles of expression, local usages, etc.). Each topic receives a fairly comprehensive treatment but nothing in Indian aesthetics has received as much attention as the concept of *Rasa*. *Rasa* has come to be accepted as the *raison d'etre* of dramatic experience—what the playwright wants to evoke, the actor tries to create, and the spectator experiences. It has proved so controversial because, as in the case of catharsis in Aristotle's *Poetics*, the author has left a lot to the reader's imagination. Of course, Bharata has devoted a full chapter (No. 6) to the *Rasa*-aspect, but his concern there is exclusively with an actor's manipulating his art to communicate the emotion being enacted. What is more, Bharata is silent on the precise process that transforms the performer's emotional mood into the spectator's thrill. *Sahridaya* does receive a whole chapter (No. 23), but, instead of elaborating the process of transmission, it seeks to initiate the man of taste about the types of women and the ways of courtship. In the absence of Bharata's word, therefore, one has to turn to his commentators; but each of them offers his own interpretation—exactly like the theories regarding catharsis. No wonder, one feels lost in the pell-mell of scholarship in the field.

Maybe, for a fuller understanding of *Rasa*, we shall have to look beyond *Nātyashāstra*; but we must start with the starting point itself—chapter 6 (*Rasa Adhyāya*) that has been rightly projected as the nucleus of the whole treatise because it is here that we have the Rasa-sūtra:

> *Vibhāvānubhāvavyabhichārisaṁyogād rasanishpattih*
> (When *vibhāvas, anubhāvas*, and *vyabhibhāvas* get integrated, there is the oozing of a *rasa*).

Obviously, to understand this formula, we must explain some basic concepts pertaining to the terminology employed here. Before doing that, perhaps it would be helpful to sum up the assumptions of *Nātyashāstra*—that poetry is manifestation of emotions; that the emotions thus manipulated are limited in numbers (eight); that some of these emotions are permanent and of primary importance, the others transitory and of subordinate nature; that permanent ones alone can be developed into *Rasas*; that feeling tones are integrated according to the laws of propriety. Now back to the *Rasa-sūtra*. In explaining it, we are follwoing the footsteps of K.C. Pandey whose approach is admirably lucid. Much of what follows in the next few paragraphs is a paraphrased summation of what he has said in this connection in his *Comparative Aesthetics*, Vol. I.

In life, an emotion may be the mainspring of a series of actions, but it is itself aroused by a situation, which may, therefore, be regarded as the cause of that emotion. Now, emotion expresses itself in various physical changes—for example, movement of eyes, change of colour, etc. These changes are, in a sense, the effects of the emotions. A persisting emotion is invariably accompanied by a number of transient emotions—for example, a lover in separation feeling apprehensive, indulging in self-disparagement, or yielding to languor. This is what happens in life. In aesthetic experience, there is no real cause, nor any real effect. For an effective communication of emotional situations, therefore, the actor has to create an illusion of being in the grip of the relevant emotion. Because of the limitations of time and space, he has to do it through minimum life-situations, symptoms of change, and the accompanying feelings. These simulated emotions called *Bhāvas*, are created through *Vibhāvas* and *Anubhāvas*. *Vibhāva* is a medium through which the actor works himself up to a certain emotional pitch and consequently shows the signs which are natural in the emotion to be depicted. It is customary to regard *Vibhāva* as a 'determinant' because it stands for the dramatic situation that serves as the medium through which an emotion arises in the actor and thus helps to build the *Bhāva*. Of course, the literal meaning of *Vibhāva* is 'imposed' feeling. It is imposed in the sense that it arouses an emotion in a manner quite different from the way emotions arise in actual life. A *Vibhāva* can have two aspects—an object which arouses emotion and the environment that stimulates emotion. They are called *Ālambana-vibhāva* and *Uddīpana-vibhāva*, respectively. The actual manifestation of *vibhāva* through an actor's gestures, language, facial expressions, etc., is called *Anubhāva*. Since the physical changes thus communicated are supposed to be the result of the emotions, *Anubhāvas* are loosely referred to as 'consequents' also. They are called *Anubhāvas* because (a) they communicate the basic emotions and (b) they make the specatator experience an identical emotion. Of course, it is through *anubhāvas* of the performer that the *sahridaya* gets to know the *bhāva* which is sought to be conveyed, but the exact nature of that *bhāva* crystallizes only in the context of the *vibhāvas*. In other words, *Vibhāvas* and *Anubhāvas* complement each other.

Now, the physical changes affected in the enactment are of two kinds—voluntary and involuntary. The former signifies imitation through the effort of will—for example, movements of eyes and eyebrows; the latter calls for a measure of inner involvement as if the emotion were actually present—e.g., perspiration, blush, horripilation, etc. Since the involuntary kind serve as expression of the feelings that stem from deep-felt emotions, they are distinguished from *Anubhāvas* by being called *Sāttvikbhāvas.*[16] While these *Sāttvikbhāvas* have been included in the 49 *Bhāvas* (besides eight *Sthāyibhāvas* and 33 *Sanchāribhāvas*), *Vibhāvas* and *Anubhāvas* have been kept out. The reason for this apparently intriguing situation is that, in *Anubhāva* and *Vibhāva*, '*bhāva*' has a different meaning from what it generally means, viz., emotion (that which effects '*bhāvana*' i.e. desire). In the case of *Anubhāva* and *Vibhāva*, '*bhāva*' comes from '*bhū*' (= to be)—that which causes something *to be* when it is not there. *Anubhāvas* and *Vibhāvas* create in the mind of the spectator the mental states which are not there intrinsically—like the lingering fragrance of musk in a container even when the musk has been removed and is no longer there.

As for the *Vyabhichāribhāvas*, they owe their nomenclature to the fact that they come, as it were, face to face with the spectator. True, they are mental states, but they appear as if embodied. Since they nurture the primary emotions, they are also called *Sanchāribhāvas*. In English, *Vyabhichāri* or *Sanchāri Bhāva* has been usually named as transient or transitory emotion because it accompanies the persisting emotion for a while before it yields place to another.[17]

These imposed, indicative or supporting emotions are all there to help realize that particular emotion which persists and is therefore called *Sthāyi-bhāva*. It is the pivotal emotion but, strangely enough, Bharata has not included it in the *Rasa-sūtra*. Perhaps he believed that that was unnecessary because, after all, as everybody knew, the entire action sprang from, and was sustained by, that persisting state of mind. The all-determining significance of *Sthāyibhāvas* is implicit in the fact that the *Rasas* derive their names from them. Indeed, *Sthayibhāva* it is which serves as the core of the emotive quality of a play. Because of this premier position, *Sthāyibhāva* has often been translated as permanent/primary emotion/sentiment/mood/ impulse/propensity.

Pramod Kale's terminology is more descriptive—Constant Mode for *Sthāyibhāva* as against Inconstant Mode for *Vyabhichāribhāva* and Spirited Mode for *Sāttvikbhāva*. He has translated *Anubhāvas* as Sensors, *Vibhāvas* as Indicators; likewise, he uses Causal Cues for *Ālambana Vibhāvas* and Causal Conditions for *Uddīppana Vibhāvas*. Consequently, his translation of *Rasa-sūtra* is: 'Rasa is derived from a fusion of Indicators, Sensors and Inconstant Modes.' Another noted scholar, Krishna Chaitanya, has offered a freer translation as follows:-

> When the prime stimuli, their congruent behavioural features, and the transient but ancillary emotional reactions they evoke, combine to activate the sentiment, the sentiment develops into aesthetic emotion.

Obviously, Chaitanya has used his own terminology: prime stimuli for *Vibhāvas*, behavioural features for *Anubhāvas*, transient and ancillary reactions for *Vyabhichāri/Sanchāri Bhāvas*, sentiment for *Sthāyibhāva*, and aesthetic emotion for *Rasa*. If one were to eschew such terminology, and put things in simpler words, one could say that relation between *Vibhāva* and *Rasa* is that of the producer and the produced, the one between *Anubhāva* and *Rasa* is that of the indicator and the indicated, even as *Vyabhichāribhāva* and *Rasa* are like the nutrient and the nourished.

Now, what Bharata means by this formula is explained through an analogy that brings dietics into the *Rasa*-theory. Configuration of the *Sthāyibhāvas*, *Sanchāribhāvas*, *Vibhāvas* and *Anubhāvas* is like mixing condiments, herbs and molasses to create a concoction or beverage: each ingredient had its own relish but the end-product has a brand new flavour/relish of its own. Bharata's implication is that just as gourmets savour food prepared with many tasty ingredients, sensitive people enjoy in their minds the permanent emotions when presented in combination with the enactment of transient emotions and their causes. But how does that configuration get effected? Instead of going into details, Bharata raises the question as to whether *Bhāvas* come from *Rasa* or *Rasa* comes from *Bhāvas* and answers it by suggesting a relationship of mutual dependence. There is no *Rasa*, says he, without *Bhāva*, nor any *Bhāva* without a *Rasa*. All the eight *Rasas* are then explained, one by one, in relationship to their respective *Sthāyibhāvas*, *Vyabhichāribhāvas, Anubhāvas* and *Vibhāvas*. What is more, each *Rasa* is assigned an independent colour and a presiding deity.[18]

So far as the categorization or the overall general tenor of the argument is concerned, there is no problem. Obviously, Bharata's contention is that emotion is a complex system through which the mind functions, that the aesthetic state is an organized system of dispositions, that aesthetic state gets created when the emotional core of an instinct is excited, that *Vibhāvas* awaken instincts and *Vyabhichāribhāvas* nourish them, that *Rasa* is an organic compound of affective and conative life, and that the process of *Rasa* implies the evolution of instincts and emotions into a coherent whole.

The problem arises when one asks how exactly the instinctive propensities and emotional apparatus are integrated to awaken them into the desired activity. Bharata is silent about the configuration—*Samyoga*, as he calls it. Surely, he could not have meant random mixing. It is strange that whereas in the context of plot (*Kārya*) and junctures (*Sandhis*), he uses such organic images as a seed's progress to fruit and the growth of an embryo in a foetus, in the case of *Rasa* he is content with the crude analogy of food-making. That does explain the relish part, but not the precise process of fusion and integration. After all, even cooking implies graded processing, if one aims at a specific taste. Surely, such expressions as 'organic arrangement,' 'harmonious combination' don't help beyond a certain point and thus create space for subjective interpretations. Perhaps Bharata did leave a hint in the use of the expression '*Rasa-nishpattih*', i.e., oozing of the Rasa. It brings to mind the image of honey oozing from the bee-hives. Collecting juice from different flowers and configurating the efforts in a hive is, even otherwise (literally), an exercise in *rasa*-making. Or could '*Rasa-nishpattih*' imply the process of distillation, drop by drop? Possibly, Bharata was visualizing an actor's extracting the essence/juice of *Bhāvas* (*Sthāyi* and *Sanchāri*), *Vibhāvas*, and *Anubhāvas* to effect an organic synthesis in his acting in such a manner as to yield the drop of the desired *Rasa*.[19]

Whether *Rasa*-business is akin to cooking, distillation or honey-making, one thing is certain: the ingredients get transformed into something new. For example, what a bee collects are not just minicule parts of different flowers but their very juices; in the honey, the juices of different flowers contribute their mite but lose their disparate entities. Ditto for the contribution of *Bhāvas* into a *Rasa*. Surely, it calls for our realizing that *Rasa* is a *Bhāva* no more; it is born of *Bhāvas* but, in the process, it becomes something other than those emotions or sentiments. In other words, *Sthāyibhāva* is not *Rasa* but its potential. What is evoked is not pain, pleasure or anything connected with emotions experienced in life; it is an impersonal state of joy, a bliss. The true nature of *Rasa* might crystallize a bit more if we say that it is *Sthāyin* awakened by its *ātman* (soul); better still if we say that *Rasa* marks the awakening of the soul of the *Sthāyin*. When the *Sthāyin* is excited, the whole body shares that state; every nerve gets strung. With the coming in and going out of *Vyabhichāribhāvas*, and with the interplay of *Sāttvikbhāvas*, *Vibhāvas* and *Anubhāvas*, things culminate into a state in which *Bhāvas* lose their personal and sensuous associations. What is left now is a relishable experience of impersonal and universal quality which is almost super-sensuous and immanent.

In life, we do have the interplay of several emotions, but they are too disorganized to have any pattern. The imagination of an artist brings law and order into this indiscriminate diversity. It keeps out the incoherent elements and picks out only the emotions, their causes and effects for representation. The emotions thus sorted out by the artist shed their individualistic peculiarities and become elemental or universal. What is more, in our ego-oriented life, we are slaves of passion and our intellect is out to dominate our actions: hence all sorts of tensions. As *Rasa* implies emotion shorn of egoism, our intellect is also willing to be dominated and the net result is a purer existence comparable to *samādhi*-situation—*sans* ego, *sans* sense, *sans* rationality. In a way, in the deconditioning process of aesthetics, our personality is deconstructed and then reconstructed. In the different being which emerges from the process, emotional and rational apparatus has learnt to accept a secondary role, thus yielding primacy to something that one could call spirit or soul.

Those oriented in the Western aesthetics, being unable to accommodate the spiritual dimension, fail to see the transcendental aspect of *Rasa*. They not only translate *Rasa* as sentiment but also insist on interpreting it as a heightened or accentuated emotion, a reflection of an emotion, a complex of emotions, or at least another kind of emotion. The fact, however, is that, in the process of aesthetic experience, an emotion is so purified by the medium that it no longer remains an emotion. It is a different quality of an experience—a state of mind which, when released from the burden of affections, finds a complete identification with the aesthetic situation itself. Emotion is a personal psychic affection, *Rasa* is an inter-personal state of the consciousness of a self which has lost its egoistic, pragmatic aspect. No wonder, even though one *bhāva* may give place to another, the same *Rasa* is maintained. Indeed, in an aesthetic experience, the feelings undergo a profound alchemic transformation. Sorrow, as a raw passion, is painful and unwelcome; but, changed into the *Rasa* of compassion, it is almost divine. This *sāttvik* dimension of passion remains dormant in life and we regard that passion as a dark force. In its search for the soul of that passion, art discovers its spiritual dimension as well, and the thrill of that discovery is the source of aesthetic joy. What makes that joy a near-ecstasy is the realization that it is something universal—belonging not just to the hero, the actor, or the spectator, but to all.

Only when one understands *Rasa* as distinct from *Bhāva*, does one realize why it is wrong to talk in terms of a *Rasa* being known, created, conveyed or suggested. It is, indeed, something that can be only experienced. It is something developed in mind. What is manifested is not *Rasa* but its relish. Rama's love for Sita cannot be produced on the stage, cognised or inferred; it is only revealed and relished. No wonder, *Rasa* is always pleasurable—a means to *Ānanda*.[20]

Indeed, if *Rasa* were only an emotional or an intellectual construct, it would not have the power of ecstasy it has. The fact is that *Bhāva* belongs to life, *Rasa* to the world of art. As such, *Rasa* has its own logic, its own laws as well as its own reality. To realize a *Rasa*, everything has to be brought to a level where it stands cleansed of the grossness of life, in a rarefied form—in the form of its essence, so to say. Indeed, properly viewed, in life there are *bhāvas* but no such thing as *sthāyi-bhāva*. Never in life is one ruled by a dominating passion that lasts or persists for a whole day—leave alone a whole life. The aesthetic process starts when one of the *bhāvas* is projected as *sthāyin*—an unmanifested *Rasa*, so to say. In the process of maturing a *sthāyibhāva* into *Rasa*, even as *vibhāvas* generate the mood, *vyabhichāribhāvas* nourish it, and *anubhāvas* manifest it, the experience moves farther and farther away from reality. Preliminary business (*Pūrvaranga*), dance, music, acting, *abhinaya*, conventions and styles—all help the process of tampering with the traces of actual life. The Western concept of imitation insists on bringing things as close to life as possible; Indian concept of *Rasa* aims at transforming the material from life into something that is life-like and yet other-than-life. As a corollary, while Western aesthetics lays so much stress on identification to facilitate catharsis, the Indian counterpart regards identification as a barrier rather than a help in effecting transcendence.

If *Rasa* is more than cathartic experience, it is because *Bhāva* is transformed into something that is a *bhāva* no more. *Rasa* is that meeting-point of the spiritual, the rational as well as the emotive, where it is none of these. No wonder, too, while the quintessence of the Western drama lies in conflict—man v universe, man v society, man v man, man v self, emotion v reason, feeling v form, old v new, tradition v modernity—Indian aesthetics thrives on the spirit of harmony. Here, reality is not apprehended rationally, emotively or spiritually but through all these simultaneously. In short, *Rasa* cannot be projected as a sentiment, as a perception, or as an ecstasy. It is neither merely this nor that; it is all these at one and the same time. That makes *Rasa* a delicately balanced experience in which involvement and detachment, *Yoga* and *Bhoga*, cognition and emotion, sacred and profane, become interchangeable terms. This delicate balance is the key to aesthetic pleasure on both the levels of creativity and receptivity. And this balance depends on the configuration of parts into a whole—a configuration in which, despite diversity, one perceives a unity. Thus the three *Gunas* configurate to let the *Sattva-guna* emerge as the first among equals. Likewise, the emotional, the intellectual, and the spiritual configurate to allow the spiritual a primacy that is felt rather than seen. In the case of *bhāvas*, too, there is at work a configuration which lets the *sthāyin* enjoy a pride of place and thus give the impression of its *Rasa* being the only one while in fact *Rasa*s of other *bhāvas* are very much there.

In saying all this, we have already gone far beyond what is contained in *Nātyashāstra*. Indeed, Bharata never talks in terms of *Yoga, Bhoga, Ātman, Ānanda, Brahmānanda, Moksha*, etc. The fact is that while *Nātyashāstra* has bare formulations and neat classification, there are no detailed examples, nor arguments. Not a single play is mentioned anywhere. No wonder, the aestheticians after Bharata had to fill the gaps through such interpretations as tend to be diametrically opposed to one another. For example, if Bhatta Lollata brought *Rasa* process so close to imitation, Sankuka injected inference into that interpretation and that crystallized into a psycho-epistemic approach (imitation-illusion-inference-recognition). Bhatta Nayaka, on the other hand, brought in the Vedantic metaphysics and thus made *Rasa* look a transcendental affair—*ānanda*. Since Abhinavagupta had the background of the Shaivite rational mysticism, his theory reflects the approach of *Shakti* as *chamatakāra* and thus *Rasa* sounds like a revelation. In fact, there are innumerable theories. Since I have neither the space nor the need—nor even the competence—to sort out these contentious issues, so far as possible, I shall try to steer clear of controversies that litter the Indian aesthetic theory and concentrate on what have come to be regarded as the essence (*rasa*) of *Rasa* theory.

Most of the problems arise from an obsession to treat *Nātyashāstra* as a *shāstra* on aesthetic theory covering all the aspects. The fact, however, is that, as mentioned earlier, it was meant to be a manual not on aesthetics in general but only on theatre arts—and that, too, on the practice rather than on the theory. It was supposed to help poets, directors and performers through the laws and rules prescribed here. It is time it was realized that Bharata was not Aristotle and *Nātyashāstra* is not an Indian version of *Poetics*. In this connection, it is worth noting that Bharata is primarily concerned not with *nātaka* (drama as literature) but with *nātya* (theatre). Furthermore, the focus is on the productional aspects rather than on the appreciation. He does bring in *Rasa* but primarily in the framework of acting—what goes into the enactment of an emotion.[21] *Rasa* as the spectator's response, as it is mostly understood now, is a later concept evolved by others in their effort to supply what was missing in *Nātyashāstra*. This *Ānanda-rasa* (as against *Bhāva-rasa* of which Bharata speaks) is perhaps what Bharata meant by such a general neutral term as *Siddhi*. Had his dramaturgy and concept of theatre been rooted in *Ānanda-rasa*, perhaps his typology of drama would have been entirely different, i.e., more generic.[22]

Of course, for our misplaced expectations, if there is any one person to blame, it has to be Bharata himself, because it is he who named the *Rasa*s after the spectator's responses. When the *vibhāvas* are curse, affliction, downfall, separation, calamity, destruction and death, when the range of *vyabhichāris* covers weariness, worry, pain, confusion, fear, depression, trembling, tears, etc., and when *anubhāvas* are such as tears, laments, sighs, change of colour, loss of memory, etc., what is it that the actor is trying to realize? Obviously he is after the emotion of sorrow with a view to extracting the essence of *shoka*. But, instead of calling it *Shoka-rasa*, Bharata calls it *Karunā-rasa* and adds rather intriguingly, '*Karunā* should be acted out by loud sobbing, fainting, lamenting, wailing, abusing the body violently and beating it.' By doing these things, one would be acting out *shoka*, not *karunā*. In calling it *Karunā-rasa*, Bharata has in mind the spectator's response rather than the performer's art. And if the ultimate aim is the *Rasa* in *sahridaya's* mind, why restrict '*Rasa*-nishpattih' to the actor's configuration of *Bhāvas* as if this were the very end itself. Indeed, it is really strange that while Bharata says so much about the way a player uses his body, costumes, make-up, speech and other modes of conveyance to create an illusion of his being impregnated with the requisite emotive state, he does not make any conscious effort to show how the essence of the emotion thus realized by the player gets related to the playgoer.[23]

Perhaps it is necessary—as the aestheticians after Bharata did realize—that a distinction is made between the two kinds of relishes. One is the *Rasa* of *Bhāva* as enacted by a player (through the configuration of Inconstant Modes, Sensors and Indicators); it implies the conversion of mental language into behaviour language. The other is the *Rasa* experienced by the playgoer whose perceptive faculties help crystallize the received images into another configuration. The difference lies in the fact that the actors go through various stages of subjective feelings; the cultivated minds of the audience go through a kind of reflex action. In short, there are two kinds of configurations in progress and the culminating point comes when the transitory feelings, coming on top of one another, create a stable mood in the performer and, in turn, a *Rasa* in the spectator. Thus seen, *Bhāva-rasa* is the feeling content embodied in the art form and *Ānanda-rasa* the culminating point of all the *Bhāva-rasas* which configurate to yield their total *Rasa*. In this connection, it must be remembered that different performers enact diverse roles and thus contribute a variety of *Bhāva-rasas*. In a sense, it is possible to say that, in the *Rasa* experienced by the spectator, actor-oriented *Rasa* has the role of *anubhāva*. One could even add that, for the audience, the hero and the heroine (as played by performers) serve as *ālambana-vibhāvas* (i.e. the source of feelings) while their situations like separation, union, season, etc., are sort of *uddīpana-vibhāvas* (exciting feelings). And if we must have a medium facilitating the process, we could turn to *sūtradhāra* whose manipulations help the transformation of *Bhāva* into *Rasa* on the one hand and *Rasa* into *Ānanda*, on the other.

What a poet creates in his play, an actor recreates on stage in conditions that are not identical; what the actor creates on the stage, the spectator recreates in his own mind, but again in conditions that are different. At each stage, there is at work a process of transformation. A character has *bhāva* only; when writing, a poet is intuitively experiencing the character's *bhāva* and deriving *rasa* out of it; an actor concentrates on crystallizing imaginatively the *rasa* of the character's *bhāva*; what is experienced by the spectator is pure *Rasa*.[24]

As an inevitable corollary to this correspondence between the acts of creation and perception, aestheticians in India always assume a close kinship between the natures of the artist and the percipient. Since the spectator is expected to recreate what the poet has created, he must have something of the poet in him. What the poet expresses is a state of his soul; it cannot produce an effect on any one except on a kindred soul. That brings us to the concept of *Sahridaya* which literally means 'of the same heart' or 'with a heart.' Putting the two senses together, it implies that *sahridaya* is a man with a sensibility that is comparable to that of the poet. The assumption possibly is that, unless the two of them are on the same wavelength, there won't be any meaningful interaction and, consequently, the right response might not be possible.

In fact, in Indian aesthetics, artist and connoisseur are supposed to be related to each other like a man and a woman. It is also described as the relationship between the lamp and the vessel: a lamp is useless without wick and oil, nor can wick and oil alone dispel darkness. A brilliant result accrues only if their interaction is made possible by a source of light. In the field of aesthetics, that source of light is *Pratibhā* which literally means a 'flash-across.' English has no exact equivalent of *pratibhā*, but, by extension, it is supposed to signify the flash of the inner eye of the spirit which gives the power of revelation to the artist and power of perception to the *sahridaya*. One could differentiate by calling them creative and responsive imaginations, respectively; but what is actually implied is the artistic sensitivity and the aesthetic sensibility. As a common name for both, *pratibhā* is, so to say, an innate faculty that serves as the common link and therefore as a bridge between the two. Inherent in the artist's ability to wring *Rasa* out of *Bhāva* on the one hand, and in the *sahridaya's* capacity to ooze *Ānanda* out of *Rasa* on the other, *pratibhā* brings them on the same wavelength. In the case of an artist, *pratibhā* manifests itself in the form of talent, imagination, intuition and inspiration, while in the *sahridaya,* it appears as taste, imagination, contemplation and transcendence. But for this sensibility, a *sahridaya* won't be able to pass through all those stages of aesthetic evolution involving feelings and contemplation, identification and detachment, ecstasy and tranquillity. To put it differently, the seat of *Rasa* is a heart that has been humanized. Anyway, since *Rasa* presupposes a degree of sensibility and capacity for imagination, withdrawal, and intuitive perception, ideally speaking, *sahridaya* must be a man of character and breeding who has power of quick understanding, interest in arts, knowledge of literature, and capacity for objectivity, concentration and identification.

From what has been said above, it should be clear that the locus of creative *Rasa* is not the performer but the play and that of aesthetic *Rasa* is not the stage presentation but the sensibility of the *sahridaya.* After this realization, it is easy to see that the *Rasa-sūtra* applies as much to *sahridaya* as to the artist. One could say that when *vibhāvas, anubhāvas* and *sāttvikbhāvas* join to excite *sthāyi-bhāvas*, it yields not only *Bhāva-rasa* in the performer's enactment but also *Ānanda-rasa* in the percipient. Indeed, *sahridaya,* too, rises above *Tamas* (darkness) and *Rajas* (passion) *gunas* and gets permeated with *Sattvaguna* (purity). Thus, thanks to his power of involvement as well as detachment, and consequently, experiencing bhoga and yoga at one and the same time, the *sahridaya* experiences a *Rasa* of his own which is an untainted impersonal joy, a form of bliss. Having thus transcended from the personal to the universal, *sahridaya* becomes totally unselfish, totally pure—very like the purification of the *Bhāva* in the play. In this state, the *sahridaya* realizes the harmony of the universe in his own being—not just intellectually but spiritually. As all looks so beautiful at this stage, *Rasa* created by art serves as a datum for *Saundarya* (beauty). *Yajna* is complete, as it were, and all the participants feel as if they had become part of the Absolute and thus shared its multiplicity.

The beauty of *Rasa* lies in the fact that, although shared by all, it is not commonplace. It might be based on an emotion that is common to all, but the process of universalization and transcendence makes it acquire the mystique of *Brahmānanda* itself. Of course, as pointed earlier, *Rasa* is only a surrogate and not the Supreme Bliss itself. Anyway, the transformation of the ordinary into something extraordinary brings in the *sahridaya* the feeling of a miracle. No wonder, Indian aesthetics refers so often to *alaukika* (wonderful) and *chamatkāra* (miracle).

When one refers to *Rasa* and *Ānanda,* it gives the impression that all arts yield the same kind of transcendental pleasure. But as anyone familiar with the variety of aesthetic experiences should testify, there are all kinds of responses. This numerality has been explained analogically by reference to a fine crystal glass that sheds multi-coloured light, a prism that splits a ray of light into a spectrum, to the six tastes of the same palate, and to the innumerable manifestations of the same *Brahmā.* Anyway, *Rasa* in the singular connotes the aesthetic enjoyment in general while *Rasa*s refer to the particular peculiarities of the responses. In the Western tradition, too, we talk of aesthetic pleasure as if it were one and the same response in all the cases and in all the arts, although a student of literature knows only too well what variety inheres an epic poem, a lyric, a tragedy, a comedy, a melodrama, a horror film, a Gothic romance, or a grotesque novel. In terms of Indian aesthetics, one could describe these various experiencs as *Vīra-rasa, Shringāra-rasa, Karunā-rasa, Hāsya-rasa, Raudra-rasa, Bhayānaka-rasa, Adbhuta-rasa, Bībhatsa-rasa*, respectively. Indeed, it is unrealistic to expect all the works of art to yield the same kind of overall impact. After all, in each experience, *Rajas, Tamas* and *Sattva guna*s are reshuffled in different ways. What is more, the four faculties of the inner consciousness—*ahankāra* (ego), *chitta* (mind), *buddhi* (intellect), and *manas* (will)—are involved and they naturally participate in varying degrees and therefore precipitate qualitatively different responses.[25]

The trouble, however, is that controversies have been created over the number of the *Rasa*s. Bharata mentioned eight; *Shānta-rasa* was included to make it nine. Vishwanatha came out with two more—*Vātsalya-rasa* (parental affection) and *Bhakti-rasa* (devotion). And there is *Shakti-rasa* (sense of power) as yet another claimant. In principle, at least, there is nothing sacred about the number of *Rasa*s mentioned in *Nātyashāstra.* Indeed, it should be possible to discover more and more such *bhāvas* as can be rendered *sthāyin* to yield more and more *Rasa*s. We should wish to eschew all such controversies including those that seek to project either *Shānta-rasa* or *Shringāra-rasa* or *Adbhuta-rasa* as the only real *Rasa*. The seed of these controversies was sown by Bharata himself when he declared *Shringāra, Raudra, Vīra* and *Bībhatsa* as the primary *Rasa*s and the rest as derivative ones. Nevertheless, we would wish to make here one point that will be taken up later.

Ordinarily, in a performance, *sahridaya* experiences several *Rasa*s but only one of them dominates; that is the principal (=*Angī-) Rasa* round which the secondary (=*Anga*-) *Rasa*s get ranged in position of subordination, as it were. *Shānta-rasa* is supposed to be one in which all the *Rasa*s have their spells but eventually cancel one another to create a situation of no pain, no joy, no love, no hatred, no desire, no thought. If such a situation is possible, should it not be possible to have another *Rasa* in which all the *Rasa*s create through their interplay a perfect equilibrium on terms of equality, without cancelling one another?

While it would be churlish to deny Bharata credit for laying sound foundation of Indian aesthetics, it must not make us blind to the limitations of his *Nātyashāstra.* Rooted in theatre practice as *Rasa* was, it needed a lot of elaboration and extension from subsequent writers before it could be seen to have universal validity for all arts. In his obsession with the actor's delineation of the *bhāvas*, Bharata almost neglected the spectator's interest—what was actually received and how it was communicated. It also meant complete neglect of the formal aspect, language, and the conveyance of meaning. Strangely enough, even though he talks about the creatively organized context of the sensuous stimuli for the communication of a feeling, he fails to see the creatively organized context of the signals received for the elicitation of an emotional reaction. How ironic that the man who was so keen on the emotive configuration for communicating the spirit of *Bhāvas* did not bother about a corresponding linguistic configuration and the way the spirit of the words was realized and their meaning communicated! No wonder, after Bharata appeared so many writers who sought to explain what he had missed—the different aspects of the art of poetry, especially the problem of cognition, the role of decorative devices, and the linguistic manipulation to facilitate it.

The history of Indian aesthetics from Bharata to Vishwanatha through Jagannatha highlights a couple of interesting points that are worth noting. In both the Western and the Eastern traditions, aesthetic formulation started with dramatic arts and came to dominate the theory of poetic arts. Whether or not the early Hindu aestheticians were aware of it, it is possible to hear in their views the echoes of the Greek formulations, even as the post-Renaissance Western aesthetics appears to be full of the dim, and at times not-so-dim, echoes of what the Indians had contributed. Indeed, when any one familiar with the Indian theory turns to the latest Western writers on literary theory, much appears to be adaptation of the Hindu aesthetics. On the other hand, there has been an equally marked trend on the part of the Indian scholars, who have been initiated into the Western tradition, to group the Indian aestheticians into 'schools' under such labels as are peculiar to the Western 'isms.' Thus Bhatta-Lollata has been credited with Generation theory (*Utpādavāda*), Sankuka with Inference theory (*Anumitivāda*), Bhattanayaka with Enjoyment theory (*Bhogavāda* or *Bhuktivāda*), Abhinavagupta with Revelation theory (*Dhvanivāda*). And then there are, of course, those other 'isms' like *Smritivāda, Anubhūtivāda*, etc., which correspond to Recollection theory, Experience theory, etc.

In both Eastern and Western traditions, one hears a lot that highlights their common concern with expression, impression, suggestion, perception, cognition, intuition, imagination, empathy, synthesis, stylistics, figures of speech, etc. Going by Shrikrishna Mishra in his *Coleridge and Abhinavagupta,* it is all a case of adaptation; only the terminology is different. But whosoever tries to have a closer look should be able to see that, in both its highways and byways, Indian aesthetics goes beyond the emotive and cognitive concerns into the spiritual realm of the soul. Certainly, *Pratibhā* is much more than just talent or imagination; Ānanda is not just pleasure dominated by ideas or entertainment. Instead of imitation, what sways here is the concept of Māyā; instead of empathy, aim is detachment; instead of catharsis we have *Rasa*; instead of generic classification, we have aesthetic categories. The basic aim in Indian aesthetics is to grasp the soul of an experience or an emotion. Thus with Bhatti, Bhamaha, Dandin, Udbhatta, Mamata, Ruyukka, *alamkāra* is not just a matter of figure of speech but a wider concern. It covers all the decorative devices pertaining to diction, style, metre, rhythm—at all levels, ranging from emotive to archetypal associations. So much so that at times it would appear as if *alamkāra* were yet another name of literary charm or even beauty in general.

In Indian aesthetics, as indeed in the Indian dramaturgy, the watchword is synthesis. In fact, that is the key concept in the entire Hindu civilization. That is why, genius and taste, poet and *sahridaya,* charm and response always go together, like Shiva and Shakti. For the Hindu aestheticians, *Rīti* is not just style—it is essentially a way of manipulating words creatively—communication determined by the laws of propriety (*auchitya*). By that is implied not a moral propriety but the laws of probability, relating parts to the whole—to the inner soul, that is. The underlying idea is that creation of beauty is not the work of unbridled imagination. Since everything has to be purposive, there must be certain propriety in the relations between aesthetic factors and the desired *Raṣa*.

In the context of *Rīti,* in the Indian aesthetics, communication through diction has three dimensions—*Abhidhā* (direct meaning), *lakshanā* (secondary meaning, as in metaphors), and *vyanjanā* (unexpressed sense). Interestingly, *vyanjana* is also a culinary expression implying the creation of a delicate taste out of the given ingredients, through a given process. In the literary field, it has come to mean a subtle, extraordinary process that creates delicate impression or conveys an unexpressed sense through a secondary significatory power. For example, in irony, the word for which is *vyangya*. An allied figure of speech which has had an absorbing fascination for the Indian aestheticians is *Vakrokti*. It means eccentric expression but what it implies is an inversion of speech—an artful turn of phrase or a deviation in expression from the commonplace. Kuntaka devoted a whole book, *Vakrokti Jivita*, to this art of creative twisting. It signifies a uniqueness of expression which helps one convey the intended meaning suggestively through minimum use of empirical linguistic mode. Aesthetic effect lies in our realizing that although the thought could have been expressed through ordinary language in several other ways, the poet has opted for a deviation which has not only communicated his intention so economically and charmingly but also made the implicit more eloquent than the explicit. What is more, somehow one gets the impression that perhaps the use of the device was inevitable because the idea could not have gone home so effectively and so completely by using any other expression. When such an adornment is made to look an inalienable part of the adorned, poetry shines forth.[26]

Great art lies in effecting the synthesis of form and content, speech and thought, sound and sense, into a unified whole. How that synthesis is effected has been the subject of much discussion. In the Indian aesthetics, besides the concept of *Rasa*, if there is anything unique, it is the concern with that medium of synthesis—*Dhvani* in the framework of *Sphota* theory. *Sphota* literally means bursting out; in the contexts of linguistics and aesthetics, it signifies an unmodulated, subtle sound or sound-unit from which the sense sprouts. In the aesthetic experience, when sound does not remain just a source of sense but becomes sense itself, it becomes an indivisible entity like the spirit and may thus be said to represent the soul of the word. It is because of that invisible quality of word that a poem says more than what is said in the poem. How that subtle, unsaid part does reach the audience is a mystery which prompted aestheticians to talk about *Alaukika* (otherworldly, wonderful) and *Chamatakāra* (miracle) in art. Of course, it is generally conceded that it lies somewhere in the organization of the parts into a whole. The configuration of words in poetry, for example, is impregnated with a subtle hint and when that is grasped, the meaning bursts forth with all its intensity. It is very like a powerful explosion when all you have done is to bring a match-stick to the ignition point. Or it is like a sudden ringing of the bell in one's mind when something altogether forgotten bursts into the consciousness on the mention of something associated with it directly or even remotely. In the aesthetic experience comes flashing to the mind that unsuspected meaning which the poet had concealed in the process of subtle organization. Since it is a suggestive business, the sudden ringing of that bell in mind has been often confused with suggestivization and thus 'suggestion' is the word used for the Indian term, *Dhvani*. But translated literally, it should have such equivalents as 'sound,' 'tone,' 'echo,' 'resonance,' etc.

Since Western aestheticians have also talked about the role of suggestion in poetry, translating *Dhvani* as suggestion does great injustice to this unique feature of the Indian aesthetics. Inevitably, it breeds a tendency to study *Dhvani* theory entirely in the context of suggestion, suggestibility and suggestivization, as understood by the West. Thus does *Dhvani* get reduced to yet another mode of cognition. The fact, however, is that *Dhvani* is not a suggestion or a mode of cognition any more than *Rasa* is an emotion heightened or reflected. Instead, *Dhvani* is a sort of hieroglyphic of poetry—lying not just in words but even in sounds. Of course, Indian poetics also makes distinction between *Vākyārtha* (meaning of the words) and *Lakshyārtha* (targeted meaning); the latter is supposed to have something over and above the former. Ordinarily, human intercourse is governed by literal meaning of the words; but whenever the implied meaning becomes primary, the effect is thrilling, almost magical. That something which on the one hand helps the poet imbue the ordinary words with a magic power and on the other enable the reader to perceive the invisible and thereby experience the thrill is *Dhvani*. Now, art always directs us to *something* felt to be *somehow* enormously important for us but inexpressible and therefore vaguely discerned; when the key to the knot is discovered, a bell rings, as it were. But, then, ringing of a bell is akin to the movement of concentric waves—one gives rise to another which produces yet another. In poetry, too, the evoked meaning comes vibrating like that echoing resonance of a ringing bell. Such is the nature of *Dhvani*. A layman may not notice that hidden meaning but, thanks to his sensibility, a *sahridaya* smells it out. When that happens, the entire framework appears to be lit with a new significance. It is like a flash of lightning—or like the igniting of a store of dynamite. Of course, there is no direct connection between *Dhvani* and *Sphota* theories, as the explosion-analogy might suggest, but the authority of *Sphota* does lend a measure of credence to *Dhvani* theory.

As *Dhvani* is a medium, a link between poem and percipient, Anandvardhana's classic, *Dhvanyāloka,* has an alternative title in *Sahridayāloka*. *Āloka* means light; thus *Dhvani* is that kind of sound which is imbued with the power of flash. Language ordinarily performs the functions of indication, denotation, implication, suggestion or communication, but *Dhvani* is a function above all these. It is a kind of illumination which dazzles the *sahridaya* so much that he stops perceiving all other functions. At that moment, the beauties of form and content lose themselves in a higher form of beauty which is perceived not by the external senses but by something within—by the soul. Now this spirited beauty is inalienably related to *Rasa*. In the *Rasa-dhvani* framework, therefore, there is a happy synthesis between the sensuous and the spiritual, the real and the ideal, the mastery of technique and a real genius. In other words, *Dhvani* it is that effects the 'togetherness' of content and form; that is what makes literature '*sāhitya*.' It brings together word and meaning, poet and poem, poem and reader. Indeed, *Dhvani* serves as a vital bond among all the factors and even among all the beings involved in the aesthetic experience. Every sentence has artistic potential; *Dhvani* makes it art. It fuses *alamkāras, rītis* and *gunas* to present a wholly new sense—a sense given not by any single element (referential, emotive or imaginative) but by all of them together. Thus seen, *Dhvani* becomes the very process of synthesizing all the modes of artistic appreciation also.

Perhaps it would be helpful to have a closer look at the relations between *Rasa* and *Dhvani*. If *Rasa* is the quintessence of art, *Dhvani* is the instrument of evoking *Rasa*—in fact, part of the process. In a sense, it is the very quintessence of *Rasa* because it is only in the face of *Dhvani* that outer elements, and whatever they stand for, stop attracting attention to themselves. Indeed, thus come into operation all those unexpressed and inexpressible but vaguely discerned thoughts and feelings which have been lying in the unconscious. With the sudden upsurge of the hidden and the unseen, one feels a thrill and thus *Dhvani* becomes a part of the *Rasa* itself. In other words, *Rasa* and *Dhvani* are complementary to each other. If *Rasa* inheres poetic content, *Dhvani* inheres poetic experience; conversely, if *Dhvani* is intuitive expression, *Rasa* is intuitive experience. Both are related to each other like *Prakāsha* and *Vimarsha* in *Trika*. Thus does word and its meaning become a unity. That is what makes poetry *sāhitya* par excellence.[27] That unity can be grasped intuitively—neither synthetically in creation nor cognitively or emotively in perception. In short, poetry, in its essence, is *Rasa-dhvani* that determines the basic mental state of the *sahridaya*, i.e. the aesthetic experience.[28] Indeed, only when *Dhvani* pervades, *Rasa* is realized. If modern poetry has often been declared unpoetic, it is because, in the absence of *Dhvani*, it fails to yield *Rasa*.[29]

Thus seen, *Dhvani* does not just effect the supremacy of suggestion over denotative and indicative functions of language. It also performs the unique function of making words and meaning, sense and sound, expressed and unexpressed, ideas and emotions, images and symbols, text and context, message and medium, mores and modes, dissolve themselves into one another. Unless a poem is imbued with this *guna*, words, meaning, emotions, images, etc. remain just what they are. Surely, this is much more than what the word 'suggestion' conveys. It is a fascinating power—something magical, miraculous, transcendental. It is not surprising that the Western rationalists are intrigued by the concept of *Dhvani* and, denying its existence, regard it as a myth. Certainly, it is something intangible and undefinable. It cannot be created; it is sui-generis. Inhering the mode of expression and, at the same time, an unseen medium of transmission, it isn't something material. Instead, it is ethereal, like sound itself—a vibration that connects the souls of the poet, the poem and the reader.

For this kind of transmission, perhaps one could use the analogy of modern broadcasting and say that *Dhvani* is what brings the artist, the art object and the recipient on the same wavelength—a sort of attuning, so to say. This broadcasting metaphor not only brings *Dhvani* to the realm of sound to which it rightfully belongs but also justifies the term *sahridaya* for the percipient. Once the relationship of attuning is established, one's attention is captured and one becomes a pliable captive in the hands of the producer who always has a palpable design on one's head, heart and soul. Holding the *sahridaya's* total being in his hand, he can melt it (*chitta-druti*), expand it (*chitta-vistāra*), and develop or illumine it (*chitta-vikāsa*). The Western aestheticians bring the creator and the percipient on the same emotional wavelength of empathy, but the Indian attuning, *Dhvani*, digs deeper than the conscious—into the unconscious which is, in fact, the level of the superconscious, too.

Of course, *Dhvani* was invented in the context of poetics—like *Rasa* in the context of theatre arts. But whereas the latter has come to be related to the wider context of aesthetics in general, *Dhvani* remains confined to poetry, possibly because *Dhvani* is a matter of sound. Can it be really accommodated in a more broad-based theory of aesthetic experience? And how about the concepts of *Ānanda, Dhyāna, Nirvāna*: can all these be related to *Rasa*, *Dhvani*, *Vakrokti*, etc., to evolve a unified concept? The questions are more easily asked than answered. In fact, thanks to these various concepts and diverse approaches, one feels as uncomfortable in the midst of Indian aesthetics as one does when assaulted on all sides by the Western theories.

Sermons from Stones
A Personal Interlude

Aesthetic theories, East and West, do yield some insights but it is as difficult to integrate them into a wholesome formulation as to adopt any one of them in its totality. Whereas the Occident interprets aesthetic theory in terms of reasoning and feeling, the Orient depends on the inner mechanism of intuition and soul. For the West, art is an exercise in communication; for the East, it is a matter of communion. For one, it is imitation of life—an experience; for the other, it is transmutation of life—a creation. As the former assumes the essence of dichotomy and incongruity, the main stress there is on drama which is a matter of conflict; the latter sees in the universe an inalienable harmony and thus the chief concern there is with theatre which is a composite art. For the Euro-Americans, the aesthetic field comprises involvement, empathy and catharsis; for the Indians, it is detachment, *Dhvani*, and *Ānanda*. When the former dig deeper, they discover the unconscious and talk about the subliminal as libido; the latter, instead, find there the superconscious and therefore project the subliminal as *Īshwara* (God). Not surprisingly, whereas for the West, art is a mode of escape, for the East, it is a kind of 'inscape.' For the former, the most important thing is form, plot-structure; for the latter, it is content, essence, plot-story. No wonder, too, the Western aesthetician proceeds, genre-wise; the Indian, *Rasa*-wise. The former is convinced that man is basically an animal using his mind for upward evolution; the latter is equally certain that he is a part of false nature imposed on his true being. Thus one proceeds from the particular to the universal even as the other moves from the universal to the particular.

As a consequence of this incompatibility, I had on hand not answers but such questions and possibilities as continued to pester me wherever I went. Even in most unlikely situations, I found myself indulging in application of the theories that I knew. In theatres, exhibitions, at home, reading or listening, walking or lying, I would draw my own deductions. Indeed, Nature had so much to offer. In fact, I did hear sermons in stones—literally, as the following few pages would indicate. Here is not a chronological account of the way my views evolved but a recapitulation of certain moments of rumination when the questions in mind clamoured for solutions.

I have been to the mountains several times and enjoyed their scenic charm. My earliest memory about these visits pertains to the thrill of seeing clouds floating at my feet because, prior to that, I had always associated them with the sky—'up above the head so high,' like the twinkling stars. There was something uncanny about clouds coming from the other direction at my own level—at times menacingly, at others smilingly as if to greet me with with a handshake—and then holding me in their embrace for a fleeting moment before proceeding further. However, all told, the first visit was a veritable wash-out because of constant raining throughout my visit. In subsequent visits, on the other hand, summer-situation invariably highlighted the brownish hues of the foliage and I would often wonder why bare, plain hills enjoyed such a high reputation for scenic beauty. However once, when I visited one of the most celebrated hill stations of India, Shimla, in the first week of August, it was all so different. It had been raining for weeks but the monsoon was still on—and I stayed on through autumn. As the rainy season rejuvenated the dry undergrowth as well as trees, the verdurous perspectives in the first few weeks were simply breath-taking. Even the familiar 'dull' spots had acquired bewitching aspects, and whenever I peeped out of my room, something would happen to me. Moving out, I would get frozen in my tracks as if spell-bound, and watch for long spells—oblivious of the poeple or the traffic around me. Often I felt as if my soul were in communion with the soul of the scene before me. The effect was electrifying to begin with, totally absorbing later, and blissful at the end. I understood then what the aestheticians meant by *Chamatkāra, Alaukika, Dhyāna, Ānanda*, etc.

One of those evenings I dare not forget. Alongwith two companions, I watched the sunset. The valley beneath us had clouds that changed their positions so oft and so fast, and assumed such a variety of shapes every few seconds that (with change in the sunlight) it appeared an altogether different locale, even though we stood rooted to the same spot. Never in my life have I missed a movie camera so much as on that day; in the course of half-an-hour I could have taken at least a hundred superb photographs—each with a unique beauty of its own. Even as one of us, a teacher of fine arts from a South Indian university, recited snatch after snatch from English poetry, and the younger companion from the North came out with his vulgar, inane, mundane, facetious, almost silly, commentary, I was itching to shout at both of them to shut up. I simply wanted to sit quietly and drink deep from that fountain of divine beauty. Here was nature at its best, unravelling the entire gamut of its most glorious treasures. Was all this beauty emerging by chance by the random changes in the positions of the clouds, or was it the result of some conscious artistic design of that master-artist called Nature? I continue to wonder till this day. Perhaps it is both—in all artistic creativity, natural or man-made.

Just a few days later, as I came out of my room, I found mist all around. I was feeling so depressed because I couldn't possibly go out for a walk. It appeared that I was doomed to waste yet another evening walking up and down the terrace. The miracle of the sunset was out of the question; in fact, it had not recurred at all. As I sighed at the prospects of another 'lost' evening, a friend emerged from the mist from the other side and exclaimed, 'What a glorious evening!' Glorious? I was intrigued by this description of the gloomy situation. More so, because here was a friend whose critical opinions I had learnt to respect. Anyway, when I turned to join him in the stroll, I noticed something that I couldn't believe. The misty spot that I had been traversing a moment ago was lit with a mercury-light overhead which had acquired an eerie power of setting the mist aglow. How can the same thing be so depressing from one angle and so exalting from another? Here was a lesson for me. I realized then that nothing is beautiful or ugly in itself, it is the angle that makes it so.

A fortnight later, rains over, the hills looked so plain again. The greenery was gone, the brown was back and the bared rocks would not mix into cluster of trees. What was earlier covered by clouds and the soft light of the shadows caused by them now appeared in its naked ugliness. Indeed, beauty lies not just in objects but in the overall effect resulting from the arrangement of those objects.

That it is a question of relating the parts to the whole in such a manner that we see not the incongruity of the parts but the integral unity of the whole, I had realized an year earlier. That was at Hyderabad—a place so radically different from Shimla in climate and natural beauty. For morning walks there, I used to prefer a certain route—not for its scenic charm but for its quiet environs that facilitated undisturbed brooding. Part of it was barren ground littered with big rock-boulders or wild growth here and there, and part of it was a road fringed with not-so-decorative plants and trees that appeared at irregular intervals. Indeed, if at all there was any charm, I didn't notice it. Anyway, the stale familiarity inhering the routine of daily passage made the locality look so dull and drab. One morning, however, I chanced to go out a bit earlier than usual, when it was still comparatively dark. And what a pleasant surprise awaited me: silhouetted against the soft and pinkish light of the dawning day, the trees appeared so charming. The wild growth afforded such a perfect background for the setting that I couldn't help asking again the age-old question: whence this beauty and that, too, in a place that had always appeared so patently commonplace? The clue to the answer came a few minutes later when things became brighter and the charm vanished. It was then that I acquired first-hand insight into the role of configuration in integrating the parts into a whole—as also into the role of such subtle effects as blur the incongruities inhering the parts. Just to have repetition of the same thrill, I started going out at an earlier hour and was duly rewarded. One day, however, I overdid that, too. In the darkness that still pervaded like a pall, all looked so somber, even frightful—until the lighting pattern changed after a while to create that coveted effect. So, beauty, I realized, is a matter of proper measure: a touch of excessive brightness can be as fatal to the total effect as a bit of disproportionate darkness. Indeed, one could say about beauty what Lord Byron had said about her cousin: 'One shade the more, one ray the less, / Had half impaired the nameless grace.' This has been confirmed again and again in different situations and times. Surrounded by subtly designed half-lights, lakes generally exude air of romance at night, but at midday they are invariably no more than vast stretches of stagnant water. Likewise, the decorative fountains on round-abouts do not have during day time even fraction of the charm they emit at night when the water-spouting is accompanied by the display of psychedelic lighting. Indeed, it is the totality that matters.

During one of my strolls I learnt yet another lesson. Physically, things were as perfect in a garden as one could wish and yet I didn't feel the joy that I expected. In fact, I very much needed that kind of thrilling impact on that particular day to restore my equanimity which I had lost because of an unpleasant exchange with a passer-by. I tried to lose myself in the spectacle, but the whole thing started looking so irritatingly ugly. Beauty, I could see, is not something objective or empirical; it lies in our response, too—in the beholder's eye, so to say, and depending on his mood. To appreciate beauty, one needs must be, or become, neutral through detachment or transcendence—something not easy to effect in a sullen mood or, for that matter, in a mood of buoyant jubilation.

Such lessons or their confirmation came my way—from Nature and elsewhere. Once I was enchanted by a view; all the trees on the slope had fallen in a pattern and appeared so beautiful. I gazed at the scene for a while and moved ahead. A few steps more and I wanted to have another glance, but it was beautiful no more. One of the trees was refusing to fit into the pattern from that angle and thus the balance was upset. Other occasion, that kind of jarring note was struck by a gap in a green perspective—a house-top that would dwarf the rest or simply draw attention to itself. On the other hand, once a single tree provided the right equilibrium and enhanced the effect by affording a contrast. Also I cannot forget a tall, bare tree which had single, hooked top-bough. Ordinarily, such a one would get lost among the other trees but, from a certain angle, it stood isolated and thus formed against the backdrop of a clear but half-lit sky, a perfect question-mark. Another situation: what appeared like a piece of sculpture turned out to be a broken tree! Yes, indeed, distance too may lend the charm. Longinus's concept of the sublime is so easy to verify on the mountains: the chaos of ranges crystallizes into a grand spectacle when seen from afar. Anyway, one does not have to go all the way to the Himalayas for learning such lessons in aesthetics. Even a single tree would do; what is more, one may see how the converse is equally true. A bunyan tree looks awe-inspiring from a distance, but a closer look and the branches are seen to be wayward in their tenor. A branch in itself may not be so repulsive but the twigs thereon can put one off because of their patternlessness. Leaves might be even more chaotic. Chaos of leaves is lost in the twigs, patternlessness of twigs into the branches, and waywardness of branches into the tree, and thus all these incongruities add up to yield a sublime spectacle.

Beauty, in short, inheres the relating of parts, incongruent or otherwise, to the whole. Ugliness lies in some incoherence between the parts and the whole. We could even go to the extent of modifying our earlier observation and say that nothing is ugly or beautiful, configuration makes it so—configuration that invests some suggestion of meaningfulness on what may otherwise appear chaotic, absurd. I recall in this connection an arch outside a theatre. Its want of symmetry intrigued me; worse, it seemed to lean precariously. Was it a case of a design ill-executed, I just wondered. Suddenly I noticed that, seen from the front angle, it appeared to greet an approaching visitor with a slight bow with folded hands. What appeared a freakish design a moment ago started looking a stroke of genius. But how if I had missed that suggestion? That absence of *Dhvani* would signify the failure of the artist. At the same time, if the greeting gesture had been made too obvious and explicit through all-too-familiar symbols, it would not be so artful. In other words, configuration is not enough; there has to be something more. One thinks in this context of *gestalt* which makes the whole more than the sum-total of the parts.

Of course, the sum total need not necessarily amount to anything beautiful. It might as well turn out to be something ungainly. Witness, on the one hand, that little girl who, at the age of three, had enough of aesthetic sense to give an approving nod to her aunt whenever the latter effected changes in the arrangement of the drawing-room and, on the other, that young bride who is fond of collecting beautifully framed pictures but whose drawing-room arrangement is so odd as to look shocking. The latter's problem is that she is concerned with the parts individually without being able to relate them to the whole. Art calls for attention to both the macro and the micro levels—parts as parts, parts in relation to one another, parts in relation to the whole, and the whole as a whole. Lapses may occur at times even in professional hands. For example, in an art exhibition, I was put off by the very first glimpse. The exhibits were pieces of great art and there was obvious effort at arranging them tastefully and yet things wouldn't click. Intrigued, I tried to find the reason and discovered that the architectural design of the exhibition-hall could not absorb the over-all quality of the exhibits.

Indeed, between garbage and collage, there is a very thin dividing line and that is why vulgarity and pornography are no more than obverse sides of the coin called high art. Ornaments admittedly signify art work but when a woman, to display her wealth and jewellery, puts on too many of them, result can be grotesque. It looks something vulgar, almost obscene. Painting of a nude woman can be a great work of art, but it might as well deteriorate into something indecent—depending on whether the sensuality is only a part of the whole or something for its own sake, whether it draws attention to itself or is subsumed in the totality. It is all the question of what is being highlighted—the body, the material aspect and its quantity, or the soul of the thing, its quality. A love story may yield sufficiently titillating stuff to become a best-seller, but, to become a classic, it has to go beyond the sensuous aspect of the experience. In saying this, I am not implying that great literature has moral or religious core; it underlines, instead, that deeper level of experience where distinctions among body, mind and soul disappear. That applies to all arts: what words are in literature, sounds are in music, line and colour in painting, instruments in a concert, movements in a dance, bricks or stones in architecture, and actors in a performance. It is always a question of so integrating the basic elements that they lose their original characteristics to yield something of greater significance. Before that transmutation takes place, we have, so to say, only the body of an element; after the transmutation, its soul. In a work of art, obscenity does not disappear; only, provided with a context, it is made a meaningful part of a significant experience.

From what has been said above, it should be easy to deduce the distinction between art on the one hand and entertainment or propaganda on the other. It is art only if the elements allow themselves to become subservient to the overall spirit of the work; when the elements tend to dominate, artistic process is incomplete and the work produced is of an inferior quality. What makes pop-music so popular with the masses is this superficial level of its appeal to the senses; Beethoven and Mozart go deeper and therefore need something of a finer sensibility. I recall a rock-show organized during the Festival of France in India. Technically, with all those lighting tricks and sound-equipment, it was so thrilling visually and aurally. No wonder, soon enough, younger participants were up in their seats, clapping and singing; not long thereafter, they could be seen near the stage, dancing and thumping in a manner that reminded one of the rats around the Pied Piper of Hamelin. In their movements, one saw neither grace nor harmony nor balance; instead, it was a display of animal vigour. Each followed his or her own rhythm in the cacophony and, at the end, all passions spent, each one looked totally exhausted. It might have been something exciting but there was obviously nothing elevating about it. Needless to add, the older among the audience found the proceedings too loud for their taste and, utterly bored, they left much before the end of the show. In a classical performance, on the other hand, it is invariably the younger people who leave early, unless there is something to gratify their sensuality in the form of the performer's physique, glamorous make-up, or minimal costuming—as in a ballet, for example. The Indian classical dances are purer forms of art insofar as they eliminate the role of body and senses to such an extent that, after a while, one tends to forget whether the performer is a man or a woman. No wonder, too, the costuming is heavy and make-up more symbolic and ritualistic than sensuously exciting. The idea is not to titillate or even involve the spectator in an emotional state, but to facilitate his detachment from the senses so that he might experience the spiritual core of the performance.

This does not mean that the proverbial Indian prudery is puritanical or hypocritical enough to shut out the sensuous completely from the aesthetics. Instead, there is in *Kāmasūtra* a whole system that treats love-making as an art—fulfilment of one's being through senses. Through proper regimentation of sexual energy, intercourse *(bhoga)* becomes a kind of *yoga*. The ideal is not so much indulgence as liberation. In this connection, it is worth noting that while in the west the sex-shows, strip-tease and cabaret dances pander to the sensual beast in man, in India, the traditional sex-joints, run by fully dressed dancing girls, were meant for the *bhadra-loka*—the cultured elite who would prove ideal spectators (*sahridayas*) in Bharata's theatre. What is more, the dance performances were accompanied by soulful singing of high poetry—*ghazals* and *qawwalis* which only the sophisticated could appreciate. Obviously, the aim was not catharsis through involvement at sense-level but *Rasa* through detachment. That is true art—so handling the gross and indelicate as to evoke an elevating response.

How a *Rasa* gets created will become clear if we notice what happens in a classical *raga* or a *ghazal*. The sounds produced in the former are rather raw, hoarse, even jarring; but gradually, through repetition in varied tones, they get refined enough to acquire a kind of sweetness. The notes, lines, phrases, even syllables, are repeated, recast and reworded again and again until the essence is obtained. It is like churning to extract the cream. Towards the end, when the *rasa* is realized, one transcends the variety; or, one might say, the variety coalesces into a unity. Thus is thought made subtle and emotion etherealized. One of the classical forms of singing in India is called *khayyal,* which literally means thought. Its progress echoes the tenor of thought-creation—how a thought crystallizes out of stray ideas which spring up one after another at different stages of thought formation.

Perhaps, for the best illustration of *Rasa*-evocation, it would be both helpful and interesting to refer to the aesthetics of *ghazal*, the most celebrated form of poetry in Urdu literature. It is the most popular form for recitation in poetic symposia called *mushairas.* In a *ghazal*, couplets do get created, but the lines of couplet don't rhyme mutually; rather, it is the even lines which rhyme throughout (aa ba ca da ea . . .). However, each couplet is a complete, self-contained unit in respect of thought. The real aim is to say something old or new in an altogether fresh way so that the listener's or the reader's whole attention is immediately captivated by the novelty inhering the thought and/or the way of presentation. Thanks to the economy of expression and the completeness of an idea in a single couplet, when the second line of the couplet is halfway through, an attentive reader or listener may be in a position to anticipate the concluding rhyme-unit. This exercise in guessing is gratifying if one is proved right in one's conjecture; it is even more thrilling if the poet comes out with something unexpected and more subtle. Since each couplet has a new thought, and since that thought is invariably feelingful, the reading or hearing of a *ghazal* implies one's passing from one realm of thought to another and from one sentiment to another, in fairly quick succession. In other words, here is a kind of situation in which both head and heart are involved in a stimulating exercise—something akin to tickling. That is why, more often than not, long after a reading or listening session, one finds oneself humming some of the more memorable verses which have left their imprint. It is like relishing the taste of food after the meal is over. The most notable aspect of *mushairas* is the instant response that the couplets receive.

Indeed, each good couplet has the quality of a flash and the power of an epiphany. One feels like joining the recitation, repeating it with the poet, or even to one's own self. This resonant echo is so like the vibration stimulated by tickling the strings of a musical instrument. This is what one might call *Dhvani.* Indeed, thus do the poet and the reader find themselves attuned to each other and therefore on the same wavelength. This situation may not last for long but the more appealing couplets do tend to become an integral part of one's aesthetic sensibility. That explains why a truly cultured Indian invariably has a verse to cite in every situation.[30] As every couplet of a *ghazal* has a touch of novelty about it, and since every line makes one exclaim either 'What an idea!' or 'How well-said!', a lover of Urdu poetry is rarely too tired of verses. That is why *mushairas* go on and on for hours on end. No wonder, in Omar Khayyam's notion of 'paradise enow,' a book of verses has such a vital role. Indeed, like the joys of Paradise, poetry knows no satiety. It is also a joy for ever.

Perhaps we should offer a few examples of verses par excellence, but we won't. In fact, we cannot, because, owing to the fact that their peculiarity lies in the way the ideas are expressed through such specific verbal tricks as create an instant rapport with the reader, they cannot be translated without losing that *Dhvani*-quality. Indeed, here is a proof—if one was ever needed—that aesthetics is not a matter of cognitive or emotive communication. Those are things that language can manage, but not that elusive, ethereal something which is at the heart of *Rasa* and *Dhvani*. In the case of translation, it is impossible to produce that magic touch which invests words with a poetic flavour. In any case, the flavour may be different in the new version—a different *Rasa*, so to say.[31]

If the flavour gets lost in translating verses in a language that is still alive, how can one be sure of retaining the charm of the poetry written in a language that is as good as dead—say, in Greek tragedy which was studded with such music and poetery as is no longer within our reach? In such a situation, can we really grasp the spirit of that genre on the bases of translations? This poser haunts me still—and so do many others. For example, what happens when a work is translated into another medium—an epic into a play, a play into a novel, a novel into a movie or a television-serial? (Witness, for example, the different versions of the *Rāmāyana*—Valmiki's epic, Tulsi's *Kathā*, that old classic movie, recent tele-serial, and the innumerable versions for children). Even otherwise, critics do have diverse opinions about the *Rasa* of the same classic—*Mahābhārata*, for example: *Vīrā-rasa, Shāntā-rasa, Karunā-rasa*, or even *Raudrā-rasa*. That might happen even when the writer himself translates or adapts his own work. In a situation like this, isn't it totally unrealistic to assume uniformity of response in the form of a particular *Rasa*? The assumption sounds all the more problematic in respect of theatrical performances in which the communicative role of language is played by such variable material as the humans—the director, the designer, the actors! In the composite art of theatre, men are what colours are in painting, sounds in music, or words in literature. To cap it all, spectators too have their human variability, and thus, with the best of breeding and culture, two *sahridayas* might not be of the same heart mutually or vis-a-vis the playwright. Perhaps that explains why occasionally the same production gets such diametrically opposed assessments by reviewers known for their competence, integrity and objectivity. In fact, on occasions, one may find oneself such a poor *sahridaya* of one's own work—at times feeling inconsolably miserable because of one's inability to evoke the response that was intended, at times deliriously marvelling at his/her own ingenuity and artful manipulation of words.

All this should make a good case for dismissing all aesthetic theories as myths. But, then, going by actual practice, it is also a fact that, invariably, despite the barriers of languages, media and human factors obtaining on the levels of both creation and perception, the difference in the responses evoked is one of degree rather than of kind. Perhaps it is possible to argue that the variation is in respect of the *vyabhichāribhāvas*; so long as the *Sthāyibhāva* is the same, the *Rasa* produced is, by and large, the same. As for the differential inhering the process of translation and adaptation, possibly it owes itself to the facts that one is keen only to retain the cognitive, the emotive or the formal aspects, and that one seldom makes allowance for that spiritual aspect which owes its existence to the mysterious and intangible element called *Pratibhā*. One may call it inspiration, intuition, fancy, imagination or chance. Obviously, something speaks through the artist—as if in spite of himself. No wonder occasionally an artist might find himself marvelling at his creative work: 'What made me say all these profound things and in such a beautiful way?' Such *pratibhā* is what a translator or adapter cannot muster, revive or reinject—not even the original artist when he does it again. Indeed, that is what makes art something a-rational, if not exactly irrational. Maybe, that accounts for people seeing kinship between madness and genius.

Can a cultivated man be of 'the same heart' as the artist who has such a touch of the a-rational about him? Possibly, the idea is that he too must be imaginative enough to transcend the literal and accept as reality (even though momentarily) what is, in fact, non-real. Like the artist, he must be capable of objectivity—that is, capable of liberating himself from the bonds of ego. At the same time, this detachment is not to be extended to all kinds of sensuous responses. So delicate is this balance between subjectivity and objectivity that disaster follows its absence. This brings to mind a spectator who made obscene remarks when

Othello throttled Desdemona—and that, too, in the famous production by E. Alkazi, one of the greatest modern directors India has produced. Obviously, the spectator was in no mood to submit himself to the illusion. On the other hand, it is common to see some child shrieking in a cinema-hall when a train appears to move straight towards him. The running train being a reality for him, his fear is real. The feeling (Bhāva) of fear turns into *Rasa* of fear for the grown-up person who knows the train to be unreal. Indeed, only a man with the right sensibility and in a balanced frame of mind can receive an emotion or an idea in such a manner as to experience its *Rasa* rather than the emotion or the idea itself. It implies discarding not of body but of its grossness—a process of transcendence in which the negatives are not negated but so intermixed with the positives that the overall result is one of affirmation. In fact, the more the incongruities, inconsistencies and tensions that get assimilated, the greater appears the art. That is precisely what we have been saying about the creative process, too.

Of course, this does not imply complete identification between the values of artistic creativity and aesthetic perception. In an original painting and its print (in the posters, for example), aesthetic values can be equally rich but the former has hardly any artistic value. However that does not mean that the artistic and the aesthetic processes can never become one. They do at times—for example, when one indulges in day-dreaming, wishful thinking or imaginative recollection. When a man lies imagining himself dying, meeting a beloved, or reliving an old experience, he is both the creator and the percipient. The identification ceases when the fancy-work is drawn on a canvas or put down in black and white. Now it becomes a frozen experience that can be relived only as an outsider, as a *sahridaya*—even when the percipient is the creator himself. In a sense, it is possible to say that when the ethos of the moment is captured, it is eternalized, but at the cost of that vibrant vitality which marks a living experience. To put it differently, to experience the soul, one must transcend the limitations as well as the fullness of body. But, then, certainly body cannot be dispensed with completely. For highlighting the feminine in a woman, the mother in her, or her spirit of sacrifice, the requisite state of her soul can be exteriorized only through the expressions on her face, her gestures, gait or postures—through her body, so to say. Indeed, for depicting the universal, one proceeds only through a particular: likewise, above all, by getting related to the unconscious does the conscious become a medium of expressing the archetypal. In day-to-day life, our interest lies in the particulars, the body, the conscious; the soul, the archetype, the universals are of interest only in the world of art.

Apropos the relationship between life and art, one is reminded of a verity enshrined in Browning's 'Last Ride Together.' Certainly, even a most cultured man stops his scrutiny of the most exquisite statue of Venus the moment a living woman, wading through water, lifts her skirt. Realizing such comparative weakness of art vis-a-vis nature, and aware also of the fact that the sensuous cannot be wished away, Indian aestheticians underplay the physical element in art so that the spiritual might come to the fore. On the other hand, in the West, where talk of soul and spirit is an anethma, the modern artists have sought to bypass the delimiting realms of body, logic and consciousness by resorting to distortive movements—e.g., the cubist or surrealistic painting, the psychological novel, the abstract dance, the theatre of the Absurd. Unfortunately, all that has turned out to be a deeper plunge into the grossness of the senses. No wonder one hears talk about evolving a new aesthetic approach as often as about the need to redefine tragedy.

Towards a New Definition

As should be clear from the foregoing, aesthetic theory has to accommodate much that is of contradictory nature—sacred and profane. While Plato, Hegel, Goethe, et. al. did perceive something divine in beauty, most other aestheticians in the West remained within the confines of the sensuous. Source of the problem lies possibly in the fact that, as the archetype of beauty, Nature has something in it that evokes worshipful attitude and yet, at the same time, represents the level of gross reality as well. Another thing that is possibly responsible for confusion in this context is the fact that the entire realm of art is usually assumed to be uniformly beautiful although, in fact, it ranges from sublime to grotesque. Likewise, responses, too, vary from ecstasy to mindlessness. In this respect, the Indian aestheticians are more realistic because their *Rasas* correspond to different aesthetic states—*Adbhuta-rasa* to the sublime, *Vīra-rasa* to the grand, *Shringāra-rasa* to the charming, *Hāsya-rasa* to the ludicrous, *Raudra-rasa* to the terrifying, *Bhayānaka-rasa* to the horrible, *Karunā-rasa* to the pathetic, and *Bībhatsa-rasa* to the grotesque.

Another usual *faux pas* is to trace the source of aesthetic value in form, medium, style, genius, cognitive content, or emotive response, individually rather than collectively. Besides, it isn't enough to see things either from the artist's angle alone or exclusively from the point of perception. Imitation, expression, playfulness, illusion, generation, etc., are important concepts in their own ways, but they don't explain all about creative process; nor do perception, empathy, inference, participation alone so far as the percipience is concerned. Also, a wholesome approach must reckon with insights afforded by both the Western and the Eastern thinkers. And that would mean accommodating at once reason and soul, imitation and transmutation, communication and communion, existential dichotomy and cosmic harmony unconscious and superconscious, mundane and divine, involvement and detachment, escape and inscape, catharsis and *Rasa*, and so on. Indeed, art belongs to a realm where one cannot, and must not, try to regard as separate such apparently distinct terms as intention and execution, intuition and imagination, impression and expression, perception and apperception, etc.

Of course, there is always a danger in yoking contradictory elements to create a synthesis. One has to be extra-careful in this particular case because accepting half-truths blindly can be as disastrous as rejecting them altogether. For example, taken individually, imitation or illusion fails to take one far enough; but one could interrelate them by saying that all art is imitation in the sense that one feels transported to a world that is not real—an illusion of a more patterned and meaningful existence. Even though the material used is familiar, there is a touch of novelty; on the other hand, despite the process of selection, there is, because of creative organization, an illusion of wholeness and completeness, too. Thus seen, it becomes a case of transformation rather than imitation. Things are not exactly what we see or hear: touched by imagination and intuition, they lose the characteristics that are associated with the purely emotive or cognitive levels and thus acquire a faculty which enables one to see deeper into their souls. Thus does imitation cease to be imitation: purged of grossness, what remains is pure essence. That explains why one has always a feeling that art has *something* to say in addition to what is visible; true appreciation begins with the discovery of that mythical 'something'. More intuitively than deliberately, the artist implants in the art object such clues as should help reveal that latent consciousness. When clues are perceived, the object suddenly ceases to be a purely physical being; instead, it appears vitalized by the principle of consciousness. That is how, even while imitating reality, art leads to the illusive world of the intangible—the spiritual.

The problem arises because the West is concerned solely with the world of material reality and the East has made the soul as the realm of its almost exclusive concern. Finding chaos and conflicts in nature, the occidentalist turns outward to the world of man for orderliness; the Orientalist, on the other hand, finds tensions in the world of man and turns inwards for harmony and order. Finding peace and enlightenment in the inner realm, the latter lauds it as the superconscious or the pure conscious, while the former rejects it as the unconscious—as the area where dark forces operate. Unless both these approaches are reconciled, things are bound to remain partial and unsatisfactory. In practical terms, such eclecticism means accommodating the validity of both body and soul, form and formlessness, realism and ritualism, individuality and totality, particular and universal, stereotype and archetype. In this connection, it would be worthwhile to recall the conciliatory tenets of the Chinese and the Japanese aesthetics—Yang-Yin and Yu-gen.

Our bringing in soul might put off the rationalist reader but one might as well question the rationality of those who are prepared to accept the Life Force of the vitalists, the Absolute Idea of Plato, and the collective unconscious of Jung, but not the concept of the supersoul. They can believe in the operation of the genes (which no body has ever seen) generation after generation but cannot see any sense in the transmigration of souls. Personally I cannot go very far with Aristotle and his ilk, nor can I follow Bharata and his tribe all the way. For me, God, Truth and Beauty are one, and thus the intellectual and the sensuous exist on the same level as the spiritual. In what follows, I do fall back on the oriental (rather, Indian) terminology, but, as will be seen, I do imply conceptual deviations. Ideally, I should coin new terms and avoid the use of such words as have acquired cliched associations, but that is something more easily proposed than executed.

Perhaps I should begin by restating the areas of my agreement—of borrowings and deductions, if you so like. Later I could indicate my deviations, reservations, or changes of focus.

(a) Beauty is a matter of wholesome relationship between the parts and the whole.
(b) Art implies making—creation of a beautiful whole out of parts, i.e., unity in diversity (*Saṁyoga*).
(c) Essence of art lies in transforming the chaotic into something patterned, creating rhythm out of discord, using lower senses and crude feelings to nourish the soul.
(d) Senses, ideas, motifs, forms do go into the making of a work of art but, in the process, they lose their peculiar characteristics.
(e) Aesthetic creativity is not merely a matter of organization alone; equally important are subject, medium and style.
(f) About the beauty of art, there is something extra-rational, inexplicable, almost magical (*Alaukika*).
(g) Creating a work of art requires talent and a certain kind of intuitive sensitivity (*Pratibhā*); likewise, proper response can come only from a man with a certain sensibility and imagination (*Sahridaya*).
(h) In aesthetic experience, one responds in spite of oneself, as if bound by a spell (*Chamatkāra*).
(i) In aesthetic experience, one feels as if mind and body had lost distinctness and one had become deconditioned and therefore incapable of thinking or feeling about oneself (*Yoga*).
(j) Aesthetic experience is not a matter of emotion and thought but something richer—involing one's entire being (*Bhoga*).
(k) This state of *Yoga* plus *Bhoga* doesn't mean escape from self but inscape—experiencing self at a deeper level when subject and object become one.
(l) In the work of art itself, there is something which makes one see more than what is visible and apprehension comes like a flash (*Dhvani*).

(m) In aesthetic experience, ideas and feelings no longer remain what they are but get refined and transmuted into something altogether different (*Rasa*).
(n) The overall aesthetic response is transcendental—a pure bliss (*Ānanda*) which is, however, momentary.
(o) While experiencing the state of *Ānanda*, one is at a level deeper than that of consciousness—not one of the unconscious but that of the superconscious; it is a kind of union with God (*Brahmānanda*).

Obviously, in the above listing, I am leaning more on the oriental side. This is not because I claim to know the Eastern aesthetics better. In fact, I don't know Sanskrit at all (a great handicap, indeed!). My partiality is rooted in the fact that my experience as a percipient leaves me even less contented with the Western theories which do explain the ideational and emotive aspects but not the magical quality of the impact. If I have to pinpoint the quintessence of the aesthetic appeal, I would prefer to start not with communication but with communion—and a lot more that falls beyond the realms of time and space. Indeed, aesthetic experience is basically extra-terrestrial (if not exactly supraterrestrial)—an affair of the soul as well as one of the head and the heart. Certainly, it is not my intention to deny the sensuous aspect of the aesthetic appeal, nor do I mean to suggest its complete identification with the spiritual, the mystic or the religious. It is both sensuous and spiritual: rooted in senses, it is experienced by the soul.

In a purely religious experience, material world is eliminated and all polarities disappear completely; here, the sensuous world is not absent but only transformed through interaction with the spiritual. What is basically a private experience becomes a publicly shared one. Besides, in the perceptive counterpart, traffic is not with ideas but with intuitions. It is a case not of message but of revelation—a flash, so to say. No wonder, as Susanne K. Langer puts it, the crux of aesthetic experience lies in intuitive activity. She goes to the extent of talking about the 'magic circle' of art. Empathy cannot be the proper word for such a relationship between the art object and the percipient; it is a much more complex, even subtle, knot of different kinds of responses—disinterestedness, detachment, contemplation, participation and evocation which appears so much like the mystic illumination. It is a response involving biological, psychological, historical, cultural and, above all, spiritual factors. In fact, the more extensive is the texture of factors involved, the greater is the beauty and the richer the experience afforded. In short, we must refrain from confusing the aesthetic experience on the one hand with emotional appeal, moral judgement or hedonistic pleasure and on the other with the mystical vision. It is sensuous in the parts, but in the process of organizing the parts into a whole, the sensuous gets transmuted into the spiritual.

In view of this approach of mine, I am not going to synthesize Aristotle and Bharata, nor am I going to follow or reject either of the two. Rather, mine is going to be a selective-cum-eclectic approach. Having stated the areas of agreement, I am going to explain or interpret certain concepts—or else reinterpret them—in my own way to broaden their scope. Indeed, it is necessary to liberate some of the accepted formulations (e.g., configuration, *Rasa*, *Dhvani*, *Sphota*, and *Ānanda* theories) from the confines of their original contexts—say, the arts of poetry and drama—so that they become universal enough to be equally applicable to the visual, plastic, performing and even functional arts. In any case, I should be keen not only to relate the usually polarized ends of aesthetic communication, viz., creation and perception, but also to discover the necessary bridges that forge or facilitate a unity between the two.

Maybe, we could start by asking again those fundamental questions: what is beauty and what is art? For answers, there could be no better guide than Nature who, as an artist par excellence, is the archetypal source of all beauty. In any case, just as, in the Platonic love, the first stage in one's union with God is seeing a beautiful woman, admiration of nature is the first step towards aesthetic appreciation. As I learnt from the 'sermons from the stones', beauty inheres a configuration in which the parts and the whole are held together by an integrally wholesome relationship. Of course, in this configuration, the resultant is more than the sum total of the parts and thus does one get the impression of an alchemic transmutation. What is more, the dimension of multiplicity gets so dissolved that one sees not the parts but the whole. If the perception of that unity in diversity is hampered, the result is ugliness. The perception of the wholesomeness of the relationship between the parts and the whole being intuitive rather than analytical, it is immediate. Of course, in case of want of proper detachment, perception can get mixed with the elements of subjectivity. This might bring into operation such other factors as would make one impervious to the sense of wholeness or else to the want of it. That also explains why every mother regards her own child as the sweetest creature ever born. No wonder, too, when the legendary lover, Qais (popularly known as Majnu), was asked what he saw in his pitch-dark beloved, Laila (literally meaning night), he reportedly retorted, 'To realize how beautiful she is, you must see Laila with Majnu's eyes'. Conversely, in the eyes of a rival, even the most stunning beauty might look quite plain.

Beauty may be natural or man-made. Art refers etymologically to making—making of beauty by man. Indeed, art is beauty concretized; if beauty is the soul, art is its form. Taking raw elements from life, an artist creates among them such a pattern of relationships as yields a composite whole—a whole which not only subsumes the individuality of parts but also transcends the identity of each of them. The elements used may be lines, colours, stones, pieces of wood, movements, sounds, words, senses, etc., but in the process of artistic transformation, they acquire new forms. What is more, they acquire also the potential of evoking such associations as suggest the possibility of a deeper meaning. Thus does everyday reality change into such an illusion as embodies Reality in its totality. What we imply by Reality-in-totality is not what Plato called archetypal Idea—the source of artistic imitation—but the quintessential *Rasa*. The manipulation of parts so as to give the impression of having expressed the whole truth is like realizing eternity in temporal terms. Thus seen, art is a way of transmuting the all-too-familiar material into something new and strange or meaningful. The process of effecting the unity in diversity involves an alchemic change—transforming chaos into something patterned, creating rhythm out of discord, using feelings and lower senses to worship the soul. Likewise, senses, ideas, motifs and forms lose their peculiar characteristics. To put it differently, in art, the main thing is a purposive organization of the parts into a whole. More properly, we could call it 'configuration'.

Of course, in Nature, too, if anything enjoys universal validity, it is the practice of configuration—right from the elements to the celestial bodies. The way electrons, protons, neutrons, etc. form themselves into an atom, and the way atoms form themselves into molecules, molecules into elements, and elements into compounds is key to the way the whole universe operates. At any given moment, as one thing occupies a central position, others take up immediately complementary or supplementary positions to produce a balanced state of an integrated whole. Even when science had not progressed far enough to analyze the natural phenomena in terms of nuclear charges, people could see the way the basic elements like earth, water, fire, air and ether configurated to produce various substances. Indeed, in any natural scene or situation, if anything is heard loud and clear, it is the process of configuration. Even in the very being of man, this law operates. Although he appears to be a single unit, in fact he is a complex organism of numerous levels—physical, mental, nervous, psychological, spiritual, etc. Despite the surface appearance of an equilibrium, these levels are always changing to produce ever-new sets of configurations in which one of the levels dominates, even as the rest adjust themselves in positions of subservience. Thus when a man sits lost in thought, his emotional level does not vanish; his nervous and psychic energies are also in operation, although all these are subservient to the functioning of the head. Similarly, while making love, his mind and other senses let the sensual apparatus dominate. In any emotional state, so many feelings get stimulated, but only one of them overtops the other; the next moment, with a new situation, another feeling might take over the charge. In short, emotions, thoughts, instincts, intentions, reflexes—all keep changing their configurative positions and yet human personality has the appearance of a balanced whole. How the law of configurations-within-configurations operates pyramidically becomes clear when it is realized that while the instincts are series of chained reflexes, the affect-charges of these instinctive forces configurate into emotions; and emotions, when organized, yield sentiments. Likewise, disposition is the sum of all instincts and impulses, temperament a complex result of dispositions, and character an overall configuration of instincts, sentiments, dispositions and temperaments. In the same way, stimuli join to produce sensations; sensations orchestrate mutually and with further stimuli to yield perceptions, which eventually get interlaced into concepts.

Indeed, whatever the relation of art with nature otherwise, at least in configuration, art imitates nature. Painting is a configuration of lines and colours, literature is one of words, music that of sounds, dance of movements, and so on. Likewise, theatre may be seen as a configuration of arts. In dramatic arts, what is a plot if not a configuration of events, what is a spectacle if not a configuration of stage properties, and what is a performance if not the configuration of action by a number of performers? A character, too, is a configuration of certain human traits and states of mind. What one is at a given moment—a father, a husband, a servant, a villain—depends on what shines forth as the pivotal core of the configuration. A change in the relationship of these traits might result in some other aspect of the personality coming to the fore and thus changing the entire pattern of configurations. It is like seeing a scene from another angle—the same constituents but a different sight. Ditto for the emotions portrayed. That is what Bharata had realized on the level of the creation of *Rasa* in an actor's performance. No wonder he used the word *'saṁyoga'* in his *Rasa-sūtra*. Unfortunately, however, he missed to see similar patterns of configuration on other levels, including that of responses. In fact, properly seen, in theatre—indeed, in all arts (as also in all life)—there is a constant process of ever-changing configurations, very like the flux of ever-changing Bergsonian 'selves' in human personality. To put it differently, in theatre we have not just the configuration of *Bhāvas, Anubhāvas* and *Vibhāvas*, that Bharata talks about but configurations of many other types, too—for example, those of objects, events, responses, relationships, attitudes. And, in each configuration, what comes to be apprehended is not the diversity of parts but a unity inhering the totality of those parts.

That totality which expresses the internal life of configuration of *Bhāvas* is what Bharata called *Rasa*. In fact, it is possible to call quintessential totality of each configuration as its spirit, its *rasa*. For example, when a poor man's plight is depicted through his looks, movements, speech and actions, we may not feel his hunger but, in the totality of the portrait or the stage-portrayal, his soul gets reflected; what registers with us is not what he looks but what he is. Likewise, when we see a father looking fondly at his child, we may not feel his pleasure but everything in his looks, movements and actions converges into the totality of his being as a father. In the first case we have the quintessential *rasa* of poverty: in the second, the *rasa* of paternal affection. Here we are referring to *rasa* not in the context of aesthetic perception but that of artistic creativity—what crystallizes in a creative configuration. In a movie, in depicting a scene, what we have are just visuals captured by the camera. The way the shots are arranged is perhaps the best illustration of the configuration business. What gets created is the totality of a situation or scene through the collage-like process of the selected pictures. The photographs may not have been taken on the same day, they may not belong to the same locale, or they may not pertain to continuous action, and yet, in the process of configuration, there gets created the feeling of continuity in respect of time, space and situation.

For an example, let us take a rape scene. A lesser artist might depict in details the entire sequence from A to Z with all its vulgarity, obscenity and crude violence; but a true artist can create it with the help of selective configuration of visuals in which the participants may or may not be in focus. This brings to mind one cinematic sequence. After a few very brief glimpses of a chase, the camera was focused for a moment on a rocking chandelier to the accompaniment of shrieks and sounds of the struggle and then shifted to the adjacent room where a birthday party was in progress. In a few seconds, when the camera returned to the rape-room, the intensity of violence and passion was writ large on everything lying there. The totality of these snippets built up, as it were, the quintessence of the entire action. We had the essence of a rape—sans the gross details. Such an expression of the internal essences of a configuration may be called its *rasa*, its soul. Obviously, in a sequence that is trying to collect realistic details, we shall have too much of gross business and therefore our response would be on the sensuous level, be it pain or pleasure; it may or may not touch our souls. In a truly artistic configuration, we receive only the *rasa* of the action; therefore, in the consequent *Rasa* of the experience, pain or pleasure comes in a rarefied manner. As the quintessential spirit or soul of the experience finds its way direct to our soul, the twin 'souls' hold, as it were, a direct communion with each other.

Indeed, even if what goes into the making of an art are sensuous elements, it would be wrong to use the word synesthesis because, in the process of configuration, two things bring about a qualitative, almost alchemic, change. First inheres the selection of the parts. Each emotion, each situation, each relationship is subjected to a rigorous selection in which the grosser elements are discarded and only such ones retained as are quintessential. Secondly, in each configuration, there operates the law of gestalt—that a whole is more than sum total of the parts. As Von C. Ehrenfels showed in the context of musical scales, a tune is not present in notes separately but springs up in the arrangement of the scales. In the same manner, as the Berlin Gestalt School proved later, impulses organize themselves into patterns in the dynamic sensory field. That elusive, indefinable 'something' of the Gestalt must be brought into the aesthetic theory if we want to understand it better. This is something that Kant called *'geist'* (soul); without it, art tends to acquire a mechanical rather than aesthetic dimension. Those who are allergic to the concept of 'soul' may call it by the more secular name of *Rasa*, but the fact remains that the quintessential *Rasa* has about it something meta-sensuous, almost spiritual. When Bharata used the culinary analogue in respect of *Rasa*, what he wanted to highlight was its quintessential quality. *Rasa* remains in mouth when food has been consumed; it is the essence of the ingredients sans their grossness. As soul, too, is what remains when the body and its elements are gone, *rasa* of the food may be regarded as its soul. Likewise, in aesthetics, when we talk of the *rasa* of an idea, an emotion, an action, a situation, an event, or a character, we imply, as it were, its soul which has been liberated from the grossness of life in the process of artistic selection.

Certainly, an artist cannot capture everything; he has to omit the inessential. What he retains is the vital essence of the whole—its *rasa*. Such a distilled concentrate is a kind of archetype. Reproduced on the titles of the Cambridge edition of Shakespeare's individual plays, Picasso's sketch captures in just a few apparently doodlesome lines the likeness of the great playwright. There are no details—just the essence which we may call the quintessence or *rasa* of the features of the Bard of Avon. Likewise, Ranga's famous cartoons of Gandhi are no more than random outlines, but they retain the *rasa* or the quintessential soul of the Mahatma'a looks. Only a common artist is too bothered with the gross details; a true artist is invariably content with a subtle hint. Indeed, every artistic communication dispenses with superficial level of senses in favour of a subtle meaning—the *Rasa*.

Of course, when Bharata spoke of *Rasa*, he was thinking of the quintessence of *Bhāva* through the configuration of *anubhāvas*, *vibhāvas, sanchāribhāva*s, etc. The fact, however, is that the entire aesthetic operation is a network of such configurations—each an attempt to dissolve some diversity into a unity. What is more, these configurations get configurated further mutually to yield still more configurations. To put it differently, we have *rasa* not only of *bhāvas* but also of objects, colours, sounds, situations, relationships, responses, senses, etc. These configurate in theatre into *rasa*s of events, characters, dialogues, etc., which, in turn, configurate to yield *rasa*s of scenes and acts and eventually the *rasa* of all *rasa*s—the *Rasa* of the play. In this business of configurations, the physical, the mental and the spiritual also configurate severally in accordance with the business-in-hand—conceding precedence at times to body, at times to mind, and at times to the soul. In the long run, however, it is the spiritual that holds the sway. Once this is realized, it is not difficult to visualize how the conscious, the unconscious and the superconscious are reconciled in a configuration—or, for that matter, *Sattva, Rajas* and *Tamas gunas*. Indeed, the configurative business it is that reconciles all, even the heterogeneous but interrelated elements. Thus are effected the configurative syntheses of content and form, words and meaning, charm and response, genius and taste, subjective and objective, *yoga* and *bhoga*, will and idea, ego and libido, Dionysian and Apollonian, the positive and the negative. And all these configurate in a kind of musical matrix—that is, individually, mutually, interrelatedly, chorally.

From the foregoing, it is easy to see how the gross gets transmuted and rarefied through a series of configurations into something quintessential, ethereal—soul-like. And since each configuration yields a 'soul', one can say that art is a business of communion among 'souls'—a business whose own soul is the ultimate *Rasa*. At each stage, on either end of this configurative business, there is a configurative *Rasa—Bhāva-rasa* on the one hand and *Ānanda-rasa* on the other. To understand the twin phenomena and their mutual correspondence, one could bring in the modern technology—electronics in general and television in particular. Just as a transmitter scans a series of lines and converts them into a train of electrical signals which the receiver reconstructs into an electronic beam, similarly, artist's 'soul' transmits those artistic signals which *sahridaya*'s soul receives. The role of integrated circuits, electronic tunnels and guns, picture tube, etc. corresponds to the role of configuration at different stages of aesthetic experience. Like the electronic waves in the air waiting for a receiver to convert them into sounds and images, an art object awaits the touch of *dhvani* to effect the aesthetic attuning of the like-hearted percipient, the *sahridaya*. Once that wave-length equation is facilitated, the process of further transmutation starts.

Now, on the relaying end, an image is split into colours that are scanned and converted into waves; those waves are captured at the receiving end and reorganized into such a new configuration of colours as gives the impression of a single image—very like the one transmitted originally. In the aesthetic process also we have a sort of deconditioning of an experience into physical, mental and spiritual stimuli which are regrouped into another configurative experience on the end of the *sahridaya.* In a telecast, what is received is not the original picture per se but the cofiguration of signals; likewise, aesthetic process does not afford exactly the same experience but its etherealized self, *Rasa*. It is something complete, a whole derived from the original but totally new—soulful, rather than emotive or cognitive. What was *bhāva* is *Rasa* now—an integrated result, not part of the process. Just as in the case of television, we feel mistakenly as if it were coming direct, in aesthetics, too, one gets the delusive feeling that all the parties involved are linked by the same sensations; in fact, it is something rarefied to such an extent that even the painful comes purified as joy.

To explain the difference, we would like to change the metaphor of our approach. Whereas God's love causes the beauty of what He loves, man's love is caused by the beauty of what he loves. An artist becomes god-like when he imbues an object with his love to cause its beauty; when an aesthete perceives that beauty, in a way, he shares the creator's divinity. This transcendence of human limitation is the source of aesthetic pleasure. In this context, it is possible to say that, in the aesthetic process, a percipient's ego does not exactly get dissolved but becomes one with God; he can thus excalim 'An-al-Haq'—'I am Truth', or 'I am I'. Of course, in this state of 'union', when the distinction between the subject and the object stands erased, 'I' is something other than the 'I' experienced in mundane existence. It is this transcendence which lends to the aesthetic experience a new meaning as well as an intensity. Obviously, it is not a meaning in the cognitive sense nor intensity in the emotive sense; it is a significance on the meta-conscious level. Unfortunately, what the West sees beyond the conscious are the levels of the subconscious and the unconscious—areas of darkness; for the spirit-familiar orientalist, this one is, instead, the realm of enlightenment on the superconscious level.

How does one reach that level? Through another configuration, of course. But this *'samyoga'* is better known as *yoga*. But before we come to that, it should be interesting to recall Aurobindo Ghosh's aesthetic formulations. Beauty, for him, is concentrated form of delight, its highest manifestation being God; artistic beauty is only a shadow of it. Art, he believes, is the alchemy that converts the gross into divine; *Rasa*, the soul's pleasure, is something pure and perfect. Aesthesis, for Aurobindo, is not merely mental, emotional or vital but something that extends to overhead levels.[32]

The Hindu view of life, from which stems Aurobindo's aesthetic fomulation, sees in life a number of layers in human existence. These layers are distinct and yet so integrally related that there is no clash among them. Western thought simply glosses over them or clubs them simplistically under the emotional and the intellectual; what is more, the two are assumed to operate not only independently but also in mutual hostility. According to the Hindus, Man and Universe are divine manifestation of the one, the Eternal.[33]

In normal life, we are engrossed in the realm of material needs to sustain life and thus seldom do we rise above the realms of the lower mind. Thus those heights of evolution, where inertia and ignorant movements of life and body may be replaced by the dynamics of the inner sources of the higher mind, remain normally unscaled. Anyway, there is something common in Matter, Life and Mind—*Jivātmā*. Called the soul or eternal self of the living being, it comes, however, from beyond the nature of mind, life and body. A part of the universal, Pure Consciousness, it belongs to the transcendental. And it is because of this soul that one can open to the higher nature beyond.[34] Nevertheless, all these operate in unison without any mutual conflict in functions or in the areas of operation. Hence the integralism of the Hindu view of life. In fact, the Hindus assume an elaborate system so far as the functioning of the three levels of existence (Matter, Life and Mind) is concerned—several divisions in the form of a ladder.[35]

Aurobindo's system extends beyond these to the overhead levels—the higher mind, the illumined mind, the intuitive mind, the overmind, and the supermind.[36] Of course, these overhead planes are not heightened operations of mental faculties—methods and ways of knowing. Instead, they are domains of being which signify grades of spiritual energy at different levels of universal consciousness. The thing most notable in this connection is that the Hindu mind sees the element of sacred in everything at every level—physical, vital, dynamic, emotional, intellectual, aesthetic and spiritual.

Ordinarily, man's enjoyment is limited to mental, vital and physical fields of consciousness, reason being the governor of life. Aesthetic enjoyment goes beyond—to the overhead level. Of course, art can be intellectual but, then, that is not great art; expression of the overhead inspiration implies spontaneity without any mental activity. At the source of art is, therefore, super-conscient cosmic mind when it comes in direct contact with the supramental truth-consciousness—not Mind but Overmind.[37]

Art starts with the sensuous and treats it as a continual point of reference, but it does not stay there. It soars into the invisible world of imagination. In other words, it signifies the release of one's being from the ego—'*Chitta-vistāra.*' Usually, our perceptions, thoughts and actions are organized by our reason; in art, reason is replaced by intuitive knowledge which overtops reason and is more luminous. As intuition finds meaning and significance in spiritual value, it brings in spirituality and one feels closer to the Divine. Since *Yoga*, too, aims at intimacy with the Divine, creativity can be seen as *yoga* and *sahridaya* as a kind of *yogin.* The artist does not seek his own personal manifestation but brings the Divine to manifest itself in matter; the percipient rises out of the ignorant world-consciousness into the divine consciousness. *Yogin* withdraws from the world step by step through *sādhanā* to reach the stage of purification before he is united with the supreme soul. Likewise, the *sahridaya* passes through the stages of detachment, release from ego, to experience the stage where material, mental and spiritual become one, and when Truth, God and Beauty comprise an indivisible triune. In fact, it is easy to see a close correspondence between the stages of a *yogin*'s progress and an aesthetic experience. Very like *yoga*, art effects detachment from the senses, breaks one's blind egoistic shells, leads to the cessation of personal desires, removes the sheaths of ignorance, reveals the invisible beneath the visible, and enables one to discover oneself as a part of some universal experience.

This idea of *Yoga*-aesthetics equation is best realized by Dr. Padma Sudhi in Volume III of her *Aesthetic Theories of India*. Here, the title of the opening chapter is also the title of the volume as a whole—'*Yoga* Activity as the Fountain-Head of Indian Aesthetics'. According to the author, *Yoga* is generally regarded as a bunch of different disciplines—a physical science that keeps the body fit, a biological system that helps evolve into a charming person, a para-psychological art that yields occult and mystical experiences, and a religious practice that yields spiritual peace. There is, according to Dr. Sudhi, one more dimension of yogic exercise—what she calls *Saundarya Yoga*.

Yoga literally means joining—when two antitheses lose their identities and transform themselves into a different, or an absoultely new, entity. In the practice of *Yoga*, it means paradoxical withdrawal from the conscious level of existence so as to experience the Pure Consciousness. Withdrawal is the first necessary step—the basic condition which enables one to control one's senses, to transcend time and space, to encounter the supersoul and thus to experience a blissful peace of mind. This is precisely what happens in the aesthetic experience, too. Thoughts, feelings and deeds are so joined into a harmonious whole that the cognitive and the emotive aspects tend to merge into a state of transcendence; at that stage, one identifies oneself with the objects of art and thus feels exalted. *Yoga* enables one to reach a stage when one's soul encounters another's without the mediation of body—very like lovers losing themselves into each other's gaze and thus becoming oblivious to the presence of others.

Art also facilitates such a rapt attention as excludes self-consciousness and facilitates identification between the self and the non-self. If the integration of body and mind in *Yoga* produces an integral personality, art too effects such an integration—of sensitivity in the artist and of sensibility in the *Sahridaya*. As popularly believed, *Yoga* is an experience in transforming emotions into a spiritual experience; that is also what happens in the aesthetic experience. Aesthetic experience, too, involves both alienation and identification—precisely in the manner a *yogin* withdraws from his own self or soul to become one with God or supersoul. Indeed, art is so akin to *samādhi*-situation: like the *dhyāna-yogin* closing his eyes to reach the pure consciousness, an artist employs his inner eyes of imagination and intuition. And as in *tantra-yoga*, artistic creation is also a manipulation of the will and other faculties. Keeping in mind the concentration that the artist effects in the process of creation, perhaps we shan't be very far from the truth if we describe him as a creative *yogin.* And since the study of an art object also implies one's staying in the 'present' for a long time, it needs an equally strong mind—the concentration of *Yoga*. Anyway, in both *Yoga* and aesthetics, the ultimate end is *Ānanda*. True, it is *ānanda* with a difference. While *yogin's ānanda*, signifying sway of the soul, is very close to the *Brahmānada* and yields utmost peace, tranquillity and joy, the *Rasa-ānanda* is a synthetic joy inhering the configuration of the cognitive, the emotive and the spiritual.

Yoga is the fountain-head of the aesthetic experience, as Dr Sudhi insists, because, without it, one cannot see the soul. It is only when one enters, through concentration, the *dhyāna*-state that one traverses from the waking conscious state of the gross mind to the dream-state of the subconscious mind (which is repository of impressions), down to the unconscious stratum of the causal mind (which computerizes past and present), through the deepest level of the Pure Conscious where time and space disappear and only *Ānanda* remains.[38]

Yoga unfolds step by step the nature of empirical consciousness to reach the goal of Pure Consciousness. Likewise, in art, the aesthetic *yogin* enters the dream state from where he plummets down into the realm of the unconscious and then deeper still into the superconscious where a flash of enlightenment awaits him. If *yoga* enables one to experience tranquillity in turmoil, aesthetics too implies self-control in self-indulgence—*yoga* in *bhoga*. True, the Western aestheticians have not talked in these terms but they have been perceiving something in aesthetics which prompts them to talk about Absolute Idea, intuition, contemplation, etc. Anyway, it is possible to say that an artist lets the material from the conscious to be transmitted at the levels of the subconscious and the unconscious until its soul is realized at the level of the Pure Conscious. The soul of the *sahridaya* receives at the level of the Pure Conscious this *Rasa* which gets related by stages (in reverse order) to his unconscious, subconscious and then the conscious.

Surely, without *Dhyāna-yoga*, an aesthete cannot reach that stage where his soul may be ready for a communion with the soul of the art-object. Only when concentration has yielded the stage of *Dhyāna* that attuning between the two is possible. That is to say, *Dhvani* depends on *Dhyāna.* Of course, *Dhvani* and *Dhyāna* act and react on each other; concentration facilitates attuning which, in turn, causes vibration in the soul. To put it differently, *Dhvani* and *Dhyāna* get yoked together—a situation of yet another *yoga*, so to say.

Even otherwise, the process of *Dhyāna-yoga* is what we should keep in mind when we want to understand what actually takes place during the process of configurations. In attaining the *dhyāna*, one shuffles the layers of the conscious, the sub-conscious and the unconscious in such a manner that they take the subordinate position and let the Pure Conscious come up. Exactly, in the same way, in the aesthetic process, the different aspects of a configuration are so adjusted that what comes up is the *rasa* of the object, the situation, the attitude, the response, or whatever it is. This goes on and on until a stage is reached when these *rasa*s comprise, as it were, a world of 'souls'. Thus our soul finds itself in communion with diverse 'souls'. That is to say, from the world of the sense, one finds oneself transported to the world of souls. Therefore, in the long run, when *Rasa* of the *rasa*s crystallizes, it is not our head or heart but the soul that tastes it. Indeed, it is our soul that sings, dances, absorbs beauty, and experiences *Ānanda*. The more the *rasa*s that are configurated, the more satisfying is the ultimate *Rasa*—and therefore the merrier is our soul. Neither the body or mind receives the *Rasa* nor has the *Rasa* anything of the sensuous about it any more. In fact, in the process, having been rarefied into 'souls', the tensions and contradictions get harmonized and lose their negative or painful aspects.

Ordinarily, our life is dominated by the senses and the spirit or soul remains dormant. What makes life full of troubles are the sensuous desires of the body; else, the irrational logic of our imperfect mind pollutes our soul. In the aesthetic experience, our faculties are reconfigurated, as it were, and the soul comes up—temporarily, of course. This liberation of the soul from body and mind is the source of aesthetic joy, *Ānanda*.

From what has been said above, in the aesthetic field, we have interaction among numerous configurative *Rasas* to evoke *Ānanda* in the soul, rather than in the head or the heart, of the *sahridaya.* The catalyst facilitating the process and the operation of the Gestalt-factor is yet to be discovered. In the context of poetry, of course, it has been suggested that it inheres the manipulation of words and planting of suggestions or figures of speech which draw attention to themselves and thus initiate the process of withdrawal. Even the terms used in this context are related to sounds—*dhvani* and *sphota*—and therefore usually their use is confined to the realm of poetics in the framework of the functions of language. But the fact is that what happens in poetry through words does take place in other arts, too—the devices being rooted in some other media. Maybe, we could broaden the bases of these theories by adapting the concepts and using the terms in metaphorical rather than literal senses.

For example, we have already used the word 'attuning' for *Dhvani*—bringing the parties involved in the aesthetic field on the same wavelength. Every artist, working within his medium, marshalls his resources via his intuitive sensitivity; this invests his creation with a soul (*Rasa*). To this responds the soul of the recipient, via his imaginative sensibility in a spirit of communion. When that happens, a vibration passes through the *Sahridaya* and his senses, mind and soul start responding to the stimuli from the artist or the art-object. That, in fact, facilitates the configuration of his responsive components into *Rasa* proper. This process of configuration climaxes in a moment when all that has preceded falls into a pattern and one realizes its rationale. In a sense, something bursts in one's consciousness. Like every explosion, this one too is accompanied by a 'flash of light'—a newer understanding that resolves one's problems without answering the questions rationally;

it seems to quench one's thirst without employing the apparatus of the senses. When this happens, every nerve of the *sahridaya* tingles in ecstasy. That is the precise moment when the differences between subject and object, beauty and pleasure, artist and percipient, positive and negative, disappear. Thus does the phenomenon of 'bursting' or 'boom', referred to as 'sphota' in the context of poetics, apply to aesthetics in general.

Of course, some other telling images have also been suggested as analogues to explain the working of the aesthetic process—especially with regard to the transfer of *Rasa* from the artist's soul to the *sahridaya's* soul. For example, poetry has been compared, on the one hand, to a fire brought to the dry-wood called the reader, and on the other to pure water which is absorbed quickly by a piece of cloth. In this context, human mind has also been likened to white linen which takes the colour of any hue in which it is dipped. In a way, this brings us back to the *rasa* as juice and to what Bharata had suggested with regard to the realization of *rasa* in terms of dietics. Perhaps one could take a hint and develop the idea along different lines.

Rasa in dietics is a matter of taste—the response of tongue to what is brought to it. What it receives may be a mixture of several ingredients, their compound, or else some form of distilled essence. Or those ingredients may as well be tasted one by one—in the form of several courses, repetitively, in the same or varying order, or even drop by drop. Before the tasting process starts, the tongue is invariably clean and therefore neutral in taste; during eating, the taste of the tongue keeps changing, corresponding to what it receives; by the end, what remains is *Rasa* of the meal—the end product of the different *rasas.* This *Rasa* lingers on for a while but after some time one realizes that the tongue has reacquired its natural, neutral state. Corresponding to the tongue, *sahridaya* receives the *rasas* created through 'soulful' configurations of *bhāvas*, objects, etc.; with the addition of every new configurative *rasa*, the responsive taste of the *sahridaya* also changes until, at the end, there crystallizes *Rasa* of the *rasas*. This *Rasa* of the play—or whatever the art-object—is also yet another configuration. Now, not all the tastes of the bites taken during a meal are sweet or pleasurable because some may be bitter, sour or astringent; still one's tongue relishes all of them. At least, in the process of mixing, some time even the unpalatable tastes lose their individual unpleasantness and even enhance the overall relish. Ditto for the relish of the aesthetic *rasas. Sahridaya* relishes all because, in the process of configuration, the less pleasant *rasas* also become subordinated to the overall *Rasa*. The ultimate *Rasa* lingers on for a while; one may prolong its duration by ruminating over it; but, after some time, *sahridaya* is neutral once again.

During a meal, if the order of administering the courses/drops is the same (as also the quality), the tastes produced tend to be almost the same. But if someone comes to the meal with a prior rather than a neutral taste, the process of taste is bound to be different—as also the nature of the ultimate *Rasa* of the meal. That may happen also when some courses are omitted and some others taken either in comparative excess or scantily, or else in a different order. Similarly, if *sahridaya* brings to the work of art a prior mood, a prior formulation or prejudice, the response may not exactly correspond to what was expected. Indeed, at times, variable results may be had during an aesthetic fare. It should be easy to recall such situations—reading random chapters of a novel, one or two acts of a play, dozing off intermittently during a concert, reaching late in a dance performance. As a corollary, one can see for oneself why controversies rage about the overall *Rasa* of the *Mahābhārata* or the *Rāmāyana*. Indeed, who can read the epics in their entirety in single sittings to taste the real overall *Rasa*? Reading a section or two, one enjoys the *Rasa* of only that part; in the next reading, one starts with a neutral taste, as it were, and so the *Rasa* of the part read now doesn't have the benefit of the taste afforded by the preceding section(s). In the context of the above, it should be interesting to realize that the Sanskrit word for character is *pātra* which literally means a vessel, a container—the instrument of tasting. Since another meaning of the word is 'capable', character is one who is capable of enabling the percipient to relish.

Of course, understandably, the process of *Rasa-svāda* (enjoyment) varies from art to art. For example, in the case of painting, it is possible to say that *Rasa* is lying ready for taste—like a cup of extracted juice in a refrigerator; one has only to sip it to get the instant relish. In poetry, *Rasa* may by imagined as filling the verses and overflowing. In music, we may say, we have the case of addition, drop by drop, while, in theatre, it is like having several courses served. To put it differently, we may have at times ready-made art object exuding aesthetic pleasure (as in painting and sculpture) and at others we may become a witness to the art-in-the-making and thus a part of the aesthetic process—as in music or dance. In theatre, our soul is in communion with not only the souls of characters but also that of the performance as a whole.

Anyway, whatever the art, the artist's prime task is to configurate the elements in hand so that they harmonize into a complete whole and forge a unity out of the multitude. It is something comparable to the formation of *Trimūrti* (Trinity) out of the three deities—Brahma, Vishnu and Mahesh. They are so different in their attributes—a creator, a preserver and a destroyer, respectively—and yet, through their interaction, an overall equilibrium is obtained in the universe. Such a unity in diversity is what the artist must create through his configurations—mind, body and soul; consciousness, dream, and sleep; *Sattva, Rajas* and *Tamas; Guna, Rīti* and *Rasa*; *Bhāva*, *Rasa* and *Ānanda; Satyam, Shivam, Sundaram,* etc. As the unity created out of diversity has a quality independent of the components, one could say that configurations have a transformative quality. Indeed, in the process of transformation, grossness gets lost, and thus do cognition and emotion, *yoga* and *bhoga*, sacred and profane, tend to become one and the same.

Indeed, every art is an exercise in transmutative manipulation—manipulating the given material to produce something new which has such attributes as are independent of the properties of the components. In this business of manipulation, the artist creates a network of configurations, invests them with archetypal quality, interlinks them into further configurations, and in the process implants such subtle devices as facilitate transmutation, communion and configurative responses. The object of art thus created acquires a kind of soul that radiates vibrant vitality which appeals to the soul of the *sahridaya.* In poetry, words are so manipulated as to yield a deeper sense than what they do in daily intercourse. Similarly, in architecture, stone or wood cease to be lifeless; the traditionally mute stuff appears to speak. Music, too, brings out soul of the sounds. What a piece of music stimulates is not our hearing sense but our soul. If one is saddened by it, the pall is not on our heart but on our spirits. To be sad in life, one needs some ground in experience, situation, mood, physical inconveniences, etc.; in music, there is no such ground—just sounds and something in their pattern and rhythm which speaks direct to one's soul. Aesthetic experience is, indeed, an affair of communion between one soul and the other—communication of what is not expressed explicitly.[39]

To sum up, through his talent and powers of imagination and intuition, a sensitive artist configurates certain elements together to create a thing of beauty; to the extraordinary charm of this creation, a like-hearted man of sensibility (*sahridaya*) responds in spite of himself via total absorption (*dhyāna*). Basically transcendental, this response makes one feel detached from one's narrow self on the one hand and abundantly enriched emotively, intellectually and spiritually, on the other. In this state of perfect attuning (*Dhvani*), experiencing both *yoga* and *bhoga*, emotions and thoughts get refined and transmuted configuratively into *Rasa*; this *Rasa*, in turn, fills the soul with such a blissful joy (*Ānanda*) as subsumes even the unpleasant and negative attributes of the aesthetic process. It is like a sitar-maestro employing the *jhāla* of cacophony in such a way that, instead of being disturbed, the harmony is enhanced. In this state, thanks to the configuration of head, heart and soul, the emotional and intellectual get so integrated into the spiritual as a unified response that it sounds rather silly to talk about emotional impact, intellectual perception and spiritual elevation as distinctive responses. In that higher level of consciousness which a performance should awaken, one receives ideas as feelings even as feelings come as ideas. Feeling and thinking are no longer compartmentalized responses; they have lost their separate entities. Likewise, one cannot say whether it has been escape from reality or a case of inscape because it has been both. Similarly detachment and involvement, subject and object, ultimately lose distinction. Indeed, who bothers to remind oneself that one is not the character one has been empathizing with, nor is character that impersonating actor whom one has been accepting in that role? The whole situation gets so universalized that the material, the vital, and the mental no longer appear three disparate planes but coalesce into one integral unity, *sacchidānanda*. Now, the existence appears the same thing as consciousness and the consciousness the same as bliss. As a corollary, one may realize that pain, death, falsehood manifested themselves simply because they are regarded as distinct; that distinction having disappeared, what remains is *Ānanda*. This is possible through the medium of the soul, only when our everyday media of senses, feelings and ideas, have dissolved themselves. That is to say, the aesthetic experience of *Ānanda* awakens our soul through self-transcendence. *Rasa Ānanda* is, therefore, a voyage of our soul: out of the happenings and contacts, their secret divine sense and essence, there is extracted a divine purpose so that, by experience, our mind grows out of the inconscience towards a supreme consciousness.

Thus seen, art becomes at once what the different Indian aestheticians have regarded it—*līlā*, *māyā*, *yoga, sādhanā, anubhava*, etc. My humble contribution lies in underlining the creation of a network of configurative *rasas,* in treating *Rasa* as an archetypal totality with a soul, in highlighting the communion among the different souls, in equating the *Yoga* and aesthetic responses, in expanding the scope of *Dhvani* and *Sphota* by liberating them from the contexts of poetics, in injecting in aesthetics a soul-activity on the metaconscious level, in providing configurative bridges between the artist and the aesthete through the analogue of electronic communication, and, above all, in projecting *Rasa Ānanda* as a triune subsuming into a unity body, mind and soul, creation, preservation and destruction.

With such an understanding of aesthetic response, when we return to tragic pleasure, there is hardly anything paradoxical. Here is *Rasa* resulting from the configuration of several *Rasas*. Some of these might not be very pleasant *per se* but, when combined with others, they lose their intrinsic unpleasantness into a most welcome relish. Here is something analogous to the role of hot condiments in pickles or curry—the more, the tastier and, therefore, the more relishable. Sugar is sweet and a confectioner may produce a whole range of wonderful sweets, but that is the stuff for infants or a grown-up with sweet tooth. A gourmet's taste buds are more appreciative of an art when they are tickled with an enigmatic preparation in which sour, bitter and/or astringent are made savoury. Surely, high art lies not so much in making sugar taste ever so sweet as in making palatable what is basically horrible in taste. Such, indeed, is the art of tragedy: all kinds of horrible happenings such as violence, incest, murders are so configurated with the heroic deeds that the overall *Rasa* tastes truly pleasurable. Since tragedy affords maximum scope for accommodating contradictory elements like conflicts, tensions, incongruities, dichotomies, and since these are the elements that serve as the very spine of drama proper, tragedy has come to enjoy the highest respectability as an art. It is, indeed, the most dramatic of performing arts!

What, then, is the *Rasa* that dominates in tragedy and makes it so deeply dramatic? *Karunā* perhaps would be the most ready answer and possibly the most popular reply. But is it, really? A doctoral dissertation submitted to the Panjab University sought to apply the *Rasa* theory to Shakespeare's plays and the position that emerged was both interesting and intriguing. According to the study, the *Rasa* that dominates in *King Lear* is, of course, *Karunā*; but in *Hamlet*, it is *Shāntā-rasa*; in *Othello*, *Bībhatsa*; in *Romeo and Juliet, Shringāra*; in *Henry IV, Hāsya-rasa*; in *Henry V, Vīra-rasa*; in *The Tempest, Adbhuta-rasa*. When the outline story of *Oedipus Rex* was narrated to an orientalist, he exclaimed immediately, 'Why, obviously, here the dominant *Rasa* is *Adbhuta*!' In the light of all this, well might one ask: how can the plays like *Oedipus, King Lear, Hamlet, Othello, Romeo and Juliet*, that belong to the same genre, have such diversity in respect of dominant *Rasa*? More than anything else, the question is a measure of our habit-criterion to regard a genre as a universal category. We forget that the Western genres were not created *Rasa*-wise, nor were Indian types of drama conceived genre-wise. In fact, the Indian typology itself doesn't correspond to *Rasas*. When we forget these facts, the result is confusion, indeed. Let us take, for example, Kalidasa's *Shākuntalam*. The Western reader would call it comedy because of the happy close of its romantic story. But those who have convinced themselves that comedy is a play in which *Hāsya-rasa* dominates are bound to feel disappointed when looking here for *Hāsya-rasa.* In reality, the dominant *Rasa* here is *Shringāra* for which we have no equivalent genre in the West, unless we were to regard romance as one of the genres. Now, if a comdey need not have *Hāsya* as its *sthāyibhāva*, why must tragedy have any one specific *Rasa*—be it *Karunā* or some other? In fact, properly seen, *Karunā*-centred plays tend to become melodramas.

What might one deduce, then? The fact is that, as the above mentioned dissertation has shown, what we call tragedies can yield, besides *Karunā, Shānta, Bībhatsa,* even *Shringāra Rasas*, too. As a closer look should reveal, *Vīra, Adbhuta, Bhayānaka, Raudra* can be equally powerful contenders for the honour. That leaves *Hāsya-rasa* as the only odd one out; but, in the hands of a master like Shakespeare, even *Hāsya-rasa* can get perfectly accommodated in a tragedy—as it does in *King Lear*, for example. To put it differently, all the nine acknowledged *Rasas* can go into the making of tragedies. Alternating in different scenes as primary *Rasas*, all of them can, at the end, clamour for the top honour of the main *Rasa*. It is possible to suggest that when a tragedy starts on a normal note, the *Ṛasa* produced can be anyone (even *Hāsya* or *Shringāra*) but gradually, as it passes through the stages of intense conflict between the microcosm and the macrocosm, the vision of the Absurd, the shock of recognition, the suffering, the affirmation, the mystery, the equipoise, the *Rasas* evoked may correspond to *Raudra, Bībhatsa, Bhayānaka, Karunā, Vīra, Adbhuta* and *Shānta.* Of course, depending on the way of presentation, the order might vary. The important thing is that since all those aspects are there in a tragedy, all those *Rasas* do crystallize at one stage or the other. The popularity of tragedy can be explained in terms of the multiplicity of *Rasas*. In drama, the more extensive and the more intricate the texture of the experience is, the greater is the satisfaction. Tragedy is the most dramatic, the most satisfying, because it affords all the *Rasas* and their ultimate composite configuration. The heroic, the awesome, the horrible, the terrible, the grotesque, the pathetic, the ludicrous, the erotic—all are there. In other words, tragic impact cannot be adequately covered under *Karunā-rasa* because pathos is by no means more basic to the tragic experience than the heroic; no less powerful are our proclivities towards fear, disgust, outrage, or supercilious contempt on the one hand and love, admiration and sense of awe on the other. In fact, they are all so powerfully balanced in their sway that conceding primacy to any one of them would be an act of irrational discrimination.

Tragedies often have death-endings which fill us with disgust or pity or admiration or relief or some of them together at the same time. Witness, the multiple deaths in *Hamlet* and *King Lear.* In this connection, it is worth noting that our total response is determined not by the death of the protagonist alone but by all the deaths. This calls for a review in the popular critical approach which habitually goes by the hero's fate alone. We must learn to accommodate the facts that what each character is, or does, evokes some kind of response and that all these disparate responses configurate to yield the totality of the play's impact. To put it differently, one's responses vary from scene to scene and from play to play. In view of all this, the only safe deduction would be that tragedy does not monopolize any one *Rasa* and that plays with practically all the *Rasas* can become tragedies. In fact, our hunch is that every tragedy has all the *Bhāva-rasas*, each of which tends to become dominant in one part or the other. There is, so to say, no dominant *sthāyibhāva* in tragedy. As all the *Rasas* are equally important and keep changing their configurative coalescence without letting any one dominate, the consequence is that the ultimate configuration yields a compact *Rasa* which is different from all of them individually. That brings to mind *Shānta-rasa*. In *Shānta-rasa*, too, we don't have any pure *sthāyibhāva;* rather several kinds of *Rasas* configurate mutually until they cancel one another in the spirit of all-passions-spent. In tragedy, on the other hand, till the end, they are all intact in perfect equilibrium to comprise a composite whole. This *Rasa*, I believe, remains unnamed. We could perhaps call it *Mānava-rasa*.[40]

Now, certainly, man has been the concern not of tragedy alone but of all literature. However, while other genres are content with specific aspects of human truth, tragedy aims at accommodating its totality. At the end of a play (or even in the course of it), we generally find ourselves exclaiming 'How pathetic!', 'How comic!', 'How terrible!', 'How ridiculous!', or 'How wonderful!' Only at the end of a tragedy, we find these labels inadequate and instead feel like exclaiming, 'How very human, indeed! Only man could have suffered this way! None but man could wrest such spiritual triumph out of such a hopeless situation!' On such occasions, we feel not only sympathy for the fellow humans that have suffered but also some kind of pride in belonging to them. Man, O man, how totally fragile and yet how very glorious in defeat! Even though touched with pity, our heart appears inebriated with positive self-respect at the spectacle of man's uniqueness; our eyes might be brimming with tears but there is a measure of such joyful satisfaction in these tears that calling the situation pitiable seems an impertinent insult to the heroic spirit that has eclipsed everything else. Witnessing the glory of man's becoming, we get so humanized that the utter insignificance of his being appears irrelevant. Indeed, we feel like singing halleluja to the glorious spirit of man!

Our saying all this is likely to provoke a typical classical orientalist into an outrage and well might he rejoin that the present suggestion of ours is contrary to what we have been maintaining earlier—theatre as a kind of *yajna* and aesthetics as a form of *yoga* and each aiming at the union of the soul with the supersoul. True, the rituals of *yajna* and the contemplation of *yoga-dhyāna* facilitate the recovery of a lost ideal, the chosen deity (*ishta-deva*). That this is not contrary to what we are saying now will become clear when we add that the *ishta-deva* propitiated in tragedy is Man; it is with the ideal self (*swaroopa*) of this deity that we learn to identify ourselves. When a basically private experience is made public, it ceases to be the experience of an individual; universalized thus, it pertains not to one man or a group of particular men but to all mankind. Hence, too, the release from ego—the *Chitta-vistāra*, as the Indian aestheticians call it. Thus seen, *Sacchidānanda* which used to imply, on the spiritual plane, the confluence of Existence, Consciousness and Bliss comes to signify, on the human plane, the convergence of Truth, Joy and Beauty. To put it differently, tragedy enables man to attain, in aesthetic terms, what he is always keen to acquire in spiritual terms, viz., self-fulfilment. Indeed, in an experience like this, he becomes more than himself and therefore a complete being—supreme consciousness in oriental terminology and Man (with capital M) in the western terminology.

As a closer look should show, the processes involved in tragic catharsis and spiritual transcendence have a lot common. For divine realization, one has to purify one's rationality; tragedy, too, makes one feel emotionally shattered and intellectually benumbed before the spiritual exaltation is facilitated. Of course, spiritual in this case pertains to human spirit and thus spiritual exaltation means celebration of the spirit of man. Suffering of tragedy is a catalyst: it purifies the spirit in the sense that the affective and the cognitive are scrubbed continually so that the spirit might get burnished. The dignity, magnanimity, endurance and will to break rather than bend are such attributes as shed dazzling glory all around and these are the attributes which only man is blessed with. Indeed, only man can be compassionate, contrite, loving (without being lustful) and beauty-soaked, as no other animal shares these qualities. Suffering purifies the hero by cleansing his soul of the earthiness of senses; he is, so to say, made all-too-human. Properly attuned via *Dhvani*, the *sahridaya* too finds himself humanized and thus is his soul purified and rendered fit for experiencing transcendental joy.

Seen thus, catharsis and *Ānanda* tend to become analogous, if not exactly identical. Anyway, since the percipient's soul has to move from turmoil to equilibrium via both detachment and involvement, he must belong to the aristocracy of passionate souls. Only then will he have the capacity to experience both sorrow in others' grief and joy in others' glory on the one hand and to transcend the bondage of material and vital beings on the other. In the absence of these capacities, it won't be possible to effect the melting of heart (*dhriti*), the attuning of mind to the wavelength of *dhvani*, and the universalization of individual grief (*shoka*) into shared pleasure (*Ānanda*). In practical terms it means that tragedy enables a *sahridaya* to drink *Mānava-rasa* to its lees and to relish it.

Now, since *Rasa*, as we have explained, denotes the quintessence inhering the material manifestation, what could possibly signify the essence of man? In the realm of human nature, there obtains such infinite variety that it appears most absurd to talk of any quintessential attribute common to all mankind. But, maybe, we could start our exploration from the other end—by asking ourselves what is so uniquely distinct about man vis-a-vis all other living creatures. The answer that comes most naturally is that he is the most paradoxical being in whom stand yoked contradictory qualities. At once an animal and an angel, most logical as well as most irrational, both enlightened and perverse, he refuses to be one-dimensional. A victim as well as a controller of the universe around him, he is, in a way, the mightiest and the meanest creature, the meeting point of the sublime and the grotesque—the humblest and the most ferocious, dignified like a god but ludicrous like a clown. He is perhaps the only creation of God in whom the demands of body, mind and soul are always struggling to control his actions. In the resulting pell-mell and consequent sway of relativity, he is ever-busy to churn spirit out of the sensuous, divine out of the bestial, freedom out of determinism, good out of evil. As that makes him source of both good and evil, he embodies in himself all that is fair as well as all that is foul. Perhaps the Hindu Trinity was created in man's own image—creator, preserver and destroyer. As the quintessence of all this, *Mānava-rasa* inevitably tastes at once bitter, sweet and sour.

In the opening section, 'Under the Western Eyes', we had seen all this in a slightly different perspective—in the context of the existential dichotomy and the concomitant reconciliation of the microcosmic and the macrocosmic, the Apollonian and the Dionysian, the infinite Nothing and the illusive glory. Anyway, whether one talks in terms of tragic vision, tragic sense of life, tragic spirit, or tragic philosophy, whether the ambit of references is Socratic, Platonic, Aristotelian, Hegelian or Nietzschean, whether we explain the impact in the framework of metaphysics, ethics, logic or aesthetics, whether we use such terms as tragic rhythm, tragic knot, tragic dialectics, or tragic net, the basic concern is Man. Whether we look upon tragic action as an exercise in relating or balancing good and evil, as an attempt to reconcile the finite and the infinite, as a paradoxical victory in defeat, as an aristocracy of passionate souls, a process of creative suffering or spiritual cross-ventilation, it is man, man all the way. Every tragedy is a hymn in praise of the spirit of man who can wrest glory in being humbled, who does not know the truth and yet embodies it all, who does not feel ashamed of being an animal but goes on to churn divinity out of his bestiality, who suffers to become wiser and even welcomes suffering as the very hallmark of his identity—'I suffer, therefore I am'. In him we find an animal with the power of choosing, a puppet that pulls its own string, a vessel of perfume that spreads fragrance when shattered, a demon who asserts his own will against God's and emerges broken but not bent from the contest. Experiencing this human spirit, one feels humanized—inebriated with the quintessence of human experience. It means tasting the human helplessness as well as the invincibility of human spirit—his mortality as well as his immortality, as it were. Indeed, tragedy is essentially humanistic and enables the audience to savour the quintessence of human potential—both its heights and depths. This is precisely what we mean by *Mānava-rasa*, too.

Because of the complex core of human nature, tasting its quintessence implies experiencing not one emotion but a number of human emotions. In fact, it accommodates the entire gamut—both the negative ones like shame, horror, disgust and rage on the one hand and the positive ones like love, enthusiasm, sympathy and laughter, on the other. When Plato and Aristotle referred to pity and fear, they were expressing their perception of the multiplicity of emotions; but, unfortunately, for the sake of argument, they confined themselves to only two most obvious ones. Had they looked at the phenomenon with a clearer eye, they might have perceived the much more complex relationship of emotions obtaining in the tragic process. Anyway, in the context of *Rasa* theory, this fact deserves a closer scrutiny.

As shown earlier, normally a *Rasa* implies a process of configuration around some principal *Bhāva* which, in a way, is rooted in a certain truth about human nature when man is seen from a particular angle. The other aspects of human nature are so subordinated that they either get eclipsed or tend to buttress the core *Rasa*. All the diversity in characters notwithstanding, there is something singularly exclusive about the overall picture of man projected in a certain *Rasa*. Witness, for example, how the puritanic hypocrisy of Malvolio, the cruelty of Shylock, the cynicism of Jaques, the monstrosity of Caliban serve as grist to the comic mill—the *Hāsya-rasa*. Likewise, in a play yielding *Vīra-rasa*, the situations, characters and dialogues tend to highlight the heroic in man; ditto for the erotic in *Shringāra-rasa*. In a mystery play, there may be some comic moments, grotesque beings or fearful situations, but it all boils down to an all-pervading mystique that one seems to savour all along. Even when *Karunā* and *Raudra* go together in a play, the overall *Rasa* is one-dimensional. *Mānava-rasa* is unique insofar as its quintessence lies not so much in its pervasiveness as in its multivalence. In its unique configuration, the other *Rasas* are neither subordinated nor neutralized (as in *Shānta-rasa*) but retained in toto, without allowing any one *Rasa* to enjoy the pride of primacy. Man, we feel, is an admirable hero, a ridiculous clown, a horrible being, a grotesque monster, a veritable mystery. All these and even more! Indeed, *Mānava-rasa* is like peppermint which tingles the taste-buds with a relish that is at once cool and sizzling, sweet and peppery.

In the Western critical tradition, if there is pivotal importance conceded to the hero in a tragedy, it is because of the assumption that our response is empathic and that catharsis is effected by what happens to the hero. Gerald F. Else has tried to rectify this imbalance by replacing 'to' by 'through'—what happens through the hero. The fact, however, is that the hero is never alone in monitoring our responses—in realizing the *Rasa*, so to say. At least in tragedy, where several *Rasas* configurate into *Mānava-rasa*, each and every character has a contribution to make. How partial and incomplete should be our understanding of man if Shakespeare had been content with Lear's family by dropping the Gloucester House altogether! By placing Oswald against Kent, Edgar against Edmund, Goneril against Cordelia, Albany against Cornwall, Shakespeare could make us savour the human spirit in its totality. As sensual Gertrude alone could not complete the picture of female humanity, there had to be an Ophelia, too; lest Rosencrantz and Guildernstern should tilt the scale of friendship on negative side, there must also be a Horatio. Likewise, the taste of human revenge would not be wholesome if it was represented either by Laertes or by Fortinbras—or by Hamlet alone, for that matter; they had all got to be there, together.

True, Shakespeare's strategy of working through comparisons and contrasts, through subplots and multiple characterization, is not a universal practice. Some choose to manipulate vertically rather than horizontally—by making the protagonist embody the human dichotomy itself. The situations of Oedipus and Medea, for example, don't need reverberating echoes. The polluted man whose banishment alone can save Thebes is the one who had come as its redeemer; the ignoramus knows absolutely nothing about himself although he was omniscient enough to resolve the riddles posed by the sphinx. Significantly, the very answer to that riddle was man who thus stands for the cosmic mystery. A most loving, tender-hearted Medea kills her own children—and that too out of her love for them! That is a situation which only a human being can pass through. Ditto about Racine's Phaedra who is perversely pure, Ibsen's Mrs. Alving who affirms the joy of living through death, or O'Neill's messiah who turns out to be a murderer.

Man being the meeting point of most contrary attributes, the human experience in its quintessence is paradoxical. The genre that affords the *Rasa* of such an experience had to have something paradoxical and intriguing about it. No wonder tragedy has baffled critics for thousands of years. In any case, it is worth noting that just as, in a paradox, the contraries don't get dissolved but balance each other, in the *Mānava-rasa*, too, the flavours of other *Rasas* persist. Of course, being an art-in-the making, drama does not afford *Rasa* ready-made; it matures by stages. Configuration after configuration, configurating the configurative, it operates via *Dhvani* (not mere empathy), until we are seeped in *Rasa*. In tragedy, we have, as it were, further configuration of *Rasas* and thus *Mānava-rasa* entails a measure of greater complexity, deeper density and keener intensity. Feeling the human at its core, sharing man's strength as well as his failings, we feel totally humanized and, in the process, the pain of existence loses its sting because it is accompanied by the pleasurable aspects as well. Anyway, what one tastes is not the physical aspect but its spirit. Thus it is our soul and not the body which experiences the essence or the 'soul' of the pain of passions; what is more, in tasting the essence of remorse, forgiveness, deliverance, etc., too, the net result is healthy and pleasuresome rather than morbid or painful.[41]

NOTES

1. Hegel does refer to the Greek tragedies for elaboration of his theories—in fact, Sophocles' *Antigone* served as his paradigm—but Shakespeare is also taken into his reckoning. He refers to the 'modern tragedy' as well, but by that he naturally meant tragedy of his own time, viz., nineteenth century. It is worth noting that even though he struck brand new chords in the theory of tragedy, he could not completely break away from Aristotle; his overall effort tends to extend the scope of the Aristotelian theory in a new direction. Indeed, Hegel's is a way of interpreting Aristotelian formulation with regard to the tragic hero—good but not too good, evil but not perfectly villainous. Anyway, Hegel exercized an enormous impact on the modern theory of tragedy: his suggestions were continually adapted and modified. A.C. Bradley, for example, produced a psychological, rather than an ethical, version of Hegelian theory when he shifted the emphasis to self-division. Thus did conflict between men come to be replaced by a conflict within. Likewise, Hegel has come handy to the Marxists who interpret the conflict between ethical forces in socio-historical terms. Rightly does Raymond Williams observe that, before Hegel, tragedy had been encolsed within the common beliefs of the age or reduced to mere technical criticism; after him, it became a system of ideas.
2. One of the favourite critical pastimes today is speculation about the form of tragedy, but so mixed are the motifs in a tragedy that discussion invariably boils down to the tragic view of life. For example, when Sewall talks about it, he says that the tragic form inheres its recognition of the inevitablility of paradox, of unresolved tension and ambiguities, of opposites in precarious balance. He then goes on to talk about Tragic Cosmos, Tragic Man, Tragic Man and Society, only to conclude: 'The same old paradoxes and ambiguities remain, but for the moment they are transcended in the higher vision.' Likewise, when T.R. Henn talks about the Nets or about the Spring-and-Trigger, the form and contents tend to lose distinction. Joyce Carol Oates, too, is not too helpful in her *The Edge of Impossibility: Tragic Forms in Literature*, because what she keeps talking about is the sense of isolation and fear born of a break between self and community.
3. Incidentally, in the history of tragic theory, Frye has the dubious distinction of seeing in tragedy the Mythos of Autumn, which stands for fall and death, rather than one of spring, which symbolizes life and rebirth. No wonder, in Frye, the phases of tragedy move from the heroic to the ironic and he declares that characterization of tragedy is very like that of comedy in reverse. Of course, in a sense, he is not totally alone in seeing in tragedy only the negative aspects. Laurence Michel in *The Thing Contained: Theory of the Tragic* also declared demonic, ir- (or anti-) rational as the essence of tragedy. Eva Figes in *Tragedy and Social Evolution* projects tragic hero as a social criminal who pollutes his environment, brings disruption on himself

and his community, and is eliminated by the community.

4. Or, maybe, an apter analogy lies in love-making—a process that strips off the sham masks of civilization and enables one to live authentically for some time in elemental state of existence. Sex, the eternal symbol of animal in man, is roused: but, after the act—during which the carnal and the spiritual become one, when victory and defeat lose significance, when pain and pleasure are rendered undistinguishable—man feels cleansed and elevated as if purged of the animal that had been causing tensions. To complete the analogy, the creative destructiveness of tragedy corresponds to the sowing of the seeds of procreation during the sexual destruction. Just as the violence of sex-act releases energy that yields the sacred outcome of a child's conception, the tragic disaster yields a spiritual exaltation.

5. Although, in our formulation, we have not quoted philosophers, critics, etc., it should be possible to hear a series of echoes from the past. That does not mean that we have attempted a conscious synthesis; only our talking about the same genre naturally suggests parallels here and there as if we were all reworking and extending one another's formulations. For example, there could be a suggestion of Aristotelian Catharsis in the way we explain the process as purgation of animalism and purification of the soul. Likewise, in our concept of existential dichotomy, there is scope for reading Sewall's 'secret cause,' Henn's Freedom v Determinism, and Ellis-Fermor's balancing of man against the universe. Perhaps there is something Hegelian in the clash between the microcosmic and the macrocosmic values, even as one might label our idea of transcendence as 'spiritual regeneration' (Maxwell Anderson) or 'spiritual cross-ventilation' (John Mason Brown). The initial shock of recognition and eventual affirmation might possibly recall Raymond Williams's 'bridge between the shores of negation and affirmation,' and Glicksberg's 'denial of the myth of nothingness.' The interrelationship of the passional, the intellectual and the spiritual is very much inherent in Nietzsche's Dionysian-Apollonian reconciliation, in Fergusson's rhythm of Purpose, Passion and Perception, in Unamuno's truths felt and truths thought, and in Gassner's 'aristocracy of passionate souls.' Similarly whether Steiner welcomes tragic suffering as a fire that hallows, or F.L. Lucas welcomes it as the experiential banquet, they are not very far from what we have been saying.

6. The 'epicality' of his epic theatre is ironic because there is nothing on epical scale either in action or in characters. In fact, the characters are figures from the lower depths of society caught in a scene of bondage and frustration. Anyway, Brecht is concerned not with characters as such but with their story which is told analytically, episode-wise (hence the name 'epic theatre'). This is a theatre of judgement which acquaints the audience with the social problems without suggesting solutions, and the audience are placed in the position of a judge to think and to find the solution. 'Change the world: it needs it'—that is Brecht's exhortation; but, having lavished all care on presenting the condition of the world, he leaves the how-part of the change to the audience.

7. That such a complete anaesthesia of the heart is impossible to achieve and that too through music which is proverbially known as the language of heart and soul, is underlined in Steiner's description of what happened during a performance of *Mother Courage.* After denying the recognition of her own dead son, when the Mother opened her mouth in soundless agony, the very silence seemed to reverberate the theatre.
8. Giraudoux mixes even much more in affording a complex experience that is at once serious, comic, extravaganzaic, ironic and pathetic, but his theatre does not make us feel uncomfortable because this is precisely what the playwright wanted—even in reinterpreting Greek myths where tragic plots are handled comically. I have seen quite a few productions of Brecht's plays (mostly in Hinudstani, of course)—*Mother Courage, Caucasian Chalk Circle, Exception and the Rule, The Good Woman of Setzwan, The Threepenny Opera*—but never have I come out of the theatre thinking too deeply about the problem. In India, at least, Brecht has come to mean high spectacle, lots of music, use of masks, etc. Perhaps the idea is to prove that Brecht is so close to the traditional theatre of India becuase he had borrowed his trappings from the East—from Peking Opera, to be more precise.
9. Tragedy is an experience and tragic is the quality of that experience. It is not necessary that the two should coincide. After all, as Elder Olson has observed, there is a difference between having an experience and grasping the meaning of an experience. Witness T.S. Eliot's lament in his *Four Quartets* that we have had the experience but missed the meaning.
10. In this connection, it would be worthwhile to recall what has been said earlier—that discussion about the form of tragedy invariably boils down to the tragic view of life. This fact seems to have bothered Aristotle, too. No wonder he uses 'praxis' for both action and experience. Likewise, on the one hand, he declares 'mythos' as the first principle (the 'arche') and on the other, in the context of plot versus character, he uses 'mythos' (plot) as equivalent of 'logos' (story). According to him, since form is the body and soul the essence of life forming that body, plot could be regarded as the soul of tragedy.
11. For example, it has been argued that our age does not satisfy Macneille Dixon's formula for the birth of tragedy, viz., the spirit of poetry meeting the spirit of enquiry. Nor does the age conform to William O'Connor's condition of restricted individuality. According to Elder Olson, tragedy failed to thrive because it fell into the hands of such poets as were not dramatists, the dramatists being too realistic to be poets. Walter Kaufmann's thesis is that the moderns are too infatuated with success to have sympathy for failure. Erich Fromm would, on the other hand, shove the blame on the modern man's suppression of the awareness of the reality of death. For Howard Mumford Jones, ours is an age of plight. Charles I. Glicksberg puts the blame on the nihilism of the age, Alan S. Downer on the want of faith and courage. For Elmer Rice, the factor responsible is anti-intellectualism and spiritual negation: we have taken apart the human machanism but have yet to discover the formula to reassemble it. And then there was that prophetic

proclamation of Joseph Wood Krutch in 1929 declaring that the modern man is groping without a moral staff in a world devoid of sustaining illusions and long cherished values. One cannot affirm life tragically, he averred, in an age without faith: one may not believe in God but one must have faith in man!

12. At the zenith of civilization and nadir of culture, the modern man felt bewildered by the forces around him. The technological advancement flattered him into believing that he was an omniscient god but all else pointed to his utter insignificance. Evolutionary forces predicted his onward progress, but the nuclear inventions threatened him with extinction. Likewise, modern psychology made suspect the very rationality of man and therefore the rationale of all human institutions—and that in an age when he claimed to have acquired a scientific outlook! On the other hand, the philosophy of the age gave existence precedence over the essence and rendered man free in a godless world to choose for the entire universe at a time when he had lost control over his own world. Social engineering reduced the individual to a social unit while both capitalism and communism tended to treat him as an economic unit.
13. Crude Density; Dynamic Ruggedness; Dynamic Ramification; Ingenuous Beauty; Comprehensive Precision; Quintessential Flower; Flower of Tranquil Equilibrium; Flower of Innermost Profundity; and Flower of Mysterious Singularity. (For details see Toshihiko, et al.)
14. Of course, in the aesthetic framework, beauty and *ānanda* don't merge but retain their identity; in fact, the former is subservient to the latter. After all, aesthetic experience is rooted not in pure *yoga* but in *yoga*-plus-*bhoga*. In aesthetics, what you transcend is not the *Leelā* of *māyā* but that of the *gunas*; the state reached is not one of *Brahmānanda* where one may exclaim, 'I am I', but that of *Rasa- ānanda* when one can go no farther than saying, 'I am; this is; I am this.' On the aesthetic experience, one may have gained both *Prakāsha* (luminous existence) and *Vimarsha* (self-consciousness), but the *Trika* absolute of *Prakāsha-Vimarsha* is not yet there. Indeed, while a *yogin* reaches the fourth state of consciousness, viz., *Turīya* (when he can oversee all the earlier three stages of waking, dreaming and deep sleep), the *sahridaya* remains just half-a-step short of it. Anyway, in transcending *bhoga*, the transcendence itself becomes a mode of cognition.
15. This religious aspect is inherent even in the theory regarding the origin of drama as narrated in *Nātyashāstra*. After all the four *Vedas* had been completed, the gods approached *Brahmā*, the Creator, with a request for the creation of a fifth *Veda* which should be accessible not merely to the people of the higher castes, but to every body, including the *Shūdras*, even the non-Aryans. As a response came *Nātyaveda* which has elements from all the four *Vedas*—recitation from *Riga Veda*, singing from *Sāma Veda*, rituals from *Yajur Veda*, and sentiments from *Atharva Veda*. The divine architect, *Vishwakarmā*, is believed to have built the stage for performance. While Shiva contributed his vigorous dance of *Tāndava*, his consort, Parvati, came out with the tender one of *Lāsya;* Vishnu invented four dramatic styles essential

for effects, and Bharata directed the first production and later laid down the rules of theatre arts in a thoroughly practical manual called *Nātyashāstra*. During the first performance, to ensure an uninterrupted and successful presentation, Indra drove the evil spirits away with his *jarjara*. In short, here was a collective effort of all the major deities, including the Trinity.

16. These *sāttvikbhāvas* or *sattvajas* are eight in number—*stambha* (paralysis), *sveda* (perspiration), *romancha* (horripilation), *svara-bhanga* (change of voice), *vepathu* (trembling), *Vaivarnya* (change of colour), *ashru* (tears), and *pralaya* (fainting).

17. *Nātyashāstra* mentions thirty-three *vyabhichāri-bhāvas* as follows: *Nirveda* (world-weariness), *glāni* (physical weakness), *shankā* (anxiety), *asūyā* (envy), *mada* (intoxication), *shrama* (fatigue), *ālasya* (laziness), *dainya* (depression), *chintā* (worry), *moha* (confusion), *smriti* (remembrance), *dhriti* (peace of mind), *vrīdā* (shame), *chapalata* (impulsiveness), *harsha* (joy), *āvega* (panic), *autsukya* (longing), *nidrā* (sleeping), *apasmāra* (apoplexy), *supta* (dreaming), *vibodha* (awakening), *amarsha* (resentment), *avahitthā* (dissimulation), *ugratā* (violence), *marana* (death), *trāsa* (fright), *vitarka* (perplexity), *jadatā* (heaviness), *mati* (learning), *garva* (arrogance), *Visāda* (defection), *vyādhi* (disease), *unmāda* (madness).

18.

STHĀYIBHĀVA	*RASA*	COLOUR	DEITY
Rati (love)	*Shringāra* (erotic)	Shining dark	Vishnu
Hasa (amusement)	*Hāsya* (comic)	White	Pramatha (Shiva's attendant)
Shoka (sorrow)	*Karunā* (compassionate)	Light grey	Yama
Krodha (anger)	*Raudra* (furious)	Red	Rudra
Utsāha (dynamic energy)	*Vīra* (heroic)	Light green	Indra
Bhaya (fear)	*Bhayanaka* (terrifying)	Black	Kāla
Jugupsā (disgust)	*Bībhatsa* (disgusting)	Blue	Shiva
Vismaya (wonder)	*Adbhuta* (awesome)	Yellow	Brahmā

19. Or may one turn for the key to the configuration to *Sūtradhāra* who, as the etymology goes, holds the strings (*sūtra*) and is thus the puppeteer manipulating the action to create a certain effect?

20. One way of explaining this would be to use the *Trika* terminology and say

that *Rasa* is the impregnation of a feeling with passive *Prakāsha* (luminous existence) as well as active *Vimarsha* (consciousness). Or, maybe, it would be more worthwhile to see things in the context of *Triguna*. According to the Indian philosophy, matter has three essential *gunas* (properties) which make up in varying degree everything in nature, both organic and inorganic, physical and mental. In fact, these *gunas* are supposed to serve as the vital bond between a body and its soul. Representing the force of inertia and unconscious in nature, *Tamasguna* signifies inaction, mental darkness, dullness, sluggishness, and is therefore represented by black or dark blue colour. *Rajasguna* stands for the principle of restlessness and activity because it represents the force of energy and motion in nature which translates itself into the qualities of passion, action, struggle and desire. Its colour is flaming red or dove grey, while the colour of the third *guna, Sattva*, is white or rosy yellow. This last *guna* signifies goodness and harmony as it represents the force of perfection, purity, equilibrium. It dominates in gods or unselfish and spiritually inclined men. In day-to-day life, everything and everyone has all these *gunas* in different proportions and one's overall nature or situation is determined by the *guna* that dominates. The power of art lies in the fact that it disturbs one's normal pattern to create a new order in which *Tamasguna* and *Rajasguna* are subordinated to give freer play to *Sattvaguna*. If we use such words as body, mind and spirit for *Tamas, Rajas* and *Sattva*, it amounts to saying that in the equilibrium created by the aesthetic experience of *Rasa*, spirit comes to dominate. Hence the spiritual thrill, *ānanda*. In this context, it should be interesting to recall the difference between *ānanda* and *jīvan-mukta*. Since *gunas* bind the soul to the world and thus limit its full propensity, real freedom of the soul should lie in transcending all the *gunas,* including *Sattva*. Indra is content with the *ānanda* of *Moksha*; Buddha must go a step farther—to the peace of *Nirvāna*.

But, then, just as F.L.Lucas had ridiculed the therapeutic interpretation of catharsis by asserting that theatre is not a hospital, one might as well ask if aesthetics is an exercise in meditation. Is *sahridaya* a mystic; is art appreciation a surrogate-*samādhi*? Well, surely, aesthetic experience involves detachment but that is the very starting point and not the final stage. True, no one decides to visit a theatre because he wants to have something otherworldly; but one does go with the expectation of an experience of such nature as cannot be had in routine existence. That is why for Abhinavagupta, the key-word in aesthetic experience is *alaukika* (not of this world and therefore extraordinary).

21. It is not for nothing that, of the 37 chapters, five (8-12) are devoted exclusively to the art of body movements (use of minor and major limbs, footmovements, choreography, gait and postures), five (20-22, 24-25) to styles of acting and theatrical representation, three (26, 35-36) to casting, distribution of roles, actor's curse and redemption, and seven (28-34) to vocal and instrumental music. On *Rasa,* there is just one chapter (No. 6); one could add the next one (No. 7) by courtesy because it deals with *bhāvas*. Even when Bharata talks about types of acting—[*Āngika* (physical gesture),

Vāchika (verbal representation), *Sāttvika* (gestures that flow from mental state)], *Ahārya* (costume and make-up), conventions (*lokadharmi* and *nātyadharmi*), types of *Siddhi* (*Mānasi*, i.e., human and *Daivī*, i.e., divine), or *Rītis,* i.e., dramatic techniques or styles [*Sāttvikī* (mental), *Ārabhatī* (violent), *Bhāratī* (vocal) and *Kaishikī* (graceful)]—references to *Rasa* are unrelated to *ānanda*-aspect.

22. Chapter 18 does deal with the ten forms of dramatic composition, but the typological basis is the structure. What is more, Bharata's concern is with the rules of composition, the material that is not to be represented on the stage, the interludes, etc. References to Rasas are on the periphery rather than seminal.

23. It is, of course, possible to offer a defence in his behalf by arguing that Bharata implied a stage-wise configuration in *sahridaya's* mind, parallel to the one in a performer's processing a *bhāva.* After all, etymologically speaking, *abhinaya* (Sanskrit word for acting) means 'carrying across,' and the word for character, *pātra,* means a pot, a container. That is to say, the actor and his acting are not the end in themselves but only the means to create, contain and communicate the *Rasa.* Maybe, Bharata's contemporaries knew all this and regarded *sahridaya's Rasa* as something automatic and almost sui-generis. Whether or not he assumed all this, his silence on the issue has raised such ghosts as continue to haunt Indian aesthetics till this day.

    The fact that *Rasa* has come to be identified with *Ānanda* has lent yet another dimension to the controversy. It is argued that while acting, an actor too enjoys his role and so in his case *Bhāva-rasa* is *Ānanda-rasa* itself. But it is a misleading argument because an actor's is the relish of playing, not of the play. While containing wine, a decanter does come in touch with it and thus, in a way, tastes it; but that is not taste in the sense of relishing. In creating the *rasa* of a *bhāva*, performer has artistic satisfaction, but it is different from the *ānanda-rasa*, the aesthetic satisfaction which a *sahridaya* would experience.

24. There may or may not be intermediary stage of an actor; the reader of a play is both the actor and the spectator rolled into one. In this connection, one may add that while, in theatre, *Rasa* is realized by stages, in arts like painting and poetry, it is instant. Indeed, the finished product of a poet's or a painter's art is already brimming with *rasa* and awaiting its relish by some reader or viewer; in the performing arts, we are witnesses to an art-in-the-making and hence the case of *Rasa*-in-the-making.

25. Thus, in *Shringāra-rasa*, *Sattva* and *Rajas* permeate and all the faculties are stimulated but mildly; *Hāsya* rests in mind, has traces of *Tamas* but is touched more by *Rajas* than by *Sattva;* in *Vīra-rasa* which is permeated by *Sattva, Rajas* is seen in traces, *Tamas* is completely out, and there is dominance of will; *Karunā* is seated in mind and dominated by *Tamas* and bears the traces of *Sattva; Adbhuta-rasa* is resplendent with *Sattva* and *Rajas* and involves intellect; *Raudra* involves ego and has traces of *Rajas* and *Tamas* to the total exclusion of *Sattva; Bībhatsa* is devoid of *Sattva*, has a little of *Rajas*, only traces of *Tamas*, and is seated in mind. In varied situations

like this, the extent to which one's *chitta* (mind) melts in sympathy (*druti*), expands to experience the universal (*chitta-vistāra*), and feels illumined (*chitta-vikāsa*), is bound to be different. It is an experience of the *chitta*, nevertheless.

26. Far from implying any distortion, *Vakrokti* is one of the many *gunas* (excellences) in the Indian poetics. Ananadavardhana calls these *gunas rasa-dharma;* but, for Kuntaka, they are ingrained in the poetic temperament. Anyway, a *guna* here is not just any quality or merit. It is a way of collocation—not of words and ideas alone but of sound and meaning, too—that would lend the poem a touch of brightness. What *Rasa* is in content, *guna* is in form. Thus seen, the position enjoyed by *Auchitya* has its counterpart in *Vakrokti*. In this connection, Kuppuswami Sastri has reproduced in his book the following graphic illustration created by V. Raghavan:

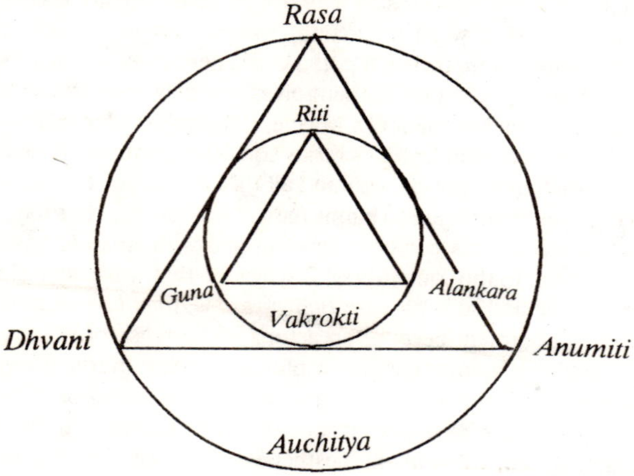

The bigger circle of the highways, enclosing the bigger triangle of content, stands for *Auchitya*, while the inner circle of the by-ways, enclosing the smaller triangle of form, pertains to *Vakrokti*. In the smaller triangle, *Rīti* is at the top, *Gunas* and *Alamkāras* are side by side but in positions of subservience; ditto for *Rasa* in the bigger triangle vis-a-vis *Dhvani* and *Anumiti*.

27. When words and meaning conjoin in *Dhvani* to bring the implicit into light, a unique beauty of unfailing appeal is obtained—a beauty radiating from within in respect of both word and meaning. As truth and beauty get interlinked in *Dhvani,* it serves, in a way, as the spiritual component, i.e., soul of the poem. It is this fusion of the conscious and the unconscious that lends to the poem a touch of the magical as well as the a-logical. Thus seen, *Dhvani* is obviously much more than meaning (*artha*) and therefore translating it as Suggestion is as unfair as translating *Rasa* as Sentiment.

28. Of course, there are *dhvanis* of other types, too—namely *Vastudhvani* (the subtle power of the word as poetic embellishment) and *Bhāvadhvani* (when

the sense serves as a transient emotion). Obviously, in these different contexts, *dhvani* is used both for word and for its meaning. Thus situated, *dhvani* helps exploit the beauty of every element in the medium of language, e.g., *alamkāras, gunas, rītis,* etc. That is the reason why *Dhvani* is equated with the whole poetic process and the entire work—rather than any one stylistic element—appears to produce a *Rasa.*

29. Art has been compared to a woman who, to please her lover, employs suggestive arts—like a veil on her face which enhances her charm by preventing it from becoming all-too-obvious. A poet, too, indulges in the artful game of subtle apprehension through partial suppression. Modern poetry, on the other hand, uses not a thin veil but a thick pall through which little is visible. One keeps groping in vain because there is no ringing of the bell. Or, to change the metaphor, we are in a dark tunnel with not a ray of light to beckon us to the other end; in this tunnel, instead of being changed into a vibrating echo, one's shout turns into a cry that gets instantly frozen into a dreadful silence. Indeed, in the absence of *Dhvani,* modern poetry appears to be more like a grotesque and parodic pastiche than an integral mosaic.

30. Of course, in this exercise, the same verse may prove serviceable in a variety of situations. Take, for example, the following couplet:

    Koi khum ke khum hai piye huey, koi ek jaam ka muntzir
    Tere rind phir bhi hain mutmayen tere maikada ke nizam se
    (Some have had jugfuls of wine, some are still waiting for a single cup. And yet these drinking clients of yours are satisfied with the management of your bar).

    It is not difficult to imagine this verse being addressed by a poor man to God, by a frustrated employee to his master, by a bachelor denied the marital felicity!

31. One may not be able to give example of the great power that Urdu *ghazal* has, but one can at least show what a different rasa might be realized in the process of translation. Let us take, for example, one of the most famous couplets:

    Tum mere pass hote ho goya
    Jab Koi doosra nahin hota

    One would be very faithful to the couplet if one translates it as: 'You are with me, as it were / When there is no one else around.' Anyone familiar with Urdu would, however, be shocked at this banal and commonplace rendition of a couplet that always succeeds in enthralling the imagination of a reader who cannot help repeating it to himself dozens of times. In fact, it is so good that Mirza Ghalib, one of the greatest Urdu poets, was so bowled over by its simplicity as well as subtlety that he offered to barter away his complete works just for this single couplet. No less enchanting is Ghalib's own couplet:

Dil-e-nadaan, tujhe hua kiya hai?
Aakhir is dard ki dava kiya hai?
(O ignorant heart, what has happened to you?
What is, after all, the remedy of this malady?)

In being translated thus, the couplet has lost every vestige of its glorious composition—its anguish, depth, and lilt. The way richly suggestive ambiguity vanishes in translation will be clear when we render yet another famous couplet by Ghalib:

Maut ka ek din muayyan hai,
Neend kiyon raat bhar nahin aati?
(The day of my death is pre-ordained;
Why don't I get sleep throughout the night?)

32. In this connection, Sri Aurobindo would discount the general belief that mind and spirit mean the same thing, that all consciousness can be spoken of either as mind or as spiritual substance, and that body is merely matter and therefore something quite different from the spiritual part of nature. It is because of the western man's tendency to confuse the spirit and mind that most of the aesthetic controversies have arisen.
33. Of course, there are two schools of thought—*Advaita* (Non-Duality, i.e., Monism) of Shankara and *Dvaita* (Dualism) of Sankhya—about the way that eternal, ultimate reality is manifested. While the former believes that it is in the form of just one indivisible energy, the latter argues that it is in the form of two forces called *Prakriti* and *Purusha.* Of these, *Prakriti* represents matter that is visible but unconscious and therefore blind; *Purusha* is that force of knowledge or consciousness which cannot manifest itself and is, therefore, a kind of cripple. Life is thus comparable to a cripple on the shoulder of a blind man. When *Purusha* and *Prakriti* join hands, intellect is born. But, in the process, there gets created, as a by-product, ego (=I-consciousness) which, in turn, creates in *Purusha* an illusion that it (*Purusha*) is *Prakriti* itself. Thanks to such ignorance about its true self, intellect is the source of all misery. Only when one transcends this level of ignorance and sees the true nature of the relationship between *Purusha* and *Prakriti,* does one regain the primordial joy. Of course, that is possible only when one gains a release from ego. That release is the aim of a *yogin* and, as we show elsewhere, the aim of art, too.
34. This *Jīva-ātman* must not be confused either with *Jīva* (i.e., spirit) or with *Ātman* (i.e., self). It is at times translated as psychic being, but it has nothing to do with psyche in the Western sense. For that western psyche, the Hindu philosophers have another term, *Mann*—one of the eleven senses that organizes all the other ten senses: five senses of knowledge called *Jnānendriyas* (viz. senses of vision, hearing, taste, smell and touch) and five motor senses called *Karmendriyas* (viz., two hands, two feet and one sex-organ). Seen thus, *Mann* is again different from *Manas* which represents will, intellect being *Buddhi*, and *Chitta* being the mirror on which the interaction of *Jīva* is

reflected.

35. In this ladder, the nethermost is the layer of physical consciousness, the material realm. It ranges from the bottom of spine down to the feet under which is the subconscient (which has its own layers); by way of its functions, it commands physical consciousness and the subconscient; and its centre is called *Mūlādhāra*. Below the navel is the lower vital being, dominated by the activities of sex and food and therefore commanding the small vital movements, e.g., greed, lusts, desire, sense-movements; its centre is called *Svādhishthāna*. Next is the higher vital layer which has centre around the navel (called *Nābhipadma*) and commands the larger life forces—passions and such-like desire-movements. Between the navel and the shoulders is the emotional being: centred round *Hridaya-padma*, it commands the higher emotional being—joy, sorrow, love, hate, etc. It has the psychic being deep within it. From throat to the crown of the head, there are numerous layers of mind, the three chief layers being centred around throat (*Vishuddha*, which externalizes mind and expresses mental forces), the mid-point between the eyebrows (*Ājnā-chakra* which is the seat of thought, sight and will) and the top of the head (*Sahasradala* which communicates the higher consciousness and intuitive mind).

36. Moving on the wings of imagination, Higher Mind signifies steady downpour of spontaneous knowledge and totality of truth-seeing at a single glance. Illumined Mind is like flaming stuff, and has more power and intensity: truth comes as a flash with minimal thinking and yields rapturous ecstasy of knowledge. Intuitive Mind is like a flash of lightning—complete in a single stroke—a supra-intellectual way of knowing. Overmind is a delegate of the Supermind consciousness—a creator of truths, knower of universal beauty, universal love, universal delight. It has no language of its own and uses language made by mind; therfore, it makes mind, life and matter as its media. Supermind is divine gnosis which needs no language, no medium.

37. As against the super-conscient, Aurobindo perceives the subconscient as that submerged part of our being in which there is no waking consciousness or coherent thought, will or feeling; it receives obscurely the impressions of all things and stores them up in itself. Habits, impressions, reflexes, nervous reactions, primitive reactions—all belong here. It is not the foundation of the nature, nor one's basic self; instead, it is a mask of false nature imposed on the true being which is the inner self that expresses the divine. This is the realm of western psychology, the subconscious, the unconscious, the racial consciousness, etc. It is worth recalling here that Aurobindo's subconscious is part of the subliminal which is not what the Freudians call libido. It is something complex enough to accommodate the superconscient as well as the subconscient. It is infinitely great with more knowledge, more power than the small self on the surface. It is, indeed, omnipresent and omniscient intelligence. Another thing which links the physical nature, the vital being and the mind—and which is in direct touch with the Divine—is the soul or the psychic being. It experiences all—the interplay of mind, body and life. As observed elsewhere, it is not the same thing as *Ātman*. *Ātman* is the self; soul

or psychic being is the self within—somewhere deep behind and in the middle of the chest. It is in the body but has no physical frame: it is part of the subtle body.

38. Perhaps it would be helpful if, in the operation of *Chitta* (total mind), we see not vertical stages but concentric circles, like the ones created by a stone thrown in a pond. Thus conceived, maybe, they correspond to the realms of *Buddhi* (intellect), *Manas* (feeling), *Ahankāra* (ego), and *Ātman* (soul). Even the Western aestheticians, who don't believe in soul or *Ātman,* concede the role of intuition which is supposed to signify a line of intersection between the conscious and the unconscious. No wonder Freud talked about art in relation to the dream and Jung visualized the unconscious as the seat of the archetypes.

39. Against the *Shabda Brahma* of literature, the *Nāda Brahma* of music, the *Vastu Brahma* of architecture or sculpture, we have the *Rasa Brahma* of dramaturgy. In this connection, perhaps it would be of interest to recall what we said earlier when talking about the origin of drama—that theatre was akin to *Yajna* ceremony. In fact, it has also been described as *Chākshusha-yajna* (*Yajna* of the eyes). In a *Yajna*, we have recitation (*Pāth* of the *Mantras*), to the accompaniment of rituals, that climaxes in oblation *(Āhuti*) and ends with the distribution of *Bhoga* or *Prasāda* that signifies the sharing of gods' benediction; in a theatrical performance, when dialogues and actions climax in our complete surrender to the spectacle, we receive, as it were, the *Prasāda* of *Rasa-ānanda.*

40. It is, indeed, strange that whereas there have been suggestions for addition to the number of the eight original *Rasas*—for example, *Shānta, Vātsalya, Bhakti*—no body has ever thought of projecting *Mānava-rasa* for this honour. And this despite the fact that the occasions when the Indian audiences have emerged totally steeped in humanism were by no means all that rare—especially in our own times when the Western literature is not only known to our *sahridayas* but has also inspired the modern writers in Indian languages.

41. Our introducing *Mānava-rasa* might appear a preposterous proposition to those who can never think of accommodating the very idea of tragedy in Sanskrit aesthetics. Well might they retort: what about the tragic view of life, the existential dichotomy and conflict between macrocosm and microcosm? It might be possible to answer back, for the sake of argument, that the Vedantist concept of *Dvaita* has perhaps the potential of supplying the corresponding equivalents in terms of *Purusha* and *Prakriti.* Indeed, one could also see in the concept of microcosm the Western mind's version of what the orientalist calls *Māyā.* One might even attempt to explore a close correspondence between the tragic process and *Rasa-nishpattih* in terms of detachment, involvement and transcendence. But, when all is said and done, these questions are irrelevant. No writer worth his salt would start with a declaration to himself, 'Let me today write a tragedy or a play with such-and-such *Rasa*,' and then go on to hunt for requisite ingredients or their equivalents. Nor does he design his strategies for evoking a set kind of

response. Only a lesser playwright would start with a palpable design on the emotional, intellctual and/or spiritual apparatus of the audience and look for objective correlatives in the form of purposive action, characters and dialogues. A true writer wants just to share an experience which he thinks is worthwhile; some view of life or *Rasa* might be inherent in that experience but that is not the motivating force. The writer's *Pratibhā* will see to it that the right cues get woven into the texture of everything that he creates. What *Rasa* dominates in a play or what kind of generic impact it yields would depend not on his prefixed intention but on what gets created. If there is conflict between macrocosmic laws and microcosmic values, if the suffering is creative, and if the close evokes affirmation, one could declare it a tragedy; on the other hand, if the conflict is on a different plane or it leads to suffering that fails to yield positive results, one might look up for other labels. Likewise, judging in terms of Indian aesthetics, one need not insist on a world-view or stages of *Rasa-nishpattih* but accept the play as a kind of *prasāda* from the creative mind, whatever the *Rasa. Rasa* lies in *sitār* and *its* interaction with the maestro's fingers via his *pratibhā*, not in aesthetic theories.

Bibliography

Abdullah, Adnan K. *Catharasis in Literature*. Bloomington: Indiana U P, 1985.

Abel, Lionel. *Metatheatre.* New York: Hill and Wong, 1963.

_______, ed. *Moderns on Tragedy*. Greenwich, Conn. Fawcett, 1967.

Adolf, Helen. 'The Essence and Origin of Tragedy.' *Journal of Aesthetics and Art Criticism* X, 2(December 1951),112-25.

Adorno, Theodore. *Aesthetic Theory*. London: RKP, 1984.

Albrecht, W.P. *The Sublime Pleasures of Tragedy: A Study of Critical Theory from Dennis to Keats*. Lawrence:University Press of Kansas, 1975.

Amur, G.S. *The Concept of Comedy: A Restatement*. Dharwar: Karnataka U P, 1963.

Anderson, David.*The Tragic Protest*. Richmond: John Knox Press, 1969.

Anderson, Maxwell. *The Essence of Tragedy*. Washington, DC: Anderson House, 1939.

Aspects of Indian Poetics (Talks on All-India Radio). New Delhi: Publications Division, 1969.

Aurobindo (Ghosh), Sri. *Lights on Yoga*. Pondicherry: Sri Aurobindo Ashram, 1935.

Bacon, Wallace A. and Robert S. Breen. *Literature as Experience*. New York: Mc-Graw Hill, 1959.

Bagchi, Amlendu. 'Aesthetics in Modern Psychology.' *Our Heritage* (Calcutta) XII (Jan.-June 1964), 1-26; XIII(Jan.-June 1965), 27-137.

Barbour, John D. *Tragedy as a Critique of Virtue: The Novel and Ethical Reflection.* Chicago, California: Scholars Press, 1984.

Barzun, Jacques. *The Use and Abuse of Art.* Princeton: Princeton U P, 1973.

Beardsley, Monroe C. *Aesthetics: Problems in the Philosophy of Criticism*. New York: Harcourt, Brace & World, 1958.

Belsey, Catherine. *The Subject of Tragedy: Identity and Difference in Renaissance Drama*. London: Methuen,1985.

Benson, Carl and Taylor Littleton, eds. *The Idea of Tragedy*. Illinois: Scott, 1966.

Bentley, Eric. *The Life of the Drama*. New York: Atheneum, 1964.

Berdyaev, Nicolas. *The Destiny of Man*. London: G. Bles, 1948.

Berke, Bradley. *Tragic Thought and the Grammar of Myth*. Bloomington: Indiana U P, 1982.

Berleant, Arnold. *The Aesthetic Field: Phenomenology of Aesthetic Experience*. Springfield: Charles C. Thomas,1970.

Berlin, Normand. *The Secret Cause: A Discussion of Tragedy*. Amhurst: Univ. of Massachusetts Press, 1981.

Berlyne, D.E. *Aesthetics and Psychobiology*. (Century Psychology Series). New York: Appleton Century Crofts, 1971.

Bhanot, Kanta. 'Dramatic Art of Shakespeare and *Natyashastra*.' Unpublished doctoral dissertation, Panjab University, 1991.

Bhat, G.K. *Tragedy and Sanskrit Drama*. Bombay: Popular Prakashan, 1974.

Bhat, S.C. *Drama in Ancient India*. Delhi: Amrit Books, 1961.

Blau, Herbert. *The Impossible Theatre*. New York: Macmillan, 1964.

Blistern, Elmer M. *Comedy in Action*. Durham, NC: Duke U P, 1964.

Block, Hakell M. 'Some Notes on the Problem of Modern Tragedy.' *Comparative Literature Studies* IX, 1 (March1972), 80-84

Boas, George. 'The Evolution of Tragic Hero.' *The Carleton Drama Review* I, 1 (1955-56), 5-21.

Bodkin, Maud. *Archetypal Patterns in Poetry*. Oxford: OUP, 1963.

Bogard, Travis and William I. Oliver. *Modern Drama: Essays in Criticism*. New York: OUP, 1965.

Booth, Wayne C. *A Rhetoric of Irony*. Chicago: Univ. of Chicago Press, 1974.

Borchardt, Donald. 'Catharsis in the Absurd.' *Southern Speech Journal* XXX, 4 (Summer 1965), 15-19.

Borev, Yuri. *Aesthetics: A Text Book*. Moscow: Progress Pub., 1981.

Bosanquet, Bernard. *The Concept of Aesthetics* (1915). Delhi: Capital Publishing House, 1980.

Bowra, C.M. *The Greek Experience*. New York: Mentor Books, 1957.

Bradley, A.C. *Oxford Lectures on Poetry*. London: Macmillan, 1950.

Brashear, William R. *The Gorgon's Head: A Study in Tragedy and Despair*. Athens: Univ. of Georgia Press, 1977.

______. 'The Power of Negative Thinking: An Essay on Tragedy.' *South Atlantic Quarterly* LXXIV, Winter 1975, 21-39.

Bredvold, Louis I. 'The Modern Temper and Tragic Drama.' *The Quarterly Review* LXI, 18 (May 1955), 207-13.

Brereton, Geoffrey. *The Principles of Tragedy*. London: Routledge & Kegan Paul, 1950.

Brooks, Cleanth, ed. *Tragic Themes in Western Literature*. New Haven: Yale U P, 1960.

______ and Robert B. Heilman. *Understanding Drama*. New York: Holt, Rinehart and Winston, 1945.

Brown, John Mason. 'American Tragedy.' *Saturday Review of Literature* XXXII (August 6, 1949), 124-29.

Buckhardt, Titus. *Sacred Art in East and West*. London: Perennial Books, 1967.

Burke, Kenneth. 'On Catharsis, or Resolution.' *Kenyon Review* XXI, 3 (Summer 1959), 337-69.

Butcher, S.H. trans. & ed. *Aristotle's Theory of Poetry and Fine Arts*. New York: Dover, 1951.

Byrski, M.C. *Concept of Ancient Indian Theatre*. New Delhi: Munshiram Manoharlal Pub., 1974.

Calarco, N. Joseph. *Tragic Being: Apollo and Dionysus in Western Drama*. Minneapolis: Univ. Of Minnesota Press, 1968.

Campbell, Joseph. *The Hero With a Thousand Faces.* New York: Meridian Books, 1956.

Camus, Albert. *The Myth of Sisyphus and Other Essays.* New York: Random House, 1955.

Carlson, Marvin. *Theories of the Theatre.* Ithaca: Cornell University Press, 1984.

Chaitanya, Krishna. *Sanskrit Poetics: A Critical and Comparative Study.* Bombay: Asia Pub., 1965.

Chamu, S.V. 'Catharsis—in the Light of Triguna Theory.' *Literary Criterion* VI, 4 (Summer 1965), 36-43.

Chandra, Rai Govind. *The Structure of Comedy.* Calcutta: Thacker Spink, 1952.

Charney, Maurice. *Comedy High and Low: An Introduction to the Experience of Comedy.* New York: OUP, 1978.

Chatterji, P.C. *Fundamental Questions in Aesthetics.* Simla: Indian Institute of Advanced Study, 1968.

Chaudhry, Prabas Jiban. *A Guide to Aesthetics.* Jijnasa: Quest Series, 1977.

_______. *Studies in Aesthetics.* Calcutta: Rabindra Bharati, 1964.

Choudhary, Satya Dev. *Essays on Indian Poetics.* Delhi: Vasudev Prakashan, 1965.

Christensen, Parley A. 'Tragedy as Religious Paradox.' *Western Humanities Review* XXI, 1 (Winter 1958), 39-58.

Clark, Barrett H. *European Theories of the Drama.* New York: Crown Pub., 1966.

Clay, James H. 'A New Theory of Tragedy: A Description and Evaluation.' *Educational Theatre Journal* VIII, 4 (Dec.1956), 295-305.

Coffman, George R. 'Tragedy and a Sense of the Tragic: In Some of its Ethical Imagination.' *Sewanee Review* L,1(1942), 26-34.

Cole, Susan Letzler. *The Absent One: Mourning Ritual, Tragedy and the Performance of Ambivalence.* University Park: Pennsylvania State U P, 1985.

Cook, Albert. *The Dark Voyage and the Golden Mean: A Philosophy of Comedy.* Cambridge, Mass.: Harvard U P,1949.

Cooper, Lane. *Greek Genius and Its Influences.* Ithaca, NY: Cornell U P, 1959.

_______. *The Poetics—Aristotle on the Art of Poetry.* Ithaca: Cornell U. P., 1947.

Corrigan, Robert W. *The Theatre in Search of a Fix.* New York: Delacorte Press, 1963.

_______, ed. *Tragedy: Vision and Form.* New York: Harper & Row, 1981.

_______ and James L. Rosenberg, eds. *The Context and Craft of Drama.* San Francisco: Chandler, 1964.

Courtney, W.L. *Idea of Tragedy in Ancient and Modern Drama* (1900). New York: Russell & Russell, 1967.

Cox, Roger L. *Between Earth and Heaven.* New York: Holt, Rinehardt and Winston, 1969.

Dahlstrom, Carl E.W.L. 'An Approach to Tragedy.' *Modern Drama* I, 1 (May 1958), 35-49.

Dave, R.A. 'Have We Lost The Tragic Sense?' *Literary Criterion* VI, 4, pp. 26-35.

Davies, Pennar, 'The Enjoyment of the Tragic.' *BARU*, 139 (May 1974), 305-6.

De, S.K. *Some Problems of Sanskrit Poetics.* Calcutta: Firma KLM, 1981.

_______. *Sanskrit Poetics as a Study of Aesthetics.* Bombay: OUP, 1963.

Dickie, George. *Aesthetics: An Introduction.* Indianapolis: Pegasus, 1971.

________. *Art and the Aesthetics: An Institutional Analysis.* Ithaca: Cornell U P, 1974.

Dixon, W. Macneille. *Tragedy.* London: Edward Arnold, 1924.

Dodd, Wayne Donald. *The Mortal Condition: A Definition of Tragedy.* Unpublished dissertation, Univ. of Oklahama,1963.

Dodds, E.R. *The Greeks and the Irrational.* California: Univ. Press, 1956.

Downer, Alan S. 'The Future of Tragedy.' *Poetry* (Chicago) LXII (1943), 344-46.

Draper, R.P., ed. *Tragedy: Developments in Criticism* (Casebook). London: Macmillan, 1980.

Dufrenne, Mikel. *The Phenomenology of Aesthetic Experience.* Evanston: North-Western U P, 1973.

Dutton, Richard. *Modern Tragicomedy and the British Tradition.* Sussex: Harvester Press, 1986.

Ellis-Fermor, Una. *The Frontiers of Drama.* London: Methuen, 1949.

Ellman, Richard, and Charles Feidelson, eds. *The Modern Tradition.* New York: OUP, 1965.

Else, Gerald F. *Aristotle's Poetics: The Argument.* Cambridge, Mass: Harvard U P, 1957.

Engelberg, Edward. 'Passionate Reverie: W.B. Yeats's Tragic Correlative.' *University of Toronto Quarterly.* XXXI, 2 (Jan. 1962), 201-22.

Esslin, Martin. *The Theatre of the Absurd.* London: Eyre and Spottiswoods, 1964.

Faber, Melvyn D. 'Analytic Prolegomena to the Study of Western Tragedy.' *Hartford Studies in Literatre* V(1973), 31-60.

Feibleman, James K. *Aesthetics: A Study of Fine Arts in Theory and Practice.* New York: Humanities Press, 1968.

______. *In Praise of Comedy: A Study in Its Theory and Practice.* London: George Allen & Windus, 1939.

Fergusson, Francis. *The Human Image in Dramatic Literature.* New York: Anchor Books, 1957.

______. *The Idea of a Theatre.* New York: Doubleday (Anchor Books), 1949.

Figes, Elva. *Tragedy and Social Evolution.* London: John Calder, 1976.

Findlater, Richard. 'No Time for Tragedy?' *Twentieth Century* CLXI, 959(January 1957), 56-66.

Fraser, G S. *The Modern Writer and His World.* Calcutta: Rupa, 1961.

Fraser, Russell A. *Shakespeare's Poetics In Relation to King Lear.* London: Routledge and Kegan Paul, 1962.

Fromm, Erich. *Sane Society.* London: Routledge, 1956.

Frye, Northrop. *The Anatomy of Criticism.* Princeton: Princeton U P, 1957.

Gallangher, Kent G. 'Emotion in Tragedy and Melodrama.' *Educational Theatre Journal* XVII, 3 (Oct. 1965), 215-19.

Garcia, Daniel Peter. 'Theories of Catharsis in Modern Literary Criticism: The Influence of Psychoanalysis, Anthropology and the New Criticism.' Unpublished Ph.D. dissertation, University of Oregon, 1962. (Microfilm).

Gardner, Helen. *Religion and Literature.* London: Faber & Faber, 1971.

Gassner, John. 'The Possibilities and Perils of Modern Tragedy.' *Tulane Drama Review* I, 3 (June 1957), 3-14.

______. 'Tragic Perspectives: A Sequence of Queries.' *TDR* II, 2(May 1958), 7-22.

Gassner, John and Edward Quinn. 'Basic Documents in Dramatic Theory.' Appendix to *The Reader's Encyclopaedia of World Drama.* Methuen, 1970, pp. 937-1030.

Gellrich, Michelle. *Tragedy and Theory: The Problem of Conflict Since Aristotle.* Princeton: Princeton U P, 1988.

Ghosh, Ranjan K. *Aesthetic Theory and Art: A Study in Susanne K. Langer.* Delhi: Ajanta, 1979.

______. *Conceptions and Pre-suppositions in Aesthetics*. Delhi: Ajanta, 1987.

Ghosh, S.K. *Tragedy.* Calcutta & London: Oxbridge Publishers, 1965.

Glicksberg, Charles I. *The Ironic Vision in Modern Literature.* Hague: Martinus Nijhoff, 1969.

______. *Tragic Vision in the Twentieth Century* (Crosscurrent Modern Critiques Series). Carbondale: Southern Illinois Univ. Press, 1963.

Gnoli, Raniero. *The Aesthetic Experience According to Experience*. Varanasi: Chowkhamba Sanskrit Series,1968.

Goldmann, Lucien. *Racine.* London: Rivers Press, 1972.

Green, Andre. *The Tragic Effect: The Oedipus Complex in Tragedy.* Cambridge: CUP, 1969.

Guha, P.K. *Tragic Relief.* Calcutta: Rabindra Bharati Univ., 1973.

Gupta, Chandra Bhan. *The Indian Theatre.* Banares: Motilal Banarsidas, 1954.

Gurewich, Morton. *Comedy: The Irrational Vision.* Ithaca: Cornell U P, 1975.

Guthke, Karl S. *Modern Tragicomedy: An Investigation into the Nature of the Genre*. New York: Random House, 1966.

Haecker, Theodore. 'Theodicy and Tragedy.' *The Criterion* XIII, 371-81.

Hamilton, Edith. *The Greek Way to Western Civilization.* New York: Morton, 1952.

______. *The Theory of the Theatre.* New York: Henry Holt, 1939.

Hathorn, Richmond Y. *Tragedy, Myth and Mystery*. Bloomington: Indiana U P, 1962.

Hegel, Friedrich. *The Philosophy of Fine Arts.* London: G. Bell, 1920.

Heilman, Robert B. *The Iceman, the Arsonist, and the Troubled Agent: Tragedy and Melodrama on the Modern Stage.* Seattle: Univ. of Washington Press, 1973.

______. *Tragedy and Melodrama: Versions of Experience*. Seattle: Univ. of Washington Press, 1968.

______. *The Ways of the World: Comedy and Society*. Seattle: Univ. of Washington Press, 1978.

Henn, T.R. *The Harvest of Tragedy.* London: Methuen, 1956.

Herrick, M.J. *Tragicomedy—Its Origin and Development in Itlay, France and England.* Urbana: Univ. of Illinois Press, 1955.

Herzel, Roger W. 'Anagnorisis and Peripeteia in Comedy.' *Educational Theatre Journal* XXVI, Dec. 1974, 495-505.

Hiriyanna, M. *Art Experience.* Mysore: Kavyalaya Pub., 1954.

Hofstadter, Albert. 'The Tragicomic: Concern in Depth.' *Journal of Aesthetics and Art Criticism* XXIV, 2 (Winter1965), 295-302.

Holland, Norman N. *Laughing: A Psychology of Humour.* Ithaca: Cornell U P, 1982.

Hook, Sidney. 'Pragmatism and the Tragic Sense of Life.' *American Review* V, 3, pp. 30-45.

Horovitz, Israel. 'Tragedy.' *Playwrights, Lyricists, Composers on Theatre*, ed. O.L.Guernsey Jr. TheDramatists' Guild, 1974, pp. 28-36.

Howarth, W.D. *Comic Drama: The European Heritage.* London: Methuen, 1978.

Hoy, Cyrus. *The Hyacinth Room.* London: Chatto and Windus, 1964.

Hutter, Charles A. 'Tragedy and Human Self-Sufficiency: Two Approaches.' *Gordon Review* XIII, 1 (Fall 1964), 34-43.

Huyghe, Rene. *Art and the Spirit of Man.* London: Thames and Hudson, 1962.

Hyman, S.E. 'Psychoanalysis and the Climate of Tragedy.' *Freud and the Twentieth Century*, ed. Benjamin Nelson. London: Allen & Unwin, 1958, pp. 163-81.

Indian Drama. New Delhi: Publications Division, 1956.

Iyengar, K.R.S. *Adventures of Criticism.* Bombay: Asia Pub., 1962.

Jaspers, Karl. *Tragedy Is Not Enough.* Trans. Reiche, Moore and Deutsch. London: Victor Gallancz, 1953.

Jauss, Hans Robert. *Aesthetic Experience and Literary Hermeneutics.* Minneapolis: Univ. of Minnesota Press, 1982.

Jepsen, Laura. *Ethical Aspects of Tragedy.* Gainsville: Univ. of Florida Press, 1953.

Jhanji, Rekha. *The Sensuous in Art: Reflections on Indian Aesthetics.* Simla: Indian Institute of Advanced Study,1989.

_______, ed. *Communication and the Arts.* Delhi: Ajanta, 1984.

Jones, Ernest. *Hamlet and Oedipus.* New York: Doubleday (Anchor Books), 1949.

Jones, Howard Mumford. 'A Case of Plight.' *Atlantic Monthly* CLXXXVII, 6 (June 1951), 51-52.

Kale, Pramod. *The Theatric Universe.* Bombay: Popular Prakashan, 1974.

Kallen, Horace M. 'The Meaning of Tragedy in the Freedom of Man.' *Journal of Philosophy* LV, 18 (Aug. 28, 1958), 772-80.

Kantak, Y.V. 'Why Do We "Enjoy" Tragedy?' *Literary Criterion* IV, 1 (Winter 1959), 1-10.

Kaufmann, Walter. *Tragedy and Philosophy.* New York: Doubleday, 1968.

Kaul, A.N. *The Action of Comedy.* Delhi: Vikas, 1970.

Keith, A.B. *The Classical Sanskrit Literature.* OUP, 1936.

Kern, Edith. 'The Modern Hero: Phoenix Or Ashes?' *Comparative Literature*, Vol. 10, pp. 325-34.

Kerr, Walter. *Tragedy and Comedy.* New York: Simon & Schuster, 1967.

Khrapchenko, Mikhail. *Artistic Creativity, Reality and Man.* Moscow: Raduga Pub., 1986.

Kitto, H.D.F. *Form and Meaning in Drama.* London: Methuen, 1956.

_______. *Greeks.* Harmondsworth: Penguin, 1951.

Knights, L.C. 'Notes on Comedy.' *Scrutiny* I, 4 (March 1933), 356-67.

Koelb, Clayton. 'The Problem of Tragedy as a Genre.' *Genre* VIII, 3(Sept. 1975), 248-66.

_______. '"Tragedy" as an Evaluative Term.' *Comparative Literature Studies* II, 1 (March 1974), 69-84.

Kott, Ian. *Shakespeare, Our Contemporary.* London: Methuen, 1967.

Kreiger, Murray. *The Tragic Vision.* Chicago: Phoenix, 1966.

Kreitler, Hans and Shulamith Kreitler. *Psychology of the Arts.* Durham: Duke U P, 1972.

Krishnamurthy, K. *The Dhvanyaloka and Its Critics.* Delhi: Bhartiya Vidya Prakashan, 1982.

_______. *Dhvanyaloka of Anandvardhana.* Delhi: Motilal Banarsidass, 1974.

_______. *Essays in Sanskrit Criticism*. Dharwar: Karnataka U P, 1974.

_______. *Some Thoughts on Indian Aesthetics and Literary Criticism.* Mysore: University of Mysore, 1968.

_______, ed. *Vakrokti-Jivita of Kuntaka*. Dharward: Karnataka U P, 1977.

Krishnaswamy, Thiru S.Y. 'Indian and Western Values in Literature and the Fine Arts.' *Journal of MadrasUniversity* I, 1 (Jan. 1978).

Krooks, Dorothea. *Elements of Tragedy.* New Haven, Conn.: Yale U P, 1969.

Krutch, Joseph Wood. *Experience and Art*. New York: Collier, 1962.

_______. *Modern Temper: A Study and a Confession*. New York: Harcourt, 1956.

Kuhns, Richard. *Structures of Experience: Essays on the Affinity Between Philosophy and Literature.* New York: Harper and Row, 1970.

Langer, Susanne K. 'The Tragic Rhythm.' *Feeling and Form.* London: Charles Scribner's Sons, 1953, pp. 351-66.

Leavis, F.R. 'Tragedy and the Medium: A Note on Mr. Santayana's Tragic Philosophy.' *Scrutiny* XII, 4 (Autumn 1944), 249-60.

Leech, Clifford. *Tragedy*. London: Methuen, 1969.

Lenson, David. *Achilles' Choice: Examples of Modern Tragedy*. Princeton: Princeton U P, 1975.

Levi, Sylvain. *The Theatre of India.* Vol. I & II. Calcutta: Writers Workshop, 1978.

Levin, Harry. *Playboys and Killjoys: An Essay on the Theory and Practice of Comedy.* New York: OUP, 1987.

Levin, Richard. *Tragedy—Plays, Theory and Criticism.* New York: Harcourt, Brace & World, 1960.

Livingstone, R.W. *Greek Ideals and Modern Life.* Cambridge, Mass.: Harvard U P, 1935.

Lucas, F.L. *Tragedy: Serious Drama in Relation to Aristotle's Poetics.* New York: Collier, 1962.

Mahulkar, D.D. 'Approach to Beauty in Art and Literature.' (Author's personal copy, unpublished).

Mandel, Oscar. *A Definition of Tragedy*. New York: New York U P, 1961.

Mason, H.A. *The Tragic Plane.* Oxford: Clarendon Press, 1985.

Masson, J.L. and M.V. Patwardhan. *Aesthetic Rapture: The Rasadhyaya of the Natyashastra.* Vol. I. Poona: Deccan College, 1970.

McArthur, Herbert. 'Tragic and Comic Modes.' *Criticism* III, Winter 1961, 36-45.

McCollom, William G. 'An Approach to Tragedy.' *Educational Theatre Journal* III, 1 (March 1951), 16-22.

______. *Tragedy.* New York: Macmillan, 1957.
McEachran, F. 'Tragedy and History.' *Criterion* IX (1922-39), 661-70.
Mead, Hunter. *An Introduction to Aesthetics.* New York: Ronald Press, 1952.
Michel, Lawrence. *The Thing Contained: Theory of the Tragic.* Bloomington: Indiana U P, 1970.
Michel, L. and R.B. Sewall, eds. *Tragedy, Modern Essays in Criticism.* Englewood Cliffs, NJ: Prentice-Hall, 1963.
Mikhail, E.H. *Comedy and Tragedy: A Bibliography of Critical Studies.* Troy, NY: Washington Pub. Co.,1972.
Miller, Arthur. 'Introduction' to *Collected Plays.* London: Crescent Press, 1958.
______. 'Tragedy and the Common Man.' *Theatre Arts* XXV, March 1951, 48-49.
Milstead, John. 'The Structure of Modern Tragedy.' *Western Humanities Review* XII, 4 (Autumn 1958), 365-69.
Mishra, H.R. *Theory of Rasa in Sanskrit Drama.* Bhopal: Vindhyachal Prakashan, 1964.
Mishra, Shrikrishna. *Coleridge and Abhinavagupta.* Mirzapur (Author), 1979.
Moore, Charles A. *Philosophy and Culture, East & West.* Honolulu: Univ. of Hawaii Press, 1962.
Morrell, Roy. 'The Psychology of Tragic Pleasure.' *Essays in Criticism* VI, 1 (January 1956), 22-37.
Moss, Leonard. *A Check List on the Theory of Tragedy 1900-1970.* Bulletin of New York Public Library.
Mukherji, Ramaranjan. *Literary Criticism in Ancient India.* Calcutta: Sanskrit Pustak Bhandar, 1966.
Muller, Herbert J. *The Spirit of Tragedy.* New York: Knopf, 1956.
Murphy, Gardner and Murphy, eds. *Asian Psychology.* New York: Basic Books, 1968.
Murray, A. Victor. 'The Divine Tragedy.' *Hibbert Journal* LIII, Oct. 1954-July 55, 19-24.
Myers, Henry Alonso. *Tragedy: A View of Life.* Ithaca: Cornell U P, 1956.
Nandi, S.K. *Studies in Modern Indian Aesthetics.* Simla: Indian Institute of Advanced Study, 1975.
Narasimhaiah, C.D. *Literary Criticism: European and Indian Traditions.* Mysore: Univ. of Mysore.
Nelson, Robert J. 'Ritual, Reality, Tragic Imitation, Mythic Projection.' *Diacritics* VI, 2 (Summer 1976), 41-48.
Nicoll, Allardyce. *The Theory of Drama.* London: Harrap, 1961.
Nietzsche, Friedrich. *The Birth of Tragedy and the Case of Wagner.* Trans. Walter Kaufmann. New York: Random House (Vintage Books), 1967.
Oates, Joyce Carol. *The Edge of Impossibility: Tragic Forms in Literature.* New York: Vanguard Press, 1972.
O'Connor, William Van. *Climates of Tragedy.* Baton Rouge: Louisiana U P, 1943.
Olson, Elder. *Aristotle's Poetics and English Literature.* Chicago: Univ. of Chicago, 1965.

______. *Theory of Comedy*. Bloomington: Indiana U P, 1968.

______. *Tragedy and the Theory of Drama*. Detroit: Wayne State U P, 1961.

Osborne, John, ed. *Aesthetics: Oxford Readings in Philosophy*. London: OUP, 1972.

Ossowski, Stanisław. *The Foundations of Aethetics*. Boston: D Reidel, 1978.

Packer, Mark. 'Dissolving the Paradox of Tragedy.' *Journal of Arts and Aesthetic Criticism* XLVII, 3 (Summer 1989), 211-19.

Palmer, J.D., ed. *Comdey: Developments in Criticism* (Casebook). London: Macmillan, 1984.

Pandey, K.C. *Comparative Aesthetics,* Vol. I (Indian Aethetics). Varanasi: Chowkhamba, 1959.

Pandit, Sneh. *An Apprcach to the Indian Theory of Art and Aesthetics*. New Delhi: Sterling, 1977.

Paul, David. 'The Immoral Gods.' *The Twentieth Century* CLIII, No. 911, pp. 59-65.

Peacock, Ronald. *The Poet in the Theatre*. London: Routledge, 1946.

Pepper, Stephen C. *Aesthetic Quality: A Contextual Theory of Beauty*. New York: Charles Scribner's Sons, 1937.

Pipa, Arshi. 'Some Remarks about Western and Eastern Aestheics.' *The British Journal of Aesthetics* VIII, 4 (Oct. 1968), 365-71.

Pole, David. *Aesthetics: Form and Emotions*. London: Duckworth, 1983.

Poole, Adrian. 'Tragedy and Diversity.' *Tragedy: Shakespeare and the Greek Example*. Oxford: Basil Blackwell, 1987, pp. 1-14.

Pottle, Frederick A. 'Catharsis.' *Yale Review* XL, 4 (June 1951), 620-41.

Potts, L.J. *Comedy*. London: Hutchinson U P, 1957.

Prior, Moody E. *The Language of Tragedy*. New York: Columbia U P, 1947.

Pronko, L.C. *Theatre East and West: Perspectives Towards a Total Theatre*. Berkeley: Univ. of California Press, 1967.

Purani, A.B. *Sri Aurobindo: Some Aspects of His Vision*. Bombay: Bhartiya Vidya Bhavan, 1977.

Raglan, Lord. *The Hero*. London: Watts, 1949.

Rai, Alok. 'The Idea of Tragedy.' *Quest* LVI, Winter 1968, 38-40.

Ramchandran, Ragini. *Indian Literary Criticism*. New Delhi: Reliance, 1989.

Rangacharya, Adya. *The Indian Theatre*. New Delhi: National Book Trust, 1971.

Rao, G. Hanumanta. *Comparative Aesthetics: Eastern and Western*. Mysore: D.V.K. Murthy, 1974.

Raphael, D.D. *The Paradox of Tragedy*. Bloomington: Indiana U P, 1960.

Ray, Nihar Ranjan, ed. *Indian Aesthetics and Art Activity*. Simla: Indian Institute of Advanced Study, 1968.

Reiss, Timothy J. *Tragedy and Truth*. New Haven: Yale U P, 1980.

Rice, Elmer. 'American Theatre and Human Spirit.' *Saturday Review* XXXVII, 9 (Dec. 17, 1955), 39-41.

Richards, I.A. 'Emotive Language Still.' *Yale Review* XXXIX, 1 (Sept. 1949), 108-18.

______. *Principles of Literary Criticism*. London: Routledge, 1961.

______, C.K. Ogden and James Wood. *The Foundations of Aesthetics*. New York: Lears Pub., 1925.

Roberts, Patrick. *The Pshcyology of Tragic Drama*. London: Routledge and Kegan Paul, 1975.

Rosenmeyer, Thomas G. *The Masks of Tragedy.* University of Texas Press, 1963.

Saisselin, Remy G. 'Is Tragic Drama Possible in the Twentieth Century?' *Theatre Annual* XVII (1960), 12-21.

Saiyidain, Zohra. *The Realm of Perception.* Simla: Indian Institute of Advanced Study, 1970.

Sankaran, A. *Some Aspects of Literary Criticism in Sanskrit: The Theories of Rasa and Dhvani*. Madras: Univ. of Madras, 1973.

Santayna, George. *The Sense of Beauty.* New York: Collier, 1961.

_______. 'Tragic Philosophy.' *Scrutiny* IV, 4 (March 1936), 365-76.

Sastri, K.S. Ramaswami. *Indian Aesthetics: Music and Dance*. Sri Venkateswara University, 1966.

Sastri, Kuppuswami. *Highways and Byways of Literary Criticism.* Madras: Kuppuswami Sastri Research Institute, 1945.

Sastri, P.P. *The Philosophy of Aesthetic Pleasure.* Annamalai University Sanskrit Series, 1940.

Sastri, P.S. *Indian Theory of Aesthetic.* Delhi: BhartiyaVidya Prakashan, 1989.

Sastri, S.N. Ghoshal. *Elements of Indian Aesthetics.* 3 vols. Varanasi: Chawkhamba, 1978.

Saw, Ruth L. *Aesthetics: An Introduction*. London: Macmillan, 1972.

Scheler, Max. 'On the Tragic.' *Cross Currents IV* (1954), 178-91.

Schopenhauer, Arthur. *The World as Will and Idea.* London: Routledge, 1949.

Schwartz, Elias. 'Detachment and the Tragic Effect.' *College English X*, 3 (December 1956), 153-56.

Schwarz, Alfred. *From Buchner to Beckett: Dramatic Theory and the Modes of Tragic Drama.* Athens: Ohio U P, 1978.

________. 'Towards a Poetics of Modern Realistic Tragedy.' *Modern Drama* IX, 2 (Dec 1966), 136-46.

Scott, Nathan, ed. *The Tragic Vision and the Christian Faith.* New York: Association Press, 1957.

Sedgewick, G. *Of Irony, Especially in Drama*. Univ. of Toronto Press, 1948.

Segal, Charles. *Tragedy and Civilization*. Cambridge, Mass.: Harvard U P, 1981.

Sewall, Richard B. *The Vision of Tragedy.* New Haven: Yale U P, 1959.

Sharma, Mukanda Madhava. *The Dhvani Theory in Sanskrit Poetics.* Varanasi: Chowkhamba Sanskrit Series, 1968.

Sharpe, R.B. *Irony in the Drama.* Chapel Hill: Univ. of California Press, 1959.

Shastri, A.C. *Studies in Sanskrit Aesthetics.* Calcutta: P. Ghosh, 1952.

Shumaker, Wayne. *Literature and the Irrational: A Study in Anthropological Background*. Englewood Cliffs, NJ: Prentice Hall, 1960.

Sidney, Sir Philip. *Apology for Poetry or The Defence of Poesy.* Ed. Geoffrey Shepherd. London: Nelson, 1965.

Singhal, R.L. *Aristotle and Bharata.* Hoshiarpur: VVRI, 1977.

Sivaram, M. *Ananda: An Experience.* Delhi: Vikas, 1976.

Skorpen, Erling. 'In Search of the Tragic Hero and After.' *Western Humanities Review* XIX, 4 (Autumn 1965), 293-300.

Sorell, Walter. *The Facets of Comedy*. New York: Grosset & Dunlap, 1972.

Sreekantaiya, T.N. *Imagination in Indian Poetics and Other Literary Studies*. Mysore: Geetha Book House, 1980.

Srinivasan, G. *Problems of Aesthetics*. Mysore: D.V.K. Murthy, 1972.

Srivastava, K.G. 'A New Look at the Katharsis Clause of Aristotle's Poetics.' *British Journal of Aesthetics* XII, 3 (Summer 1972), 258-75.

Stanford, W.B. *Greek Tragedy and the Emotions: An Introductory Study*. London: RKP, 1983.

States, Bert O. *Irony and Drama: A Poetics*. Ithaca: Cornell U P, 1971.

Steinberg, M.W. 'Arthur Miller and the Idea of Modern Tragedy.' *The Dalhousie Review* XL, 3 (Fall 1963), 329-40.

Steiner, George. *The Death of Tragedy*. London: Faber, 1961.

Styan, J.L. *The Dark Comedy*. London: CUP, 1962.

Sudha, T.N. 'The Comic Mode in Classical Indian and Western Dramatic Theory with Special Reference to the Plays of Bhasa and Shakespeare.' Unpublished doctoral dissertation, Kerala University, 1983.

Sudhi, Padma. *Asethetic Theories of India*. Vol. I. Poona: Oriental Research Instt., 1983.

_______. *Aesthetic Theories of India*. Vol. II. New Delhi: Intellectual Publishing House, 1988.

_______. *Aesthetic Theories of India*. Vol. III. New Delhi: Intellectual Pub. House, n.d.

Swabey, Marie Collins. *Comic Laughter: A Philosophical Essay*. New Haven: Yale U P, 1961.

Sypher, Wylie. *Comedy*. New York: Doubleday, 1956.

Szeliski, John Von. 'Pessimism and Modern Tragedy.' *Educational Theatre Journal* XVI, 1 (March 1964), 40-46.

________. *Tragedy and Fear: Why Modern Tragic Drama Fails?* Chapel Hill: Univ. of North Carolina Press, 1962.

Tarlekar, G.H. *Studies in Natyashastra*. Delhi: Motilal Banarsidas, 1975.

Thompson, Alan Reynolds. *The Anatomy of Drama*. Berkeley: Univ. of California Press, 1942.

________. 'The Dilemma of Modern Tragedy.' *Humanism and America: Essays on the Outlook of Modern Civilization*, ed. Norman Foester. New York: Farrar, 1930, pp. 127-48.

________. *The Dry Mock: A Study of Irony in Drama*. Berkeley: Uni.v of California Press, 1948.

________. 'Melodrama and Tragedy.' *PMLA* XLIII, 810-35.

Thompson, William I. 'Freedom and Comedy.' *TDR* IX, 3 (Summer 1965), 216-30.

Thorndike, Ashley H. *Tragedy*. Boston: Houghton, Miffin, 1908.

Toshihiko and Toyo Izatu. *The Theory of Beauty in the Classical Aesthetics of Japan*. Hague: Martinus Nijhoff Pub., 1981.

Tymieniecka, Anna-Teresa, ed. *The Existential Co-ordinates of the Human Condition: Poetic—Epic—Tragic: The Literary Genre*. Dordrecht: Reidel, 1984.

Unamuno, Miguel de. *The Tragic Sense of Life*. Trans. J.E.C. Flitch. New York: Dover, 1954.

Vatsyayan, Kapila. *Traditional Indian Theatre: Multiple Stream*. New Delhi: National Book Trust, 1980.

Vaughan, C.E. *Types of Tragic Drama*. London: Macmillan, 1936.

Vickers, Brian. *Towards Greek Tragedy.* London: Longmans, 1973.

Vivas, Elisco and Murray Krieger, eds. *The Problems of Aesthetics: A Book of Readings.* New York: Rinehardt, 1953.

Wadiyar Bahadur, Sri Jaya Chamaraja. *An Aspect of Indian Aesthetics.* Madras: Univ. of Madras, 1956.

Waldeck, Peter B. *Weighing Delight and Dole: A Study of Comedy, Tragedy and Anxiety.* New York: Peter Lang, 1988.

Warbeke, John M. *The Power of Art.* New York: Philosophical Library, 1951.

Watts, Harold H. 'Myth and Drama.' *Cross Currents* V (1955), 154-70.

Weisinger, Herbert. *Tragedy and the Paradox of the Fortunate Fall.* London: Routledge, 1953.

Weitz, Morris. *Problems in Aesthetics: An Introductory Book of Readings*. London: Macmillan, 1953.

Williams, Raymond. *Modern Tragedy.* London: Chatto and Windus, 1966.

Wilson, H.H. et. al. *Theatre of the Hindus.* Calcutta: Susil Gupta, 1955.

Wimsatt, W.K. and Cleanth Brooks. *Literary Criticism: A Short History.* New York: Knopf, 1957.

Yeats, W.B. 'Tragic Theatre.' *Essays and Introduction.* London: Macmillan, 1961, pp. 238-45.

Zink, Sidney. 'The Novel as a Medium of Modern Tragedy.' *Journal of Aesthetics and Art Criticism*, XVII, 2 (1958-59), 169-73.

Index